P9-EFJ-919

FEB 2 0 2013

DATE DUE

East Side Branch
Bridgeport Public Library
1174 East Main Street
Bridgeport, CT 06608

ADVANCE ACCLAIM

"In an artfully crafted exposé, *Worried?* considers a collection of vignettes of the modern world likely to have roused implicit concern. Anyone who has reconsidered ordinarily accepted elements of our existence will find this guide a beacon. The authors' ability to weave science and statistics together with clarity cleverly reveal those anxieties which should bubble to the level of our awareness and those which we should not lose sleep over."

—Kurt Weaver, Ph.D., Assistant Professor of Radiology, Instructor, Human Form and Function Thread & Mind, Brain and Behavior Block, University of Washington School of Medicine

"Few of us are able to make sense of the scientific literature for ourselves, but Johnson and Chudler have done the spade work for us; assembling the most reliable findings about the things that worry us all. They apply scientific reasoning to everyday situations in a fun and accessible way. The authors' wry tone and winsome humor brought a smile to my face even as I read about things that might kill me some day."

—Adam Baker, Ph.D., Adjunct Assistant Professor, University of North Dakota

"With new technologies and fads arriving daily, Drs. Johnson and Chudler use the principles of scientific research to investigate common worries ranging from asbestos to microwaves to gluten. As a pediatrician, I frequently encounter parents with these fears. I appreciate the humor and scientific rigor with which they sort through the cacophony of available information to advise us which anxieties are worth our attention—and which are not."

—Carrie Nedrud, M.D., Pediatrician

"Don't worry. Or, rather, worry sometimes, but only a certain amount, and only if you can do something to control the situation. From airplane crashes to sugar, *Worried?* walks us through common fears of the contemporary world, providing simple answers to the often challenging question: 'Should I be worried?' Anchored by science and simplified with diagrams, *Worried?* is an elegant and fun guide to navigate our era of information overload."

—Nathan Insel, Ph.D., Department of Psychology and Center for Structural and Functional Neuroscience, University of Montana

"In *Worried?*, Dr. Johnson and Dr. Chudler have created an absolutely delightful guidebook to help all of us, from the casually anxious stray-thought worriers to the deeply obsessed safety-checklist warriors, deal with the stressors of the modern world. Rigorously researched, appropriately fact-checked, and uproariously witty, this little tome is a must-have quick reference for that age-old nagging question, 'How bad is that, really?'"

—Devapratim Sarma, Ph.D., Scientist & Neural Engineer, Rehab Neural Engineering Labs, University of Pittsburgh, Center for the Neural Basis of Cognition, Carnegie Mellon University

WORRIED?

Worried?

Science investigates
some of life's common concerns

LISE JOHNSON
ERIC CHUDLER

Illustrations by **KELLY CHUDLER**

W. W. NORTON & COMPANY

INDEPENDENT PUBLISHERS SINCE 1923

NEW YORK   LONDON

Important Note: *Worried?* is intended to provide general information on the subject of health and well-being; it is not a substitute for medical or psychological treatment and may not be relied upon for purposes of diagnosing or treating any illness. Please seek out the care of a professional healthcare provider if you are pregnant, nursing, or experiencing symptoms of any potentially serious condition.

For information about permission to reproduce selections from this book, write to Permissions, W. W. Norton & Company, Inc., 500 Fifth Avenue, New York, NY 10110

For information about special discounts for bulk purchases, please contact W. W. Norton Special Sales at specialsales@wwnorton.com or 800-233-4830

Manufacturing by Lake Book Manufacturing, Inc.
Book design by Daniel Lagin
Production manager: Katelyn MacKenzie

ISBN 978-0-393-71289-6

W. W. Norton & Company, Inc., 500 Fifth Avenue, New York, N.Y. 10110
www.wwnorton.com

W. W. Norton & Company Ltd., 15 Carlisle Street, London W1D 3BS

1 2 3 4 5 6 7 8 9 0

CONTENTS

MEDICINE

ENVIRONMENT

CHEMICALS

ANIMALS

TRAVEL

MISCELLANEOUS

We thank Steve Johnson and Sandy Chudler for their careful reading of this book and for their many helpful comments and suggestions.

INTRODUCTION

For most of human history, people lived in pretty much the same way. No one was born in a hospital, because there were no hospitals. There was no such thing as organic farming, because there were no synthetic pesticides. Nothing was made of plastic. There were no microwaves or cell phones or airplanes or antibiotics or energy drinks. Not coincidentally, no one worried about these things. There were, of course, lions and tigers and bears, but our relationship to these animals was more straightforward. Overall, the potential threats, while arguably much greater in magnitude, were much easier to identify. But as the ever more numerous miracles of technological innovation continue to improve our lives, they also make it more complicated. Now, not only do we have things we didn't have before, we know things we didn't know before. There are clearly some things to worry about, but what are they? News media, social media, and every mom blog in the world will give you plenty of things to put on your list of worries. At the same time, there are many more places to get information than there have ever been. When these sources conflict, whom should you trust? As we struggle to make healthy and responsible choices for ourselves and our families, all of this ambiguity can be very stressful.

Here's the thing: stress, in and of itself, can cause health problems. Chronic stress can lead to digestive complaints, sleep problems, headaches, depression, irritability, high blood pressure, cardiovascular disease, diabetes, and stroke. It can also suppress your immune system so that you are frequently ill and make you look haggard and prematurely old. You can treat some of these symptoms with medication, but it would be much better to treat the underlying cause of the problem. Namely, it would be better to stop being so worried. There are a few things that can help. For example, some people find that regular exercise, meditation, or prayer helps them cope. These approaches might help with your stress level, but they don't address the underlying problem, which is that there are lots of potentially dangerous things in the world. But there is another complementary approach you can try, and that is to take control of the situation.

In this case, taking control means critically evaluating potential threats, determining what poses the greatest danger, and prioritizing your actions to minimize adverse outcomes. Knowledge is power. This is a good strategy because a sense of personal control is associated with positive mental health and lower levels of anxiety and depression. At the same time, you will reduce your overall risk of harm. It's a two-for-one deal.

The central task then becomes evaluating potential threats, which can be difficult. The world is a complicated place and becoming more complicated all the time. Unfortunately, evolution did not prepare your brain for the world it lives in. Humans tend to be tribal; we trust members of our own groups more than we trust outsiders. In addition, we are motivated much more strongly by stories than we are by statistics. These features were highly adaptive when most of us lived in small family groups, and they are still important today. But these instincts can also lead us to make bad decisions when they are applied to complex issues. Science is here to help, but only if you understand how to use it.

Science is a tool that helps us to understand why things happen. Further, it helps us predict what will happen in the future. Science is not magic; it is in fact the opposite of magic. There is no mystery about it. Fundamentally, science is a formalized way to evaluate cause-and-effect relationships rigorously. In a way, we are all scientists because babies learn to understand the world through cause and effect. But scientists bring some powerful tools to this fight: controlled experiments and math. A controlled experiment is one that eliminates potential confounds; this allows us to attribute the right cause to the effect. Math, particularly statistics, is how we know whether an effect is likely to be real, or whether we are observing something by mere chance. These points may seem nitpicky, but they allow us to draw appropriate conclusions when our intuitions might otherwise lead us astray. This is not to say that scientists are never wrong. Scientists are people, and people make mistakes and have biases that will sometimes lead to inappropriate conclusions. But the scientific method is a very reliable way to reveal underlying cause-and-effect relationships. If you are skeptical, remember that science is what puts airplanes in the sky, mobile phones in our pockets, and, for most of us, food on our tables.

We, the authors, believe that using scientific evidence is the best way to systematically evaluate potential sources of worry. We are also people living in the same dizzyingly complicated and confusing world as everyone else, and are therefore subject to the same concerns and questions. This is, in fact, what motivated us to write this book. We are both scientists, but most of the topics discussed in this book are outside our area of expertise. In writing this book we relied on our scientific training to identify credible sources, to read and understand scientific publications, and to interpret data. In the following chapters we present our findings in the hope that they will be useful to others, but we do not claim to have the final word on any topic. We are research scientists, not medical doctors; we do not provide any medical advice. If you have medical concerns, you should consult your health care provider. We encourage readers to investigate issues that interest them further.

The selection of topics covered in this book is by no means comprehensive. Indeed, there are so many things one could choose to worry about that this is an impossible task. What all of the chapters have in common is that they discuss ordinary everyday concerns. Some compelling issues have notably been left out. For example, there is no chapter about nuclear war. This is not to say that this should or should not be a real concern, but it is certainly beyond the scope of this book. We have also left some topics like vaccinations and global warming unaddressed. This is not because these issues are unimportant, but because they have been so frequently and thoroughly covered elsewhere. Of course, some things have been left out simply for lack of space and time. If, for whatever reason, you do not find the topic that you are looking for covered in this book, or if there is something you would like to know more about, we encourage you to research it on your own. In Appendix A (Do-It-Yourself) we have some suggestions about how to undertake this task.

For each topic that we cover, we have assigned a worry index. This is a way to quickly understand the relative risk posed by each issue. Please recognize that this is a subjective score meant to be illustrative, not definitive. Of course, individuals will have different priorities and may emphasize different factors accordingly. This is absolutely appropriate. In general, we believe that you should only worry about things that are (a) likely to happen, (b) have the potential to do great harm, and (c) can be avoided or mitigated through personal action. You will find that some things are very unlikely to happen, and therefore you can stop worrying about them, as there is no need. There will also be some things that are very likely to happen, but which you cannot stop. You can stop worrying about these things too, as worrying will not help. Finally, there are some things that are likely to happen, but the consequences won't really be so dire. We recommend that you also stop worrying about these things, because life is short.

We found this book tremendously interesting to write and hope that you will find it interesting to read.

HOW TO INTERPRET
THE WORRY INDEX

You will notice that for every topic reviewed in this book we have assigned a three-dimensional worry index. The three components of the index are preventability, likelihood, and consequence, defined as follows.

Preventability: The preventability score refers to your ability to avoid or mitigate a specific outcome. If there is something you can do, then you have some control. The more you can do to prepare, the higher the preventability score.

Likelihood: The likelihood score refers to the chance of a negative outcome should you be exposed to a particular element of risk. The greater the odds of an adverse result, the higher the likelihood score.

Consequence: The consequence score refers to the potential magnitude of harm. The more dire the consequence, the higher the consequence score.

In all cases we have assumed that the issue is relevant to you. We have also assumed a typical level of exposure. Obviously, these assumptions aren't appropriate for everyone all the time.

For each topic, we have provided a plot that represents these three factors graphically. The vertical axis (the y-axis) represents preventability; the horizontal axis (the x-axis) represents likelihood; and the size of the marker represents the consequence. Each plot is broken into quadrants. If you follow our suggestions, you will focus most of your effort addressing the large points in the upper-right quadrant. These are the problems that are preventable, likely to happen, and potentially serious. These are the things you should worry about.

If you're wondering how we came up with this scoring method, the answer is: we made it up. If you're wondering how we assigned the values, the answer is: we discussed and debated the scores for each topic until we agreed. You are free to disagree with us.

In most cases, it was difficult to assign a real number to the preventability, likelihood, and consequence of a particular risk factor. Almost all the time the answer seemed to be "it depends." You may find, as we did, that this is very unsatisfying. Therefore, we have done our best to make an estimate. We like to think of these estimates as a good first pass. But we strongly caution you against reading too much into the score.

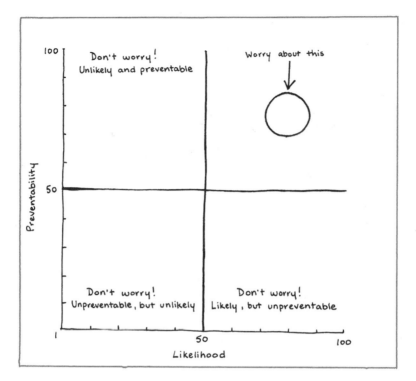

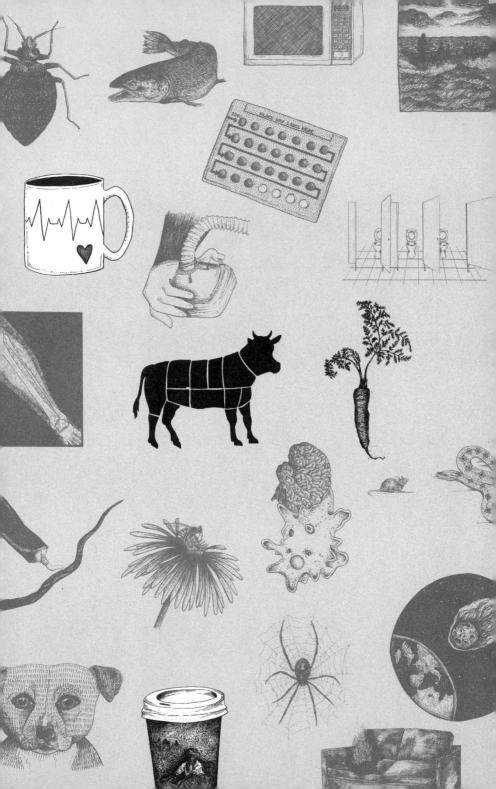

Food

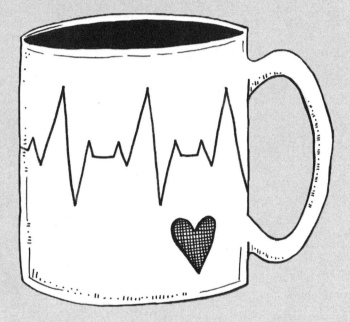

1. CAFFEINE

Caffeine is a naturally occurring drug with a number of physiological effects including diuresis, vasoconstriction, heart rate modulation, and smooth muscle contraction. But really, most of us are interested in it because of its psychostimulant properties. Oh, humans love caffeine. It is the world's most popular psychoactive substance. It is completely legal, and it is very effective. It suppresses sleepiness, improves performance, and helps us to concentrate. Without it, many of us wouldn't achieve a vertical posture in the morning or survive the 2 p.m. doldrums. But as much as we rely on it to facilitate our modern lives, many of us suspect that it is bad for us.

Although it occurs naturally, caffeine is a drug that can have some negative side effects. Caffeine works by nonselectively blocking adenosine receptors. Adenosine is an important molecule in the body, not just in the central nervous system, and blocking its effects can have widespread results. Caffeine increases acid production in the stomach and can cause heartburn and acid reflux. As a vasoconstrictor, it can lead to or exacerbate high blood pressure. Because it stimulates smooth muscle contraction, it can give you diarrhea. It is also a diuretic and can contribute to dehydration. Caffeine is notorious for causing rapid heart rate, insomnia, and headaches, and it can make anxiety worse. It can also interfere with the body's ability to absorb calcium, which is problematic for people at risk of osteoporosis. Caffeine can change the rate of metabolism for some medications and because of this property, it is included as an ingredient in some pain medications. However, this is clearly not always a desirable effect. As many of us know, caffeine can cause dependency. Cutting back on your caffeine intake can lead to a couple of really cranky, tired, headachy days. It is also worth pointing out that an acute overdose of caffeine can be fatal. Caffeine is generally recognized as safe, but that doesn't mean it is safe no matter how you use it. So, there are certainly some things to be concerned about.

But don't put down your coffee yet. There are some good things to say about caffeine. For example, it is ergogenic, which means it can enhance stamina and athletic performance. So, you might get more out of your morning run if you start with a cup of coffee (assuming it doesn't rankle your stomach or give you diarrhea, which will slow you down). More surprisingly, caffeine intake is associated with a lowered risk of Parkinson's disease, Alzheimer's disease, and stroke. It is also inversely correlated with suicide risk. Most people would consider that a nice bonus to their daily perk.

It turns out that it is also important how we get our caffeine, which is most commonly consumed in coffee, tea, cola, and chocolate. Coffee can stain your teeth and give you bad breath, but it has also been associated with a decreased cancer risk, a decreased risk of type 2 diabetes, and reduced all-cause mortality. Similarly, tea is reportedly good for cardiovascular health and reduces cancer risk. Chocolate is also high in antioxidants and may have benefits for cardiovascular health. In addition to containing caffeine, coffee, tea, and chocolate are all made from plants. These plants contain other phytochemicals that may promote good health, either on their own or in conjunction with caffeine. This is not to say that coffee and tea are appropriate for everyone at all stages of life. But if you're a healthy adult who isn't pregnant and doesn't have stomach problems or osteoporosis, you don't need to beat yourself up about indulging in a few cups of coffee or tea every day. You can even feel good about it.

But many of us also consume caffeine in soft drinks and energy drinks, which contain synthetic caffeine. Synthetic caffeine isn't a problem in and of itself, but there is very little good to say about the nutritional content of soft drinks. They are high-calorie and highly acidic, and contribute to tooth decay, obesity, and type 2 diabetes, among other things. But as bad as soft drinks are, energy drinks are potentially even worse. Energy drinks can contain large quantities of caffeine but may not disclose the actual caffeine content. In addition, energy drinks often mix caffeine with other herbal supplements that have not been tested for safety on their own or as part of an energy drink cocktail. Of course, many energy drinks are also boosted with a whopping dose of sugar. An especially disturbing trend is the mixing of energy drinks with alcohol. This might feel invigorating, but it is a bad idea. The caffeine can reduce your perception of how much you have had to drink, making it more likely that you will drink more. Contrary to popular belief, caffeine does not sober you up or make you less impaired by alcohol—it just makes you more alert while you're drunk. This can be extremely dangerous, even fatal.

When consumed within normal limits, and especially when imbibed in a cup of coffee or tea, caffeine can give you a healthy boost. Some people are more sensitive to caffeine than others, so the key is to be attentive to how your body reacts. Children can be very sensitive to caffeine, so they shouldn't consume a lot of it. Pregnant and nursing women should also limit their caffeine intake, and people with chronic health conditions or taking medications should talk about consuming caffeine with their physicians. Finally, if you are regularly consuming caffeine to keep yourself awake and alert, it is worth addressing the underlying cause of your fatigue. Although many of us treat caffeine as if it were a substitute for sleep, it is not. Chronic sleep deprivation is bad for you, and no amount of coffee can compensate for the sleep you miss.

SUMMARY

Preventability (100)

Caffeine is easy to avoid if you want to.

Likelihood (15)

Some people are sensitive to caffeine and some will develop dependency with regular use.

Consequence (3)

Assuming you do not consume a toxic dose or combine it with alcohol, the consequences of caffeine consumption are mild.

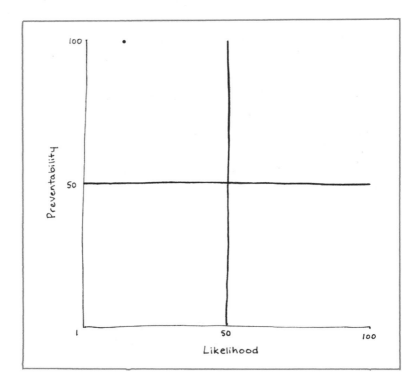

REFERENCES

Arendash, G. W., & Cao, C. (2010). Caffeine and coffee as therapeutics against Alzheimer's disease. *Journal of Alzheimers Disease, 20*, S117–S126.

BBC News. (2017, May 16). US teen died after drinking caffeine too quickly, coroner says. Retrieved from http://www.bbc.com/news/world-us-canada-39932366

Centers for Disease Control and Prevention. (2017, June 9). Fact sheets: Alcohol and caffeine. Retrieved from https://www.cdc.gov/alcohol/fact-sheets/caffeine-and-alcohol.htm

Kawachi, I., Willett, W. C., Colditz, G. A., Stampfer, M. J., & Speizer, F. E. (1996). A prospective study of coffee drinking and suicide in women. *Archives of Internal Medicine, 156*, 521–525.

Kerimi, A., & Williamson, G. (2015). The cardiovascular benefits of dark chocolate. *Vascular Pharmacology, 71*, 11–15.

Kerrigan, S., & Lindsey, T. (2005). Fatal caffeine overdose: Two case reports. *Forensic Science International, 153*, 67–69.

Khan, N., & Mukhtar, H. (2013). Tea and health: Studies in humans. *Current Drug Metabolism, 19*, 6141–6147.

Kim, B., Nam, Y., Kim, J., Choi, H., & Won, C. (2012). Coffee consumption and stroke risk: A meta-analysis of epidemiologic studies. *Korean Journal of Family Medicine, 33*, 356–365.

MedlinePlus. (2017, July 17). Caffeine. Retrieved from https://medlineplus.gov/caffeine.html

National Cancer Institute. (2012, May 16). NIH study finds that coffee drinkers have lower risk of death. Retrieved from https://www.cancer.gov/news-events/press-releases/2012/CoffeeProtectiveDCEG

National Center for Complementary and Integrative Health. (2017, September 24). Energy drinks. Retrieved from https://nccih.nih.gov/health/energy-drinks

Park, S.-Y., Freedman, N. D., Haiman, C. A., Le Marchand, L., Wilkens, L. R., & Setiawan, V. W. (2017). Association of coffee consumption with total and cause-specific mortality among nonwhite populations. *Annals of Internal Medicine, 167*, 228–235.

Rivera-Oliver, M., & Díaz-Ríos, M. (2014). Using caffeine and other adenosine receptor antagonists and agonists as therapeutic tools against neurodegenerative diseases: A review. *Life Sciences, 101*, 1–9.

Ross, G. W., Abbott, R. D., Petrovitch, H., Morens, D. M., Grandinetti, A., Tung, K.-H., . . . White, L. R. (2000). Association of coffee and caffeine intake with the risk of Parkinson disease. *JAMA, 283*, 2674–2679.

Spriet, L. L. (2014). Exercise and sport performance with low doses of caffeine. *Sports Medicine (Auckland, N.Z.), 44*(Suppl. 2), 175–184.

van Dam, R. M., Willett, W. C., Manson, J. E., & Hu, F. B. (2006). Coffee, caffeine, and risk of type 2 diabetes: A prospective cohort study in younger and middle-aged U.S. women. *Diabetes Care, 29*, 398–403.

2. DIETARY SUPPLEMENTS

Dietary supplements are exactly what they sound like: products that are consumed in addition to a regular diet in order to provide an extra benefit. In some cases, they clearly do provide a benefit. For example, all women of childbearing age are encouraged to take a folic acid supplement to reduce the incidence of spina bifida, a serious birth defect. But in many cases, the benefits of dietary supplements are unclear. This, however, has not deterred people from buying into dietary supplements. Upward of 70% of the American population takes some sort of supplement, supporting a sizeable industry to the tune of $41.1 billion in 2016. This is potentially problematic because beyond being simply unhelpful, some dietary supplements are actually dangerous.

The most familiar and widely used dietary supplements are vitamins. These compounds are vital to human health, but our bodies can't make them. Instead, we have to consume them, traditionally through food. Vitamins are especially abundant in brightly colored fruits and vegetables such as broccoli, kale, carrots, and blueberries. But conveniently, they now come in pill form. Traditionally, the category of vitamins does not include essential fatty acids, amino acids, or minerals. This keeps the list fairly short. The essential human vitamins are A, B_1, B_2, B_3, B_5, B_6, B_7, B_9, B_{12}, C, D, E, and K. We know that these are essential vitamins because deficiency leads to disease. For example, vitamin D deficiency causes rickets, vitamin C deficiency causes scurvy, and vitamin A deficiency is the leading cause of blindness in the world.

Minor vitamin deficiencies can result in less severe, but real, health implications. Certainly, if you have a vitamin deficiency, a vitamin supplement will help. But thanks to the Nobel Prize–winning chemist Linus Pauling, who advocated for the immune-boosting powers of vitamin C, many of us go for vitamin C tablets whenever we get a cold. Unfortunately, this is at best a placebo. There is no convincing evidence that well-nourished adults enjoy any benefit from extra vitamin supplementation. This includes benefits in terms of general well-being, cardiovascular health, cancer, cognitive decline, and all-cause mortality. On the other hand, overconsumption of vitamins can have some negative health outcomes. This is especially true for the fat-soluble vitamins (A, D, E, and K) because they are more difficult for your body to clear. Acute vitamin overdoses can, in fact, be fatal. So if you have them around your home you must keep them out of the reach of children. Iron overdose is actually a common cause of accidental poisoning in children, although iron is not technically a vitamin. All of this is somewhat disappointing, but there is good news. Those brightly colored fruits and vegetables do have demonstrated health benefits, some of which may have to do with the interaction between vitamins and other compounds in the plant. It's also very difficult to overdose on carrots, although they might turn you orange.

Another popular dietary supplement is fish oil. Fish oil is high in omega-3 fatty acids, which are essential for humans. You can find omega-3s in a number of sources including seeds, nuts, eggs, meat, and, obviously, fish. Omega-3s are thought to have positive impacts on cardiovascular health and to be cancer protective. In addition, with the possible exception of fishy-tasting burps, these supplements are well tolerated by most people.

Protein is another important dietary component that is frequently supplemented, especially by athletes. Typically, these supplements are either dairy based or soy based. Dairy-based protein is generally safe, unless you are allergic to milk. Soy proteins, on the other hand, are the subject of ongoing controversy due to their potentially estrogenic effects. However, the data do not present a clear picture of whether this is a problem or not.

The dietary supplements listed above are really just that: things you need to consume, whether you get them in a supplement or from some other dietary source. But there is another category of dietary supplements that are marketed as providing some sort of bonus. For example, supplements are commonly marketed as body-building and weight-loss aids, sleep aids, sexual and fertility aids, immune boosters, memory enhancers, mood enhancers, hair, skin, and nail strengtheners, and, most disturbingly, alternative or additive treatments to pharmaceuticals. It's questionable whether these products should really be categorized as dietary supplements, since they don't have a lot to do with diet. However, it is clearly to the supplement manufacturer's advantage to have this designation because the FDA regulates dietary supplements as food, not as medicine or drugs. This is important.

The FDA requires that drug manufacturers demonstrate both safety and efficacy before a product can be brought to market. This requires extensive and expensive clinical trials. Supplement manufacturers, on the other hand, are not required to demonstrate efficacy. In return, supplements are not meant to be marketed as treatment or prevention for any particular disease. However, the claims of general health improvement can be made if the packaging includes the following disclaimer: "This statement has not been evaluated by the FDA. This product is not intended to diagnose, treat, cure, or prevent any disease." Safety does not have to be demonstrated for ingredients that were on the US market before 1994 because their historical usage makes them "generally recognized as safe." If a manufacturer wants to introduce a new ingredient, it must provide the FDA with notice and reasonable evidence that it is safe for human consumption. But since the safety of a new product does not have to be demonstrated to the FDA before it is brought to market, the product is considered safe until proven otherwise. Once it is on the market, the FDA will track any adverse events that are reported. But unless the symptoms are acute and specific, it can be very difficult to trace these events to the source.

Furthermore, the manufacturer is responsible for accurately labeling ingredients and performing good quality control. But the FDA does not test products for quality. Several research studies have shown that a large percentage of dietary supplements either do not contain the ingredients they claim or contain them in the wrong quantities, contain other unlisted ingredients, and/or in some cases are contaminated with heavy metals or pesticides, or adulterated with pharmaceuticals (e.g., anabolic steroids). Some third parties will provide certification for supplements. However, these certifications are only meant to ensure that the product is accurately labeled and do not indicate that the product is safe or effective.

People tend to assume that if products are commercially available in the United States they are safe, and this is particularly untrue in the case of dietary supplements. Supplements have been linked to liver damage, cardiovascular problems, psychiatric symptoms, gastrointestinal symptoms, bleeding, and stroke. People have died.

Another thing to consider when you are taking supplements is that they can interact with prescribed and over-the-counter medications. If you are taking a supplement—any kind of supplement—you need to disclose it to your doctor. And remember, most of the time you're better off with the broccoli in your refrigerator than the supplement in a jar.

SUMMARY

Preventability (95)

There are some situations (like pregnancy) in which a vitamin supplement is called for, but most of the time dietary supplements are optional.

Likelihood (30)

The dietary supplement industry is enormous, and most people do not suffer any ill effects. But if you take certain kinds of supplements you increase your risk.

Consequence (87)

Some dietary supplements are effectively drugs that have not been reviewed by the FDA. The consequences of taking these substances should not be underestimated. They can be fatal.

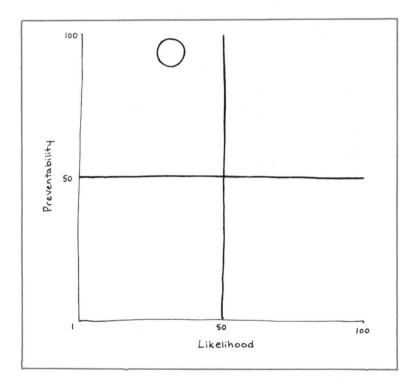

REFERENCES

American Cancer Society (2015, March 31). FDA regulation of drugs versus dietary supplements. Retrieved from https://www.cancer.org/treatment/treatments-and -side-effects/complementary-and-alternative-medicine/dietary-supplements/fda -regulations.html

National Center for Complementary and Integrative Health. (2014, June). Using dietary supplementswisely.Retrievedfromhttps://nccih.nih.gov/health/supplements/wiseuse .htm

National Institutes of Health, Office of Dietary Supplements. Multivitamin/mineral supplements. (2015, July 8). Retrieved from https://ods.od.nih.gov/factsheets/ MVMS-HealthProfessional/#en3

Nutrition Business Journal. (2017, June 9). 2017 supplement business report: The new (not-so) normal. Retrieved from http://www.newhope.com/market-data-and -analysis/2017-supplement-business-report-new-not-so-normal

Oakley, G. P. (2009). The scientific basis for eliminating folic acid-preventable spina bifida: A modern miracle from epidemiology. *Annals of Epidemiology, 19,* 226–230.

Ronis, M. J. J., Pedersen, K. B., & Watt, J. (2017). Adverse effects of nutraceuticals and dietary supplements. *Annual Review of Pharmacology and Toxicology, 58,* 583–601.

3. FOOD ADDITIVES

Food additives are a self-descriptive category. They are substances that are added to food for the purpose of enhancing color, flavor, texture, or nutritive value, and to extend shelf life. Some of these substances are familiar, like baking soda, salt, vinegar, and vitamin C. Others are synthetically derived, like sodium benzoate and aspartame. We need at least some food additives, because most of us no longer live on farms and grow our own food, nor could we if we wanted to. The world's population prohibits subsistence farming as an option. Food additives allow us to live in urban settings while enjoying a wide variety of foods from all over the world during every season of the year. This is great, as long as what we are eating is safe.

A 1958 congressional amendment to the Food, Drugs and Cosmetics Act of 1938 gave the FDA responsibility for regulating new food additives. The FDA allows thousands of different substances to be added to our food, including preservatives, dyes, emulsifiers, bulking agents, foaming agents, antifoaming agents, anticaking agents, antibrowning agents, stabilizers, thickeners, flavor enhancers, and sweeteners. According to the FDA's website, "Consumers should feel safe about the foods they eat," because "food and color additives are strictly studied, regulated and monitored." But it can be difficult to feel safe, even if the FDA thinks you should. Some food additives that were previously legal have now been banned. Some that are legal in the United States are illegal in the European Union and vice versa.

Some currently legal substances have been accused of being harmful, and consumers are left in a state of confusion about the whole issue.

On the top of many people's list of concerns are food colorings. Some foods, especially candy, are wildly unnaturally colored on purpose. Other foods are colored to make them look more like we think they should. But for whatever reason, coloring is often added to food. Synthetic dyes have a bad reputation; health concerns associated with artificial colors include cancer, asthma, learning and memory problems, and hyperactivity. But despite extensive study, the results are controversial, conflicting, and unclear. Some of the most controversial colorings, tartrazine (Yellow No. 5), fast green (Green No. 3), and allura red (Red No. 40), are still permitted by the FDA. But people have become wary of them, and consumer pressure has increasingly driven the market to develop natural alternatives including annatto, paprika, and carotenoids.

Unlike colorings, preservatives are important to ensure the safety of some foods. Nevertheless, there are some concerns that these substances are harmful. Sodium benzoate is an antimicrobial that is commonly used in both foods and cosmetics to inhibit the growth of bacteria, fungi, and yeast. This preservative is one of the additives on the FDA's Generally Recognized as Safe list. However, there are still some concerns about its toxicity and carcinogenic effects in animal models. Furthermore, a 2007 study found that consumption of a combination of artificial food colorings and sodium benzoate increased hyperactivity in children. But because it was administered with other additives, it is difficult to know whether this effect was dependent on sodium benzoate, the food colorings, or some interaction between the two. Another area of concern is the potential for sodium benzoate to react with vitamin C and form benzene, a known carcinogen. In fact, benzene has been found in some soft drinks that include both of these ingredients.

Many people are used to worrying about parabens in cosmetics, but they are also used as preservatives in food. Parabens have recently become controversial, with some studies showing an effect on male fertility and a relationship with breast cancer in women. On the other hand, some studies have shown parabens to be safe. The FDA thinks that they are safe when used within recommended limits, so if you want to avoid parabens you need to check labels.

Nitrites and nitrates have also received a lot of attention lately. These compounds are used in the curing of meat and give foods like ham and salami their pink color (it is also what makes Himalayan pink salt pink). Nitrites and nitrates inhibit botulism, a pathogen that will kill you in a jiffy, which accounts for their widespread use. Unfortunately, there is some concern that they are converted to carcinogenic nitrosamines in the body. Processed meats are thought to be cancer causing, and nitrites and nitrates may be part of the reason why. But these compounds are also present in unprocessed vegetables like spinach, and we don't usually consider spinach to be carcinogenic. Some argue that nitrites and nitrates are actually healthful.

Noncaloric sweeteners have been subject to suspicion for a long time. Saccharin, one of the first artificial sweeteners, was at one time implicated in bladder cancer. This has since been shown to be false, but saccharin has never recovered in the court of public opinion. Aspartame has been extensively investigated, but again, the results have been mixed. This can be frustrating, but you may not need to think about it too much, because low-calorie sweeteners don't actually help people to lose weight.

Of course, these examples are just a small subset of the potentially concerning substances that are added to our food. And at least all of these examples have been reviewed by the FDA. The really disturbing additives are the ones that have never been examined by the FDA at all. A 2013 report by the Pew Charitable Trust uncovered some grim facts about the FDA's oversight of food additives. One of the major problems is the GRAS (Generally Recognized as Safe) loophole. The Food Additives Amendment of 1958 included an exemption for common ingredients like salt and vinegar. The basic idea was that if most knowledgeable scientists would consider the additive safe, then the FDA didn't need to review it. The problem is, the manufacturers of food additives have been allowed to make this determination themselves. The manufacturers don't even have to report new GRAS-designated additives to the FDA. Pew estimated that 1,000 chemical additives in the American food supply were self-affirmed as GRAS and were not reviewed by or reported to the FDA. This is an incredible and troubling finding.

Pew identified a series of problems with the regulatory process for food additives including (1) the inherent conflict of interest involved in allowing additive manufacturers to select the scientists that review their products, (2) the lack of information available to the FDA about existing food additives (not only those that are GRAS) and the inability of the agency to demand this information, (3) the outdated science the FDA uses to evaluate safety, and (4) the FDA's failure to meet the deadlines set by the FDA Food Safety Modernization Act of 2011. The Pew report is equal parts terrifying and embarrassing: the United States is the only developed country that permits untested and undisclosed additives to enter its food supply. In 2017, a group of consumer, health, and safety groups sued the FDA to challenge the GRAS loophole, which was reaffirmed by the FDA in 2016.

If all of this puts you off chemical food additives, no one could blame you. But in your search for natural alternatives, remember that natural choices are not always safer, and they are no better regulated. Your best bet is to try to reduce the number of processed foods that you eat.

SUMMARY

Preventability (54)

You can try to minimize your exposure to food additives, but they are so prevalent that, short of growing all of your own food, you can't completely avoid them.

Likelihood (33)

It's difficult to know how likely any of us is to suffer an adverse event from a food additive, because they don't have to be reviewed by the FDA before they are added to our food. On the other hand, most food additives do not cause serious health problems.

Consequence (41)

It is unlikely that anything acutely toxic will be intentionally added to food, but some additives could be allergenic or cause more subtle behavioral problems.

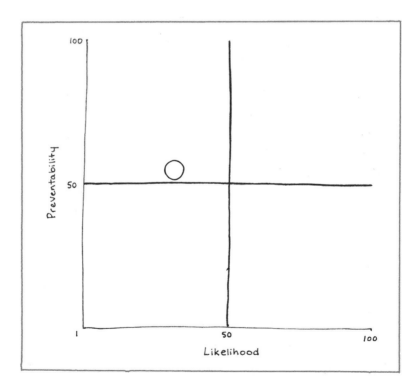

REFERENCES

Carocho, M., Barreiro, M. F., Morales, P., & Ferreira, I. C. F. R. (2014). Adding molecules to food, pros and cons: A review on synthetic and natural food additives. *Comprehensive Review of Food Science and Food Safety, 13*, 377–399.

Center for Food Safety. (2017, May 22). Groups sue FDA to protect food safety. Retrieved from https://www.centerforfoodsafety.org/press-releases/4956/groups-sue-fda-to-protect-food-safety#

McCann, D., Barrett, A., Cooper, A., Crumpler, D., Dalen, L., Grimshaw, K., . . . Stevenson, J. (2007). Food additives and hyperactive behaviour in 3-year-old and 8/9-year-old children in the community: A randomised, double-blinded, placebo-controlled trial. *Lancet, 370*, 1560–1567.

Pew Charitable Trust. (2013). Fixing the oversight of chemicals added to our food. Retrieved from http://pew.org/2yJXHbu

U.S. Food and Drug Administration. (2006). How U.S. FDA's GRAS notification program works. Retrieved from https://www.fda.gov/food/ingredientspackaginglabeling/gras/ucm083022.htm

U.S. Food and Drug Administration. (2010, April). Overview of food ingredients, additives and colors. Retrieved from https://www.fda.gov/food/ingredientspackaginglabeling/foodadditivesingredients/ucm094211.htm

U.S. Food and Drug Administration. (2018, January 24). Questions and answers on the occurrence of benzene in soft drinks and other beverages. Retrieved from https://www.fda.gov/Food/FoodborneIllnessContaminants/ChemicalContaminants/ucm055131.htm#q6

4. FAIR TRADE

There are some commodities, like coffee and chocolate, that most people really like, but only rich people can afford. The vast majority of the world's coffee is consumed by people in affluent countries, but coffee is mostly grown in developing countries, often by people who live in poverty. The traditional political and economic establishments in these countries can work to trap growers and farm workers in poverty and sometimes slavery. Knowing this can make it difficult to fully enjoy a mocha latte while relaxing on a Sunday morning. It would be nice if there was a way to remove that uncomfortable pang of guilt so that we could all go back to relaxing. Fair trade is marketed, sometimes aggressively, as the very solution to this problem.

Fair trade (two words) is a social movement that seeks to combat poverty in developing countries. In the 1980s, the first of a number of labeling initiatives was started to connect socially conscious, affluent consumers with small-scale producers in developing countries. Fairtrade (one word) is the largest of these agencies: its label certifies goods that are produced to a certain standard. In this case the standard guarantees: (1) growers receive a minimum price (the fair-trade price) even when the market is low; (2) growers participate in a democratically governed cooperative; (3) these cooperatives receive a surplus which they decide how to use for their corporate benefit; (4) all producers are small-scale operations; and (5) growers use environmentally friendly farming practices. The idea is that consumers voluntarily pay a higher price (a premium) so that producers can earn a living wage. In practice, the premium can be much higher, but many people are willing to pay it. As far as good intentions go, it's difficult to argue with this scheme. Fair trade, however, remains very controversial. This is primarily because global economies are extremely complicated, and interventions always have unintended consequences.

Several criticisms have been leveled at fair trade. First, fair trade is an inefficient way to fight poverty. Although consumers pay a huge premium, most of that money doesn't make it into the hands of the farmers. In addition, fair trade tends not to benefit the poorest countries, farmers, or members of society. The poorest farmers are not the poorest people in a society, because they still own property. The poorest people are hired laborers, who typically do not enjoy any fair-trade advantages. Certification requires farmers to form a cooperative and pay a fee, which means the poorest farmers cannot participate. The highest rates of fair-trade production are in Mexico and South America, but in general, these countries are much better off than African nations producing the same crops.

But the greatest concerns with fair trade have to do with the economic underpinnings of the system. Fair trade is basically a subsidy, and subsidies can create inappropriate incentives, thereby interfering with regular market dynamics. For example, paying an above-market price can increase overall production, which causes a glut in the market, which lowers the free-market value. Because fair-trade producers are guaranteed a minimum price, this cost is borne by farmers who are not part of the fair-trade label, perhaps because they can't afford to be. It can also cause a quality issue, because not all of the product a farmer produces can be sold as fair trade. If there is a guaranteed minimum price for a percentage of the crop, the rational thing to do is to sell the worst of your crop as fair trade and everything else for the best market value. Finally, there is an ongoing debate about whether, after accounting for the certification fees, fair-trade producers really make a significantly greater profit in the long run (although the reliability of a price floor is inherently valuable).

On balance, it appears that fair trade is good—although it is difficult to know how good—for the farmers who are certified. It isn't the best solution for every community, and it isn't a very good long-term strategy. But fair trade doesn't make up enough of the market to really impact global prices, so it probably doesn't hurt other farmers. In at least some communities, the spillover effect has been shown to be positive. If you buy fair-trade chocolate, it will not (at least in theory) have been harvested by child slaves in West Africa, which is good. However, fair trade is not the only way to identify ethically sourced cocoa, and it may not be the most efficient way to help children in these communities. If you spend your money on fair-trade products, you're probably not getting much bang for your buck in terms of combating poverty, and you're probably not getting the best-quality product, but you're probably not doing any damage either.

SUMMARY

Preventability (73)

There are a lot of fair-trade products available, but you may not be able to afford them.

Likelihood (25)

There is plenty of inequity in global trade, but buying fair trade doesn't do much to combat it. The likelihood of doing any harm by not buying fair-trade-certified products is low.

Consequence (50)

If you don't buy fair-trade products, you might end up eating chocolate (or another product) that was produced with slave labor. That might not be bad for you, but it is certainly bad for them.

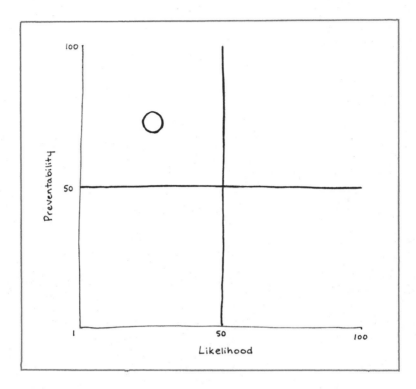

REFERENCES

de Janvry, A., McIntosh, C., & Sadoulet, E. (2015). Fair trade and free entry: Can a disequilibrium market serve as a development tool? *Review of Economic Statistics*, *97*, 567–573.

Dragusanu, R., Giovannucci, D., & Nunn, N. (2014). The economics of fair trade. *Journal of Economic Perspectives*, *28*, 217–236.

Dragusanu, R., & Nunn, N. (2014). The impacts of fair trade certification: Evidence from coffee producers in Costa Rica. Retrieved from http://scholar.harvard.edu/nunn/publications/impacts-fair-trade-certification-evidence-coffee-producers -costa-rica

Mohan, S. (2010). Fair trade without the froth. Institute of Economic Affairs Monographs, Hobart Paper no. 170. Retrieved from https://papers.ssrn.com/abstract= 1721469

Narlikar, A., & Kim, D. (2013, April 4). Unfair trade. *Foreign Affairs*. Retrieved from https://www.foreignaffairs.com/articles/africa/2013-04-04/unfair-trade

5. GLUTEN

Gluten is a combination of two kinds of storage proteins, prolamins and glutenins, found in the seeds of some grasses. In the normal life cycle of the grass, these proteins provide nutrition to the seedling. While that is at least somewhat intrinsically interesting, what makes gluten especially important is that it is found in some of the grasses we like to eat, such as barley, rye, and, most of all, wheat. In fact, gluten proteins constitute about 75% of the protein in wheat flour. When you knead wheat dough, these proteins cross-link to form an elastic network. This helps the dough stick together and gives it structure. Furthermore, when yeast fermentation fills the dough with gas, it stretches and becomes spongy. This is what gives wheat bread its texture. In general, the more gluten there is in the dough, the more chewy and airy the bread will be. Development of gluten is, therefore, a desirable property in bread, and not a desirable property in pastry (which is why you are supposed to avoid working pastry dough too much).

Bread has been popular for a long time. It is famously known as the staff of life, and the word "bread" has become a stand-in for "food." As you would expect from something that has become a dietary staple, most people can eat it without getting sick. But not everyone. In some people, gluten causes an immune reaction that causes inflammation in, and damage to, the small intestine. This can lead to diarrhea and nutrient malabsorption, the classic symptoms of celiac disease (CD). However, some of the symptoms of CD can be extraintestinal, and sometimes CD can be completely asymptomatic. Unfortunately, the absence of symptoms doesn't mean that no damage is being done to the intestines. The side effects of untreated CD include iron and vitamin deficiency, osteoporosis, infertility, and neurological problems. Fortunately, once it is diagnosed, CD can be effectively treated with a strict gluten-free diet.

People with CD have a genetic predisposition to the disorder, but not everyone who is predisposed develops the disease. Therefore, environmental factors are likely also at play. It is estimated that 1% of the U.S. population has CD, but these people are often undiagnosed. Interestingly, for reasons that are unclear, the number of people with CD has been increasing dramatically over the last 50 or so years, making it a public health issue.

There is another category of people for whom gluten might pose a problem: those with so-called non-celiac gluten sensitivity (NCGS). These people do not test positive for CD, but have gastrointestinal complaints that get better on a gluten-free diet. Whether or not NCGS exists is somewhat controversial. But a research group at Monash University in Australia has provided some evidence that (1) NCGS is a real thing, and (2) NCGS might not be caused by gluten. Their study showed that another component of wheat, a fermentable, poorly absorbed, short-chain carbohydrate called fructan, was responsible for their subjects' symptoms. This accounts for the title of their report, "No Effects of Gluten in Patients With Self-Reported Non-Celiac Gluten Sensitivity After Dietary Reduction of Fermentable, Poorly Absorbed, Short-Chain Carbohydrates," which was published in the journal *Gastroenterology*. Other plants also produce these proteins, and a diet low in these sources minimized symptoms. The study was small, but suggests that at least some people with NCGS aren't really sensitive to gluten.

One percent of the population is a fairly sizable group of people with CD, and there are potentially even more people with gluten sensitivity. But the overwhelming majority of the population easily tolerates gluten consumption. Yet many people are choosing to go gluten free anyway. This is partly because gluten has been popularly demonized. Depending on whom you ask, gluten is responsible for a huge range of maladies including acne, Alzheimer's disease, heart disease, and everything else that ails you. In some cases, there is a kernel of truth behind these headlines, but it is usually a much more nuanced issue. Most experts don't believe that a gluten-free diet provides any real health benefits to most people. It is popular to hate gluten, but there isn't a lot of scientific support for it.

Humans have been cultivating wheat and other gluten-containing grasses for thousands of years. This is short in evolutionary time, but long in epidemiological time. It's true that humans did not eat a lot of grains until the advent of agriculture, and that therefore the species did not evolve eating bread. On the other hand, if gluten was responsible for all of our health problems, we likely would have noticed by now. It is certainly true that our modern Western diets include too much refined white flour. But they also include too much sugar, salt, and saturated fat. It seems unfair to blame everything on gluten.

Of course, if you don't want to eat gluten, there is no reason that you need to. A gluten-free diet can be very healthy. But you need to be careful what you use to replace your gluten-full products. White rice is not really better for you than white bread. Thanks to the gluten-free diet craze, there are plenty of gluten-free versions of old standby processed foods such as cookies, crackers, and pasta. These products are not healthy just because they don't have gluten in them. In fact, they are more likely to be high in fat, sugar, and salt than their traditional counterparts (and also more expensive). Gluten-free diets also tend to be low in fiber and some of the vitamins (e.g., folic acid) with which flour is fortified. So, if you're going gluten free for health reasons, you need to be eating beans, lentils, wild rice, unsalted nuts, sweet potatoes, green veggies, and fruits. Actually, that's what we should all be eating anyway, gluten free or not.

SUMMARY

Preventability (100)

There are very few products for which you can't find gluten-free versions, but they'll cost you. Even if you can't find cookies, beans are always an option.

Likelihood (23)

Some people may be gluten sensitive, but if you don't have celiac disease, eating gluten is unlikely to cause you any problems. The bigger issue is that many people who have celiac disease are unaware of it, which can be a problem.

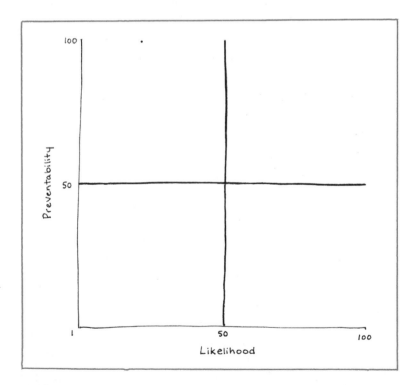

Consequence (1)

If you don't have celiac disease or sensitivity, eating gluten will not hurt you. If you replace gluten-containing foods with a lot of gluten-free processed foods, you may end up doing yourself more harm than good.

REFERENCES

Biesiekierski, J. R., Newnham, E. D., Irving, P. M., Barrett, J. S., Haines, M., Doecke, J. D., . . . Gibson, P. R. (2011). Gluten causes gastrointestinal symptoms in subjects without celiac disease: A double-blind randomized placebo-controlled trial. *American Journal of Gastroenterology, 106*, 508–514; quiz 515.

Biesiekierski, J. R., Peters, S. L., Newnham, E. D., Rosella, O., Muir, J. G., & Gibson, P. R. (2013). No effects of gluten in patients with self-reported non-celiac gluten sensitivity after dietary reduction of fermentable, poorly absorbed, short-chain carbohydrates. *Gastroenterology, 145*, 320–328.

Celiac Disease Foundation. (n.d.). What is celiac disease? Retrieved from https://celiac.org/celiac-disease/understanding-celiac-disease-2/what-is-celiac-disease/

Di Sabatino, A., & Corazza, G. R. (2012). Nonceliac gluten sensitivity: Sense or sensibility? *Annals of Internal Medicine, 156*, 309–311.

Leonard, M. M., Sapone, A., Catassi, C., & Fasano, A. (2017). Celiac disease and nonceliac gluten sensitivity: A review. *JAMA, 318*, 647–656.

Rubio-Tapia, A., Kyle, R. A., Kaplan, E. L., Johnson, D. R., Page, W., Erdtmann, F., . . . Murray, J. A. (2009). Increased prevalence and mortality in undiagnosed celiac disease. *Gastroenterology, 137*, 88–93.

Shewry, P. R., Halford, N. G., Belton, P. S., & Tatham, A. S. (2002). The structure and properties of gluten: An elastic protein from wheat grain. *Philosophical Transactions of the Royal Society B: Biological Sciences, 357*, 133–142.

Vriezinga, S. L., Schweizer, J. J., Koning, F., & Mearin, M. L. (2015). Coeliac disease and gluten-related disorders in childhood. *Nature Reviews: Gastroenterology and Hepatology, 12*, 527.

6. GENETICALLY MODIFIED ORGANISMS

Genetically modified organisms (GMOs) have had their genomes directly altered through biotechnology. Genetic manipulation isn't really a new thing: humans have been using selective breeding to mess around with DNA since the beginning of agriculture. That's just about 15,000 years. It should be self-evident that things like seedless fruit and dachshunds were not delivered to us by nature. Their unique traits give them no evolutionary advantage. However, humans have found some of those maladaptive traits desirable and have nurtured them into existence. We're all used to that, and it isn't the sort of thing we protest unless someone tries to cross a human with a chimpanzee (yes, people have tried that). It's safe to say that on some level we're all okay with genetic manipulation (because grape seeds are the worst).

However, modern genetic engineering techniques introduce a couple of new twists. First, they allow us to edit a single gene at a time. Selective breeding selects for suites of genes because most of the observable characteristics of an organism (its phenotype) are controlled by more than one gene. In addition, biotechnology allows for DNA mixing in organisms that could never sexually reproduce (like spiders and goats). This is the part that tends to freak people out—a lot.

Before we get into that, let's ask why someone would even want to do anything so bizarre. Lots of reasons. For example, most of the insulin sold to diabetics is made by bacteria. Bacteria do not naturally make insulin (they don't have pancreases), but genetically engineered bacteria can. This is huge, because prior to the invention of biosynthetic human insulin in the early 1980s, insulin had to be animal sourced, commonly from pigs. Taking insulin from a pig's pancreas kills the pig. So, from the pig's perspective, genetic engineering provides an alternative that is clearly better.

But the most common application of genetic engineering, and the one that draws the most criticism, is in agricultural crops. Genetic modifications can confer insect and herbicide resistance, higher nutritional content, the ability to withstand drought and freezing, and longer shelf life.

Many different kinds of genetically modified crops have been developed, but Bt corn, soybeans, and cotton are the most widespread. Bt crops have had some genes inserted from the soil bacterium *Bacillus thuringiensis* into their genomes, which is where the name Bt comes from. As a result of this modification, these plants produce some of the insecticidal compounds that are naturally produced by the bacterium, and the insects that would otherwise eat them are destroyed. Farmers no longer have to spray with insecticide (or at least they need far less of it) because the insecticide is built in. Yes, that means people who eat the genetically modified produce are eating the insecticide, and yes, that does sound scary. But keep in mind that many plants, including food crops, already produce insecticides. The war between plants and insects has been going on for a long time. Insecticidal compounds are not necessarily dangerous to humans, because insects are very different from us. It is also worth bearing in mind that Bt is considered to be one of the safest pesticides in the world. If you eat organic produce to avoid GMOs, you are still exposed to a lot of Bt.

Herbicide resistance is another common attribute of genetically modified crops. The idea is that if the food crop is immune to the herbicide, that herbicide can be used as a weed killer. Most genetically modified crops are resistant to glyphosate, commonly known as Roundup.

Proponents say these modifications increase crop yields, decrease pesticide and herbicide use, and contribute to economic stability for farmers and food security for everyone. Critics claim that GMOs have adverse health consequences (e.g., allergies, cancer, digestive issues) for consumers and negative environmental impacts (e.g., effects on nontarget organisms, extinction of original species, and insect and weed resistance).

The anti-GMO movement is, without exaggeration, huge, and it's having a significant impact on public perception. According to a survey by the Pew Research Center, 57% of the general public considers GMO foods generally unsafe to eat. This is especially striking because 88% of AAAS scientists think they are generally safe to eat. In case you're wondering, the AAAS is the American Association for the Advancement of Science, the world's largest general scientific society and the publisher of the highly regarded journal *Science*. A 2012 statement from the AAAS board of directors states that GMOs are not inherently more dangerous than the same foods modified by conventional techniques such as selective breeding. This statement points out that this opinion is shared by the European Union, the World Health Organization (WHO), the American Medical Association, the U.S. National Academy of Sciences, and the British Royal Society. That's a highly credentialed set of sources, and if you believe that science is a fundamentally useful way to know things, then this should ease your mind about GMOs. Genetically modified crops are extensively tested before they are approved for use, and there is no evidence that they are dangerous to the humans or animals that consume them.

But it is difficult to make sweeping generalizations about GMOs because there are many of them, and the number is increasing. In addition, the technologies that are used to create GMOs are changing, and government regulations aren't always keeping up. To examine some of these issues, in 2016 the National Academy of Sciences (NAS) commissioned an expert panel to prepare an extensive review of GMOs. The committee reviewed the scientific literature, listened to the testimony of many speakers, and read hundreds of public comments. They produced a 600-page report that is freely available online and a four-page brief on the topic.

The NAS committee publicized several key findings. First, they found no conclusive evidence that GMOs harm the environment. In fact, there is evidence of environmental benefits in terms of reduced pesticide use and enhanced insect biodiversity. However, the NAS did couch this statement with the caveat that definitive conclusions are difficult to reach because of the complex nature of the problem. They also noted that while there is good evidence that genetically modified crops do legitimately increase yields, the rate at which these increases have developed is not significantly greater than what is expected through conventional breeding strategies. In terms of health, the committee found no evidence that genetically modified foods pose a greater health risk than their conventional counterparts. Again, however, the committee added the caveat that these effects might be very subtle, or they may take a long time to develop. The 1980s might seem like a long time ago, but it may not be long enough to capture all of the long-term effects. The committee found that the impact on social and economic variables was mixed and context dependent. They did stress that while genetic engineering may have a role to play, it would not, in and of itself, ensure future food security. Finally, the committee recognized that both genetic engineering and conventional breeding can result in negative outcomes. Their recommendation, therefore, was that all new plant varieties with potentially hazardous characteristics be subject to safety testing.

This last point about regulation is important, not just because there is little oversight of conventionally bred organisms, but because some of the newer technologies for genetic engineering do not fit into the definitions used by some regulatory agencies.

So the report offers neither a ringing endorsement nor a resounding condemnation for GMOs. All technologies (including fire and the wheel) have the potential for good, bad, and unexpected outcomes.

SUMMARY

Preventability (77)

There are GMO-free versions of many, but by no means all, foods. Of course, even if you go completely GMO free, the environment you live in may still be affected by GMO crops.

Likelihood (13)

The most common GMO crops do not appear to cause health problems, but that doesn't mean there can't be any problems down the line.

Consequence (21)

At present, GMO crops are more likely to have environmental impacts than they are to have individual health impacts.

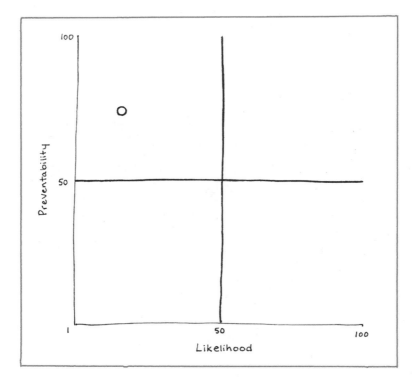

REFERENCES

Funk, C. (2015, January 29). 5 key findings on what Americans and scientists think about science. Pew Research Center. Retrieved from http://www.pewresearch.org/fact-tank/2015/01/29/5-key-findings-science/

National Academies of Sciences, Engineering, and Medicine; Division on Earth and Life Studies; Board on Agriculture and Natural Resources; Committee on Genetically Engineered Crops: Past Experience and Future Prospects. (2016). *Genetically engineered crops: Experiences and prospects.* Washington, DC: National Academies Press.

Servick, K. (2016, May 17). Once again, U.S. expert panel says genetically engineered crops are safe to eat. *Science.* Retrieved from http://www.sciencemag.org/news/2016/05/once-again-us-expert-panel-says-genetically-engineered-crops-are-safe-eat

7. ORGANIC PRODUCE

Organic produce is pricey, and sometimes very pricey. But increasingly, we are buying it. Not surprisingly, we are doing this because we think it is better. Surveys show that when we pay a premium for organically grown produce, we think we are making a choice that is healthier for ourselves and for the environment. This message is heavily reinforced by celebrities, peer pressure, internet consensus, and, of course, advertising. Critics, however, confidently assure us that this is propaganda, and that only suckers pay the extra cost. Nobody wants to be a sucker, but nobody wants to feed their child a pesticide cocktail disguised as an apple either. Unfortunately, a dig into the literature on this topic turns up a contradictory mess.

The idea of organic farming emerged in the early 20th century when some people noticed that the use of synthetic fertilizers was depleting the microbial community of the soil (which is bad). This led to the concept of holistic farming: considering all the parts of the farm as an organism rather than focusing exclusively on crop production. This is where the confusing and unfortunate name "organic" comes from. For those wondering, it is not derived from or related to the chemical definition of "organic" (carbon based). Moreover, the opposite of organic is conventional. There is no such thing as an inorganic carrot. In any case, one of the driving forces behind the organic movement was the idea that natural is better. Over time, nostalgia and anticorporate sentiment have worked their way into the mix.

Consumers started to get on board with this idea, but for a long time it was up to farmers to decide what counted as organic. In 1990, Congress created the National Organic Program, which rolled out standards for organically grown crops in 2000. At present, "organic" is defined as a set of agricultural practices regulated by the government. Any product carrying the U.S. Department of Agriculture (USDA) organic mark should meet the standards outlined by that agency. According to the USDA's website, "organic operations must demonstrate that they are protecting natural resources, conserving biodiversity, and using only approved substances."

That sounds good. But wait, detractors say, not so fast. What are those "approved substances"? Well, the USDA tells us, "the use of most synthetic pesticides and fertilizers" is prohibited. So, here is an important point: contrary to popular belief, the organic mark does not mean that no fertilizers and pesticides have been used. It means that *most synthetic* fertilizers and pesticides have not been used. One of the top reasons consumers give for choosing organic is that they want to reduce their exposure to pesticides, and that is a reasonable goal. Synthetic pesticides have a bad reputation, for good reason. However, their natural counterparts are not necessarily better for you, and in some cases they may be worse. You might love nature, but that doesn't mean that nature loves you. Plants can produce toxins that are inadvisable to eat (hemlock, anyone?). Likewise, it may be inadvisable to distill these toxins down to powder and dust your food crops with them. Rotenone, a pesticide and piscicide (fish killer) naturally found in jicama, among other species, is the example people like to give. Rotenone is naturally derived, but it's also a fairly toxic chemical that has been associated with Parkinson's disease. Notably, it is approved for use in organic farming. Furthermore, the use of synthetic pesticides in the United States is very tightly regulated. The concentrations of these compounds found in the American food supply are far below the levels that would pose a health risk.

And is organic farming really better for the environment? Some say no. One of the biggest issues is crop yield: you can't grow as much food using organic practices. This means you need to devote more land to agriculture—which could lead to deforestation. Not to mention that if all farms used manure as fertilizer, we would need a lot more manure. If we don't have the land for crops, we definitely don't have the land to raise animals, and methane is a greenhouse gas. Many critics say that if everyone converted to organic methods, we wouldn't be able to feed the world's population. Most people will agree that widespread famine is a bad thing.

These critiques are valid, and they bring up some important points that are worth acknowledging. First, we should not conflate "natural" and "healthy." Many times these two categories overlap, but they are not synonymous. Furthermore, using a natural product in a highly unnatural way isn't really natural. For this reason, the organic guidelines may be misguided. Second, the local good and the global good are not always compatible. Organic practices may be best for the ecosystem of any individual farm, but that doesn't mean it will be best for the environment as a whole. Likewise, what is best for an individual consumer is not always best for everyone in the world. If a few people in affluent countries enjoy better health while many people in poorer countries go hungry, it's difficult to call that a positive outcome.

Nevertheless, critics of the organic movement are also painting an incomplete picture. A review by Seufert and Ramankutty (2017) summarizes the potential benefits and costs of organic agriculture. It is a well-balanced review, and worth reading. The authors outline the following points. Organic farming produces lower yields than conventional farming, but the difference is variable: it depends on the crop and on specific management techniques. For some crops, organic management makes more sense than for others. It is clearly better from a biodiversity perspective, but there may be a trade-off between this benefit and crop yields. Organic management does seem to have a positive impact on soil quality. Greenhouse gas emissions are lower per unit area, but higher per unit of production, but again, the magnitude of this effect depends on the crop. A great deal of uncertainty remains about the relative impact of organic farming on water quality as well as the overall quantity of water used. Farmworkers and people who live on and around organic farms are exposed to fewer pesticides, and the higher price of organic produce turns a higher profit for farmers, many of whom live in low-income countries. Unfortunately, that (much) higher price is paid by consumers. In some cases consumers are paying 50% more for organic produce than they would for the conventionally grown equivalent—far more than the 7–8% premium that would be required to compensate for the reduced yield. Consumers who can afford the price are enjoying food with demonstrably reduced pesticide residues and arguably (if marginally) better nutrient profiles. However, at least in high-income countries where pesticide residues are already far below safe thresholds, it's unclear whether this adds up to any real health benefit. The feasibility of scaling up organic agriculture is unclear. The nitrogen (fertilizer) issue is a problem, although the magnitude of the problem is under debate. The overall message is: organic farming has some advantages and some disadvantages, and the balance depends on context. Also, more data are still needed. In any case, it doesn't appear that organic farming is the magic bullet to solve all of our food-related problems.

The USDA organic regulations are not intended to provide safer or healthier options to consumers. Instead, these regulations are designed to provide options that are more natural and have a lower impact on the local environment. No matter what anyone says, there is a good argument for natural practices: they have gone through extensive empirical testing. That does not mean, however, that what worked in the past is going to continue to work forever. If, as a society, we don't want to use pesticides, we might need to think about genetically modified organisms. If we don't want chemical fertilizers, we might need to accept the use of sewage sludge. Both of these practices are prohibited by organic regulations. If you find these things anathema because they are unnatural, remember, there isn't anything particularly natural about farming to begin with. Humans are the only species on earth that engage in agriculture, and we have only been doing it for about 15,000 years. To have a farm at all is a novelty. If you would like to eat organic but can't afford it, you should still eat conventionally grown produce, and you should eat a lot of it. You should believe that it is safe, because studies show that it is. Whatever kind of produce you buy, you should wash it before you eat it. Even if no pesticides were ever used on your food, your fruits and vegetables were grown in dirt, have almost certainly come into contact with something's poop, and have been handled by several sets of hands. *E. coli* is organic, but you don't want to eat it. Finally, this discussion pertains to organic produce only, not to organic meat, eggs, and dairy. There are some good reasons (discussed elsewhere) for going organic for these products.

SUMMARY

Preventability (91)

If you can afford it, you can buy the organic version of almost everything.

Likelihood (3)

You are very unlikely to suffer negative health outcomes from eating conventionally grown produce.

Consequence (2)

Pesticides and fertilizers can have negative consequences for farmers and for the environment, but they are unlikely to affect consumers. In addition, buying organic produce doesn't mean that no pesticides and fertilizers were used in crop production.

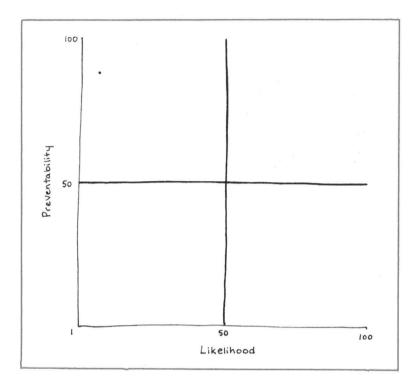

REFERENCES

Betarbet, R., Sherer, T. B., MacKenzie, G., Garcia-Osuna, M., Panov, A. V., & Greenamyre, J. T. (2000). Chronic systemic pesticide exposure reproduces features of Parkinson's disease. *Nature Neuroscience, 3*, 1301.

Brantsæter, A. L., Ydersbond, T. A., Hoppin, J. A., Haugen, M., & Meltzer, H. M. (2017). Organic food in the diet: Exposure and health implications. *Annual Review of Public Health, 38*, 295–313.

Coats, J. R. (1994). Risks from natural versus synthetic insecticides. *Annual Review of Entomology, 39*, 489–515.

Food Safety News. (2016, December 23). Few pesticide worries in latest California sampling data. Retrieved from http://www.foodsafetynews.com/2016/12/no-pesticide-worries-in-latest-california-sampling-data/#.WL-aizsrlvg

Hartmann, M., Frey, B., Mayer, J., Mäder, P., & Widmer, F. (2015). Distinct soil microbial diversity under long-term organic and conventional farming. *ISME Journal, 9*, 1177.

Lotter, D. W. (2003). Organic agriculture. *Journal of Sustainable Agriculture, 21*, 59–128.

Magkos, F., Arvaniti, F., & Zampelas, A. (2006). Organic food: Buying more safety or just peace of mind? A critical review of the literature. *Critical Reviews in Food Science and Nutrition, 46*, 23–56.

Moyer, M. W. (2014, January 28). Organic shmorganic. *Slate*. Retrieved from http://www.slate.com/articles/double_x/the_kids/2014/01/organic_vs_conventional_produce_for_kids_you_don_t_need_to_fear_pesticides.html

Reeser, D. (2013, April 10). Natural versus synthetic chemicals is a gray matter. *Scientific American Blog*. Retrieved from https://blogs.scientificamerican.com/guest-blog/natural-vs-synthetic-chemicals-is-a-gray-matter/

Reganold, J. P., & Wachter, J. M. (2016). Organic agriculture in the twenty-first century. *Nature Plants, 2*, 15221.

Seufert, V., & Ramankutty, N. (2017). Many shades of gray: The context-dependent performance of organic agriculture. *Science Advances, 3*(3), e1602638, doi:10.1126/sciadv.1602638

U.S. Department of Agriculture. (n.d.). Organic standards. Retrieved from https://www.ams.usda.gov/grades-standards/organic-standards

Wilcox, C. (2012, September 24). Are lower pesticide residues a good reason to buy organic? Probably not. *Scientific American Blog*. Retrieved from https://blogs.scientificamerican.com/science-sushi/pesticides-food-fears/

8. PASTEURIZED MILK

To pasteurize milk, you need to heat it to 72 degrees Celsius (161.6 degrees Fahrenheit) and keep it there for at least 15 seconds. It's a mild process because milk doesn't boil until it reaches 212.3 degrees Fahrenheit, about the same as water. This gentle heating is sufficient to dramatically reduce the bacterial load of raw milk. It doesn't make the milk sterile, but if you keep it in the refrigerator it won't spoil for a few weeks. The adoption of milk pasteurization in the United States has led to a dramatic decline in food poisoning. In 1938, milk was estimated to be responsible for up to 25% of all foodborne illness in the U.S. Now it accounts for less than 1%. This is why it is illegal to sell unpasteurized milk in many states and restricted in most others.

Being sick less frequently seems like an unambiguously good thing. However, a small (but growing) number of people still insist on drinking unpasteurized (raw) milk. In fact, they are willing to pay a huge premium and, in some cases, drive to a farm to buy it. Proponents of raw milk claim that heating milk changes its taste and damages its nutritional quality. They further claim that consumption of raw milk is good for asthma, allergies, and digestive health. Sanitation, they say, is key to safety and as long as the milking process is clean, then the milk is not dangerous.

But science is not on their side. Science clearly shows that drinking raw milk is dangerous. Bacteria can get into milk in a number of ways. Contamination can occur if the cow has an infection. For example, milk can become contaminated if the cow has a systemic infection that is circulating in the bloodstream (and thereby gets into the milk), or a local infection of the udder (mastitis). Tests show that this can be the case even in clinically healthy cows. Bacteria can also get into milk if it comes into contact with human skin, like the hands of someone milking the cow. The most likely source of contamination, however, is fecal. If you have ever seen a cow up close, you know that they are not particularly fastidious about their toilet habits. Depending on how close you are, you might also notice that a cow's udders are located underneath(ish) the anus. For this reason, it is very difficult, some say impossible, to eliminate fecal contamination from milk. Good sanitation can certainly help, but it isn't a guarantee. Contamination is a sporadic event, so periodic testing doesn't tell you all that much. A contamination event could happen the day before or the day after testing and it wouldn't be detected.

This type of food poisoning is serious—it goes far beyond a bellyache. Some of the most common milk-borne infections are *Listeria* (which is especially dangerous in pregnant women because it crosses the placenta) and *E. coli*, which can easily put you in the hospital and is sometimes fatal, especially in children. The consequences, therefore, can be devastating.

The purported health benefits of unpasteurized milk are scientifically unsupported. The nutritional profile of pasteurized milk is basically the same as raw milk, and the evidence for specific health benefits is spotty and sometimes contradictory. At present, there is no scientific justification for consuming raw milk. The CDC and the FDA both have web pages with colorful infographics devoted to enlightening people to this fact.

Raw milk does taste different from pasteurized milk. Cheeses made from raw milk are especially prized, and many French cheeses, for example, are not pasteurized (oh the irony; Louis Pasteur was French). If you must have unpasteurized dairy products, then you partake at your own risk. However, the dangers of raw milk products (including cheese and yogurt) are well documented, so it's best not to serve these foods at the kiddie table.

SUMMARY

Preventability (41)

In some states it is legal, if more difficult and expensive, to buy unpasteurized milk. However, in other states it is illegal.

Likelihood (1)

Unless you have a milk allergy or intolerance, it is exceedingly unlikely that you will suffer any adverse health outcomes from drinking pasteurized milk.

Consequence (1)

The consequences of drinking unpasteurized milk are potentially much more severe than those of drinking pasteurized milk.

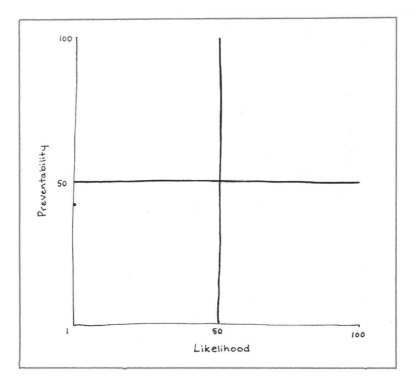

REFERENCES

Centers for Disease Control and Prevention. (2015, March 10). Raw milk. Retrieved from https://www.cdc.gov/foodsafety/rawmilk/raw-milk-index.html

Claeys, W. L., Cardoen, S., Daube, G., De Block, J., Dewettinck, K., Dierick, K., . . . Herman, L. (2013). Raw or heated cow milk consumption: Review of risks and benefits. *Food Control, 31*, 251–262.

Lucey, J. A. (2015). Raw milk consumption. *Nutrition Today, 50*, 189–193.

Macdonald, L. E., Brett, J., Kelton, D., Majowicz, S. E., Snedeker, K., & Sargeant, J. M. (2011). A systematic review and meta-analysis of the effects of pasteurization on milk vitamins, and evidence for raw milk consumption and other health-related outcomes. *Journal of Food Protection, 74*, 1814–1832.

Verraes, C., Vlaemynck, G., Van Weyenberg, S., De Zutter, L., Daube, G., Sindic, M., Uyttendaele, M., & Herman, L. (2015). A review of the microbiological hazards of dairy products made from raw milk. *International Dairy Journal, 50*, 32–44.

9. SALT

In chemistry, a salt is a compound that is formed when you neutralize a negatively charged molecule (an acid) with a positively charged molecule (a base). Examples include potassium chloride, which is used in fertilizer; magnesium sulfate, which is used to soothe sore muscles; and sodium cyanide, which is a rapidly acting poison. However, when most of us talk about salt we're referring to a particular compound—sodium chloride.

Sodium chloride is found in seawater, in crystal deposits, and in your salt shaker. Table salt, kosher salt, fleur de sel, and Himalayan pink salt are all primarily sodium chloride. Salt is useful for all sorts of things. It is a good cleaner, de-ices sidewalks and roadways, raises the boiling point of water, puts out fires, soothes a sore throat, and preserves food in the absence of refrigeration. Oh, and it enhances the flavor of food.

Salt boosts flavors because you have specialized cells in your mouth that respond to sodium. Along with sweet, sour, bitter, and savory (umami), salty is one of the five basic qualities of taste. A little bit of salt tastes good, and it makes other things, even sweet things, taste better. You may have special sodium detectors on your tongue because, physiologically speaking, sodium is very important to you. It is, in fact, very important to all animals, possibly because it is a major component of seawater.

Sodium, chloride, and potassium are the electrolytes primarily involved in the cellular resting membrane potential. The resting membrane potential is the result of different concentrations of these charged particles on the inside and the outside of the cell; sodium and chloride are relatively abundant in the extracellular space whereas potassium is relatively abundant in the intracellular space. These concentration differences lead to the inside of the cell having a negative charge with respect to the outside. This is important for nervous, muscular, and cardiovascular function. A full discussion of the membrane potential and how it works is beyond the scope of this chapter, but suffice it to say, it is very, very important, and the body spends a lot of energy maintaining it. Because sodium is abundant in the extracellular space (outside cells), it is very important in determining blood pressure and volume. As a result, the body tightly regulates sodium concentrations via the kidneys.

So, you need to eat some salt. According to the U.S. Institute of Medicine (IOM), if you are a moderately active adult, you need to consume about 1.5 grams of sodium every day. This will compensate for the salt you lose through sweat and elimination. The good news is, basically everyone is eating enough salt. The bad news is, we're actually eating way more than enough. According to the Centers for Disease Control and Prevention, Americans eat 3.4 grams of sodium per day.

Our level of salt intake is a problem because excessive salt is probably bad for our health. This is not news. Americans have been hearing, and ignoring, the warning that salt causes hypertension (high blood pressure) and cardiovascular disease for decades. The newsier part of this is the "probably." For many years, the public health mantra has been that we should get our sodium intake down to 1.5–2.3 grams per day. This recommendation is based on a great deal of research showing a positive relationship between higher levels of sodium consumption and hypertension and cardiovascular disease. But the real health benefits of cutting back on salt are difficult to measure, partly because individuals respond differently to sodium. Salt sensitivity varies between people, which is to say that some people will see a greater difference in blood pressure in response to sodium intake than others. This variability is attributable to a number of different factors including genetics, environment, and sex. What's more, the evidence for the current sodium recommendations is somewhat sparse. A 2013 report by the IOM ("Sodium intake in populations: Assessment of evidence") found that while the effort to lower excessive sodium intake was appropriate, the evidence did not support lowering the recommended daily intake to 1.5 grams per day. They further commented that it would be difficult to make recommendations about a target sodium intake range for the general population. In addition, while most studies support the relationship between elevated sodium consumption and adverse cardiovascular events, some studies conflict. Notably, a large international study published in the *New England Journal of Medicine* in 2014 ("Urinary Sodium and Potassium Excretion, Mortality, and Cardiovascular Events") found the lowest risk of death and cardiovascular events for a consumption level of between 3 and 6 grams of sodium per day. People consuming more or less than that amount increased their overall risk. Nevertheless, most health agencies (for example, the National Heart Association and the CDC) maintain that the totality of the evidence favors a reduction in salt.

It probably won't hurt you, and will likely help you, to cut back on your dietary salt. If you're looking to reduce your sodium intake, you're going to need to pay attention to labels, because salt can be found in some surprising places. Most of the salt in our diets doesn't come from the salt shaker; it comes from processed foods. Bread, cereal, condiments, canned goods, lunch meats, and cheese are all high in salt. A sandwich can be a serious salt bomb. The good news/bad news on that front is that it is a good idea to cut back on processed foods anyway. Eating more fresh vegetables, beans, and (unsalted) nuts is likely to do you good on a number of fronts.

On a side note, potassium intake is also related to hypertension—but unlike sodium, it is inversely related. Good news! Those low-sodium fruits and veggies are often high in potassium.

SUMMARY

Preventability (63)

You can make a conscious effort to reduce your salt intake, but it is a very common food additive.

Likelihood (51)

The weight of the evidence suggests that consuming excess salt is likely to have adverse health effects.

Consequence (60)

High blood pressure is a serious risk factor for cardiovascular disease. It is common, but not trivial.

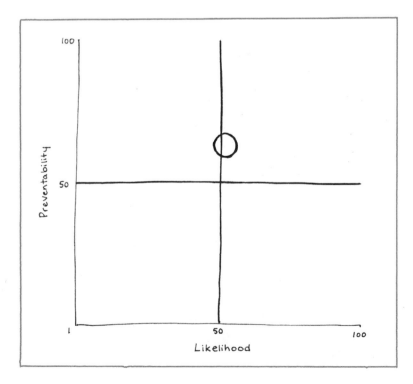

REFERENCES

Aaron, K. J., & Sanders, P. W. (2013). Role of dietary salt and potassium intake in cardiovascular health and disease: A review of the evidence. *Mayo Clinic Proceedings*, *88*, 987–995.

American Heart Association. (2017, April 21). Sodium and salt. Retrieved from http://www.heart.org/HEARTORG/HealthyLiving/HealthyEating/Nutrition/Sodium-and-Salt_UCM_303290_Article.jsp#.WZpsblGGPZv

Centers for Disease Control and Prevention. (2017, October 18). Sodium and the National Academies of Science (NAS) Health and Medical Division (HMD). Retrieved from https://www.cdc.gov/salt/sodium_iom.htm

Institute of Medicine. (2013). *Sodium intake in populations: Assessment of evidence*. Washington, DC: National Academies Press. Retrieved from https://www.nap.edu/read/18311/chapter/2

National Institutes of Health. (2010, February 12). Salt taste cells identified. Retrieved from https://www.nih.gov/news-events/nih-research-matters/salt-taste-cells-identified

O'Donnell, M., Mente, A., Rangarajan, S., McQueen, M. J., Wang, X., Liu, L., . . . Yusuf, S.; PURE Investigators. (2014). Urinary sodium and potassium excretion, mortality, and cardiovascular events. *New England Journal of Medicine*, *371*, 612–623.

Oh, Y. S., Appel, L. J., Galis, Z. S., Hafler, D. A., He, J., Hernandez, A. L., . . . Harrison, D. G. (2016). National Heart, Lung, and Blood Institute Working Group report on salt in human health and sickness: Building on the current scientific evidence. *Hypertension*, *68*, 281–288.

Wenner, M. (2011, July 8). It's time to end the war on salt. *Scientific American*. Retrieved from https://www.scientificamerican.com/article/its-time-to-end-the-war-on-salt/

Whoriskey, P. (2015, April 6). Is the American diet too salty? Scientists challenge the longstanding government warning. *Washington Post*. Retrieved from https://www.washingtonpost.com/news/wonk/wp/2015/04/06/more-scientists-doubt-salt-is-as-bad-for-you-as-the-government-says/?utm_term=.960d2ce4e4b3

10. SUGAR

To a chemist, sugars are rings of carbon atoms decorated with hydrogens and oxygens, sometimes chained together into strings. In other words, they are carbohydrates. Sugars can be simple or complex, depending on how many rings are strung together. Simple sugars have just one ring and are called monosaccharides. Likewise, if two monosaccharides are strung together you get a disaccharide, and if you add any more than that you just call it a polysaccharide.

Sugars taste sweet, and we like to eat them. This is likely because sugars are extremely important biomolecules. Notably, glucose, a monosaccharide, is the human body's primary source of energy. It is circulated throughout the body in the bloodstream and is particularly important for the brain, which demands glucose as its exclusive fuel. Sugars serve critical functions elsewhere in the body as well. Most other organisms also rely heavily on sugars. For example, the disaccharides starch and cellulose are used by plants to store energy and provide structure, respectively. Historically, humans had to either make sugars themselves or ingest them from plants. Sucrose, a disaccharide consisting of a glucose and another monosaccharide, fructose, is found in many plant sources, especially fruits. One plant that is particularly high in sucrose is sugarcane.

Sometime in the distant, murky past of civilization, someone in

India figured out how to refine sucrose crystals from sugarcane. This new product (and technology) gradually spread around the world, reaching Europe during the medieval period. Everyone, everywhere, liked sugar, just as we do now. So there was clearly a demand. But extracting sucrose from sugarcane was difficult and expensive. Unfortunately, it wasn't until the mid-18th century that anyone realized you could get the same product from a humble beet. And in pursuit of that valuable market share, Europeans began cultivating sugarcane in the New World on huge plantations made possible by slave labor. This made sugar more broadly accessible, and sugar transitioned from an exotic spice to a household staple. It's not exactly a sweet legacy, to put it mildly.

In modern Western society, refined sugar is a ubiquitous ingredient. It is still derived from sugarcane, but also from beets and corn. It is no longer expensive, and it still tastes great. It is a prime ingredient in all manner of desserts, sauces, condiments, and, of course, sugary drinks. Sugars included in prepared food are called added sugar. We eat a lot of added sugar. Way, way too much.

There is some debate about how bad for us sugar really is, but everyone agrees it's bad. Sugar consumption is linked to tooth decay, obesity, type 2 diabetes, and heart disease. These conditions lead to risk factors for other diseases, like cancer and blindness.

So how did something that is vital to life turn into something that is making us flabby and slowly killing us? Sucrose is naturally found in fruit, and fruit almost always gets a nutritional thumbs up. The problem arises when you remove the sugar from the fruit and consume it in a different context. In addition to sugars, fruit is full of fiber and other vitamins and beneficial compounds. This is important in at least two ways. First, fiber slows down absorption of sugar. Second, it limits the amount of sugar you can eat in one sitting without getting full or experiencing gastrointestinal distress. In contrast, a can of soda has no fiber, no protein, no vitamins, and can contain up to 12 teaspoons of sugar, which causes a huge spike in blood sugar. Sugary drinks are especially problematic because, in addition to having high caloric loads, the body doesn't register those calories in the same way as it does with food. The same number of calories is not equally satiating, and therefore it is very easy to consume a lot of calories without even realizing it. Humans evolved in an environment where calories were scarce, and therefore our bodies store them rather than eliminate them when we overconsume.

One of the more common added sugars, high-fructose corn syrup, may be extra bad for us. This is because, as the name implies, this sugar has a slightly higher ratio of fructose to glucose than table sugar. Unlike glucose, fructose has to be metabolized by the liver before it can be used by the body. Some of the by-products of fructose metabolism are undesirable, like triglycerides—fats that are associated with heart disease. This is somewhat controversial, but regardless, most of us need to cut back on the refined sugar that we eat (and drink). This includes natural sweeteners like evaporated cane juice, honey, agave nectar, and maple syrup.

As it happens, sugars are not the only compounds that taste sweet. Some sweet-tasting compounds like ethylene glycol and lead acetate are incredibly poisonous, but others are innocuous. This latter category is appealing to people looking to reduce their sugar intake. Aspartame, saccharin, stevia, and sucralose are examples of nonnutritive sweeteners. They are sweet, much sweeter than sugar, but they usually don't taste quite the same. Nevertheless, they can make a passable substitute and have become very popular among the calorie conscious. Unfortunately, they don't appear to have any positive impacts in terms of body mass index or cardiovascular health. On the contrary, they are sometimes associated with increased weight gain, high blood pressure, diabetes, and cardiovascular problems. That sort of defeats the point, so at present there does not appear to be a good alternative to curbing the sweet tooth, except in the case of tooth decay. Sugar-free gum is unambiguously better for your teeth than sugar gum, as it even helps to prevent cavities.

The easiest way to reduce your added sugar consumption is to stop drinking sweet beverages such as sodas, blended coffee, energy drinks, powdered drink mixes, and even fruit juice. The next categories to tackle are candy, desserts, and processed foods. For healthy people, whole fruits are a healthy food. However, not all fruits are created equal, and some will have more sugar than others.

Sugar isn't really bad for you, per se. It's the quantity that's important. It's okay to indulge in sugar as an occasional treat—as long as you don't define occasional as several times every day.

SUMMARY

Preventability (77)

Sugar is in most processed foods. You can cut back, but it is hard to cut it out completely.

Likelihood (75)

Eating too much sugar is very likely to damage your health.

Consequence (65)

Obesity, heart disease, diabetes, and tooth decay are all quite common. They can also be quite serious.

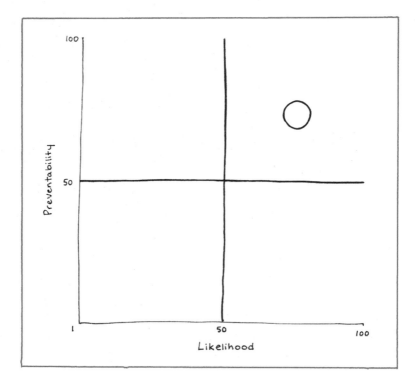

REFERENCES

Azad, M. B., Abou-Setta, A. M., Chauhan, B. F., Rabbani, R., Lys, J., Copstein, L., . . . Zarychanski, R. (2017). Nonnutritive sweeteners and cardiometabolic health: A systematic review and meta-analysis of randomized controlled trials and prospective cohort studies. *Canadian Medical Association Journal, 189,* E929–E939.

Centers for Disease Control and Prevention. (2016, September 27). Know your limit for added sugars. Retrieved from https://www.cdc.gov/nutrition/data-statistics/know -your-limit-for-added-sugars.html

Corliss, J. (2016, November 30). Eating too much added sugar increases the risk of dying with heart disease. *Harvard Health Blog.* Retrieved from https://www.health.harvard. edu/blog/eating-too-much-added-sugar-increases-the-risk-of-dying-with-heart -disease-201402067021

Lustig, R. H. (2013). Fructose: It's "alcohol without the buzz." *Advances in Nutrition, 4,* 226–235.

Mintz, S. (1985). *Sweetness and power: The place of sugar in modern history.* New York: Viking.

Mouth Healthy. (n.d.). Chewing gum to prevent cavities. Retrieved from http://www .mouthhealthy.org/en/az-topics/c/chewing-gum

Rippe, J. M., & Angelopoulos, T. J. (2015). Fructose-containing sugars and cardiovascular disease. *Advances in Nutrition, 6,* 430–439.

11. TEFLON

Teflon is one of those brand names, like Xerox and Kleenex, that has become emblematic of a whole category of things. Teflon represents a nonstick coating known as polytetrafluorethylene, or PTFE, which was invented accidentally in 1938 by Roy Plunkett, a chemist working on refrigerants for the DuPont Company. Analysis of PTFE showed that it was heat resistant, chemically inert, and really slippery. DuPont called it Teflon, but PTFE is now made by many different manufacturers.

PTFE's qualities make it very useful for nonstick cookware, which is the application familiar to most people. However, it is used in many other products. For example, PTFE is widely used in the electronic, automotive, construction, aerospace, and medical industries. It is also used in waterproof clothing (Gore-Tex), ski wax, and stain-resistant carpets and upholstery. An early use of PTFE was in the Manhattan Project, where it served as a corrosion-resistant insulator for pipes and valves. PTFE is so commonplace that it has become a political slur (first applied to President Ronald Reagan).

Recently, PTFE has acquired a bad reputation, especially when it comes to nonstick pans. Reports have circulated that PTFE-coated pans leach carcinogenic chemicals into food as it cooks. The chemicals in question are polyfluoroalkyl substances

(PFAs), sometimes also known as polyfluorinated compounds (PFCs). Specifically, PTFE has historically been made with PFOA (perfluorooctanoic acid, also known as C8). There are some very good reasons to be concerned about PFAs in general and PFOA in particular, but the nonstick pan issue is a bit of a red herring. First, while PFOA is part of PTFE synthesis, it is almost entirely burned off in the process. PTFE is inert, and also heat stable up to about 500°F, which is why it is such an attractive material in the first place. PTFE is not suspected of being carcinogenic, and when used as recommended, nonstick cookware is considered safe. That being said, you really need to use it as recommended, which means never heating nonstick cookware up to 500°F. When PTFE gets too hot, it starts to degrade and release noxious vapors that will kill your pet bird and give you something called Teflon flu (or polymer flu, to be more equitable about it). For the most part, stovetop cooking won't take you over the 500°F limit, but you should never leave an empty pan on a hot burner. But just because nonstick pans are considered safe doesn't mean that PFAs aren't a problem—it just means that cookware isn't the major route of exposure. In addition to being used to manufacture PTFE and other polymers, PFAs are used in a variety of applications where water and oil resistance are desired, for example, cleaners, textiles, paint, fire-fighting foam, wire insulation, cosmetics, and food packaging.

There are literally thousands of different kinds of PFAs, and many of them are persistent organic pollutants. This means that they don't break down easily, they have negative health effects in humans and other animals, and they bioaccumulate. PFAs have been manufactured since the 1940s, and they are now ubiquitous in the environment (even in the Arctic) and are present in basically everyone's blood. This is somewhat distressing because some studies have linked PFAs to cancer and a number of other health problems including low birth weight, thyroid disease, and high cholesterol. The two PFAs that have received the most attention are PFOA and PFOS (perfluorooctane sulfonate, an ingredient in Scotchgard, among other things). Both of these chemicals belong to the category of long-chain PFAs, so called because they have more carbons as part of their chemical structure. Recognizing the potential health problems associated with these chemicals, U.S. manufacturers worked with the EPA to phase out production of these and other long-chain PFAs by 2015, although they are still manufactured overseas. Neither Teflon nor Scotchgard is currently made with long-chain PFAs. But imported goods may still contain these chemicals, and most of us will have legacy products in our homes.

If products like Teflon and Scotchgard are no longer made with long-chain PFAs, you might wonder what they are made with. The answer is, short-chain PFAs. These chemicals are very similar to their longer cousins, which is why they can serve as substitutes. They are, at least in theory, less toxic, have shorter half-lives, and are less bioaccumulative. However, some preliminary studies have raised red flags suggesting that there are still environmental and health concerns related to short-chain PFAs. These studies are preliminary, but this is in itself a point of concern. These chemicals are being widely used for industrial and consumer applications, but their safety has not been fully characterized.

It makes sense to try to limit your exposure to PFAs, but this is very difficult to do. PFAs are in places you wouldn't expect. For example, a study in 2017 found that PFAs were common in fast-food packaging (even otherwise healthy(ish) fast food), particularly in the food contact paper. This was the case even when the fast-food companies believed their packaging materials were PFA free. Even if you never eat take-out pizza or microwave popcorn, you still have to live on the same planet as the rest of us. According to the EPA, PFAs really get around in the air. People can be exposed to PFAs manufactured thousands of miles away. According to the American Cancer Society, "Because the routes by which people may be exposed to PFOA are not known, it is unclear what steps people might take to reduce their exposure."

You can buy water filters that will reduce the concentrations of long-chain PFAs, and if you have reason to believe your water supply is highly contaminated, this is probably a good idea. You can also reduce your exposure by not purchasing stain- or water-resistant products and abstaining from fast food.

SUMMARY

Preventability (15)

It is easy, if inconvenient, to avoid nonstick cookware. But PFOA in particular was used in many different applications, and PFAs as a category are very difficult to avoid.

Likelihood (23)

Studies that have linked PFAs to health problems have done so in populations with high occupational or environmental exposure. Even in these situations the increased risk was small. It's difficult to say what the likelihood of an adverse event is for more typical levels of exposure.

Consequence (70)

Some studies have connected exposure to some PFAs with testicular, kidney, thyroid, prostate, bladder, and ovarian cancer.

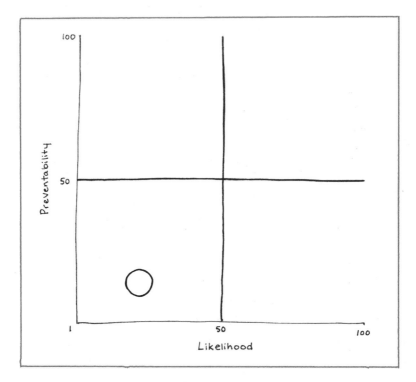

REFERENCES

Birnbaum, L. S., & Grandjean, P. (2015). Alternatives to PFASs: Perspectives on the science. *Environmental Health Perspectives, 123*, A104–A105. Retrieved from https://ehp.niehs.nih.gov/1509944/

Blum, A., Balan, S. A., Scheringer, M., Trier, X., Goldenman, G., Cousins, I. T., . . . Weber, R. (2015). The Madrid Statement on poly- and perfluoroalkyl substances (PFASs). *Environmental Health Perspectives, 123*, A107–A111.

Conder, J. M., Hoke, R. A., de Wolf, W., Russell, M. H., & Buck, R. C. (2008). Are PFCAs bioaccumulative? A critical review and comparison with regulatory criteria and persistent lipophilic compounds. *Environmental Science and Technology, 42*, 995–1003.

Lindstrom, A. B., Strynar, M. J., & Libelo, E. L. (2011). Polyfluorinated compounds: Past, present, and future. *Environmental Science and Technology, 45*, 7954–7961.

Naftalovich, R., Naftalovich, D., & Greenway, F. L. (2016). Polytetrafluoroethylene ingestion as a way to increase food volume and hence satiety without increasing calorie content. *Journal of Diabetes Science and Technology, 10*, 971–976.

Schaider, L. A., Balan, S. A., Blum, A., Andrews, D. Q., Strynar, M. J., Dickinson, M.

E., . . . Peaslee, G. F. (2017). Fluorinated compounds in U.S. fast food packaging. *Environmental Science and Technology Letters, 4,* 105–111.

Science History Institute. (2017, December 14). Roy J. Plunkett. Retrieved from https://www.chemheritage.org/historical-profile/roy-j-plunkett

U.S. Environmental Protection Agency. (2017, July 25). Basic information about per- and polyfluoroalkyl substances (PFASs). Retrieved from https://www.epa.gov/pfas/basic-information-about-and-polyfluoroalkyl-substances-pfass

12. ALCOHOL

Colloquially, when people talk about alcohol they are referring to ethanol, which is what is found in alcoholic beverages. Chemically speaking, ethanol is only one member of a large family of compounds known as alcohols. You are probably familiar with some of the other family members, such as isopropyl alcohol, also known as rubbing alcohol, or ethylene glycol, which is commonly used in antifreeze. But as useful as these other compounds are, ethanol's combination of disinfectant, psychoactive, and nontoxic properties have made it humanity's longtime favorite. It is the only kind of alcohol that you should consider imbibing, and you should consider it carefully.

Ethanol is the by-product of the fermentation of sugar by yeast. Humans have been taking advantage of this process to make alcoholic beverages since time immemorial. Alcohol has been used medicinally, ritually, and recreationally for thousands of years. It continues to play a social role in many cultures worldwide and is a huge global industry. But for as much as we like it, humanity's relationship with alcohol has been fraught with struggle, and alcohol consumption has a very dark side.

As a drug, alcohol has system-wide effects on the body. Notably, it reduces inhibition and increases sociability, impacts judgment, impairs motor function, increases reaction time, acts as a diuretic, and dilates blood vessels. In high doses it can cause vomiting, dizziness, unconsciousness, amnesia, respiratory depression, and decreased heart rate. Acute alcohol poisoning can be fatal. It is, in fact, fatal for about six Americans every day. Of course, alcohol is also addictive and is the most commonly abused substance in the United States.

Heavy alcohol use taxes the liver, and cirrhosis is a common and well-known side effect. Wernicke-Korsakoff syndrome is a less well-known but equally serious condition that is secondary to chronic alcoholism. This disorder, which is a type of dementia, is the result of thiamin deficiency. Alcohol interferes with the body's ability to absorb B vitamins, such as thiamin and folate. Malabsorption of folate may partially account for another of alcohol's adverse side effects—increased cancer risk. Alcohol consumption increases the risk of a number of cancers including breast, colon, rectum, liver, mouth, esophagus, and larynx.

In addition to these direct physiological effects, alcohol is associated with a range of negative social outcomes. Domestic violence, child abuse, sexual assault, and accidents, especially motor vehicle accidents, are all made more likely by alcohol. Pretty much any way you look at it, the world would be a safer place without alcohol.

Even so, as a species, humans are very unlikely to give up alcohol. And at this point, you might be mentally protesting that some positive health outcomes are associated with moderate alcohol use. Everyone has heard somewhere that drinking a glass of red wine is good for the heart. It's true that alcohol may have protective benefits against stroke, diabetes, and coronary heart disease. Some studies have shown that moderate drinkers have a reduced mortality risk compared to both heavy drinkers and abstainers. Unfortunately, reanalysis of some of these studies has shown that when other factors are accounted for, moderate drinkers really don't have any mortality advantage. Furthermore, the risks associated with alcohol consumption are so great that they outweigh any potential cardiovascular benefits. This being the case, no one is recommending that anyone start drinking alcohol for health reasons. If you have safe drinking water available, there really aren't a lot of medically sound reasons to drink alcoholic beverages. The only reason to drink alcohol is because you enjoy it. But drinking isn't really going to be fun if it kills you, so you should drink in moderation.

You might think you're a moderate drinker, but are you? The recommendation for moderate alcohol consumption is one standard drink a day for a woman and two drinks a day for a man younger than 65. If you're a man older than 65, you also only get one drink a day. This doesn't seem fair, but physiology isn't fair. Women and men metabolize alcohol differently because of different body composition; this is the same for older people as compared to younger people. And back to that idea of a standard drink. One drink is 12 ounces of 5% alcohol by volume (ABV) beer, 5 ounces of wine, or 1.5 ounces of liquor. If you drink a pint of craft beer with 7% ABV, you are having more than one drink. If you are a woman and drink four or more drinks in two hours, or if you are a man and drink five or more drinks in the same amount of time, you are binge drinking.

Of course, there are some times in life when you should abstain completely. There are some medications, painkillers and allergy pills for example, that do not mix well with alcohol. If you're taking any medications—prescription, over-the-counter drugs, or herbal—ask your doctor before you imbibe. Another time to teetotal is during pregnancy. This has been standard medical advice for many years, but recently women have been feeling a bit more relaxed about having one glass of wine. It is understandable to want to relax with a buttery chardonnay, but it's probably not a great idea. The official medical line is, "there is no known safe amount of alcohol during pregnancy." That doesn't mean there isn't a safe amount, but we don't know what it is, and it would be unethical to run a clinical trial to find out. That is because it is well known that alcohol can have profound, life-long consequences for an unborn child, including fetal alcohol syndrome. In addition, pregnancy isn't a static condition but a complicated process. There may be some times during gestation that alcohol will be more likely to do damage to the fetus than at other times. It probably isn't worth the risk. Reference the above comment about the general unfairness of physiology. Once that baby is born, he or she should also refrain from drinking alcohol until adulthood. Teenagers may have already achieved their adult height, but they have not yet achieved their adult brains. Drinking during this period of life can have permanent negative impacts on cognitive function.

If you enjoy wine tasting or martinis or craft beers, all of the above can seem like a downer. Life can be that way. In the end, you have to define your own priorities for your life and balance health concerns with life's pleasure. Cheers.

SUMMARY

Preventability (85)

Unless you already have an alcohol dependency, you can choose whether you want to imbibe and how much. So the preventability score is high. On the other hand, you can't control whether other people drink, and other people's drinking habits can have profound effects on your life, so preventability isn't perfect.

Likelihood (65)

Many people enjoy the occasional drink without a problem, but the incidence of alcohol-related trouble is quite high.

Consequence (90)

The consequences of excessive alcohol consumption range from a bad headache, to liver damage, to domestic violence, to death. The potential negative outcomes are so many and so severe that the consequence score is high.

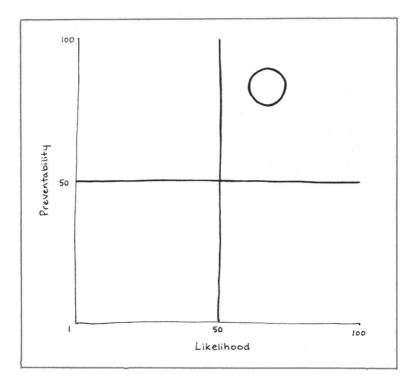

REFERENCES

Centers for Disease Control and Prevention. (2015, January). Alcohol poisoning deaths. Retrieved from https://www.cdc.gov/vitalsigns/alcohol-poisoning-deaths/index.html

Centers for Disease Control and Prevention. (2017, June 8). Alcohol and public health: Frequently asked questions. Retrieved from https://www.cdc.gov/alcohol/faqs.htm

Fernández-Solà, J. (2015). Cardiovascular risks and benefits of moderate and heavy alcohol consumption. *Nature Reviews, Cardiology, 12*, 576.

Hiller-Sturmhöfel, S., & Swartzwelder, H. S. (2003). Alcohol's effects on the adolescent brain—what can be learned from animal models. National Institute on Alcohol Abuse and Alcoholism. Retrieved from https://pubs.niaaa.nih.gov/publications/arh284/213-221.htm

Jayasekara, H., English, D. R., Room, R., & MacInnis, R. J. (2014). Alcohol consumption over time and risk of death: A systematic review and meta-analysis. *American Journal of Epidemiology, 179*, 1049–1059.

MedlinePlus. (2018, February 6). Alcohol. Retrieved from https://medlineplus.gov/alcohol.html

National Council on Alcoholism and Drug Dependence. (n.d.). Facts about alcohol. Retrieved from https://www.ncadd.org/about-addiction/alcohol/facts-about-alcohol

National Institute on Alcohol Abuse and Alcoholism. (n.d.). Drinking levels defined. Retrieved from https://www.niaaa.nih.gov/alcohol-health/overview-alco hol-consumption/moderate-binge-drinking

National Institute on Alcohol Abuse and Alcoholism. (n.d.). What is a standard drink? Retrieved from https://www.niaaa.nih.gov/alcohol-health/overview-alco hol-consumption/what-standard-drink

NIH MedlinePlus. (2016). Alcohol, medicines and aging. Retrieved from https://med lineplus.gov/magazine/issues/summer16/articles/summer16pg5.html

Stockwell, T., Zhao, J., Panwar, S., Roemer, A., Naimi, T., & Chikritzhs, T. (2016). Do "moderate" drinkers have reduced mortality risk? A systematic review and meta-analysis of alcohol consumption and all-cause mortality. *Journal of Studies on Alcohol and Drugs, 77*, 185–198.

World Health Organization. (2006). Child maltreatment and alcohol. Retrieved from http://www.who.int/violence_injury_prevention/violence/world_report/factsheets/ fs_child.pdf

World Health Organization. (n.d.). Intimate partner violence and alcohol fact sheet. Retrieved from http://www.who.int/violence_injury_prevention/violence/world_ report/factsheets/ft_intimate.pdf

13. MEAT

Consuming the flesh of other animals has arguably been important to human evolution. About 2.5 million years ago, hominins started eating larger quantities of meat and marrow. Initially they used their tools to slice the meat into small, chewable pieces. At some point, they also learned to cook their meat, making it softer and easier to digest. Over time, this led to the evolution of smaller teeth and jaws and a smaller gut. Animal proteins are also calorie dense, protein rich, and chock-full of micronutrients. When your main occupation is finding food, these are all positive qualities, and this is likely why meat tastes good. Our very early ancestors probably scavenged their meat, but humans later domesticated animals that they used for milk and eggs, and occasionally butchered for meat. Today, the meat industry is huge. Although meat is popular all over the world, Americans in particular are big consumers, eating an estimated three times more meat than the global average. As a group, Americans eat more than enough meat. In some cases, we may, in fact, be eating a lethal dose of meat. Too much red meat increases the rate of all-cause mortality.

For the generations of people who were brought up to think of meat as a health food, this is a bit surprising. Doesn't meat help you to grow up big and strong? What about all of those proteins and micronutrients that prompted our ancestors to start eating dead things in the first place? So yes, meat is a good source of some dietary requirements. Animal proteins, unlike most plant proteins, are complete. That means that they contain all of the amino acids that you need to consume all in one place. Meat is also high in iron, zinc, and some vitamins. Notably, vitamin B_{12} is found only in animal products (including milk and eggs), and vegans need to take B_{12} supplements. Eating some meat can be healthy; we run into trouble with the quantity, the type, and the way we cook our meat.

Fundamentally, there is a difference between eating the meat of mammals and eating the meat of other animals like fish and birds. The muscles of all mammals are called red meat. We also need to distinguish between processed meat and unprocessed meat. Meat processing includes salting, smoking, canning, and fermenting. Basically, anything beyond grinding or pounding is considered processing. Examples of processed meats are ham, bacon, smoked turkey, hot dogs, and beef jerky.

Processed meat is classified as a known human carcinogen by the International Agency for Research on Cancer (IARC), a part of the World Health Organization (WHO). This means that there is sufficient evidence from scientific studies in humans to conclude that eating processed meats causes cancer. Specifically, it causes colorectal cancer and may cause stomach cancer. There are hypotheses for why this is the case. For example, the addition of nitrates may be a factor. But there is no conclusive evidence yet. There are, of course, different ways of processing meat, and it is possible that some of these methods are safer than others. But this has not yet been determined. Eating processed meat, even a large quantity, does not increase cancer risk by that much (the relative risk is 1.18), but it isn't negligible. So far, the WHO has not offered any guidance about how much processed meat is safe to eat, if indeed there is a safe amount.

In addition, the IARC has classified red meat as a potential human carcinogen. The data about the cancer-causing effects of red meat are not conclusive, but they are suggestive. Again, the cancer of concern is colorectal cancer, and there are no specific guidelines about how much is safe to eat. One additional note about red meat: it may matter how you cook it. Cooking over high heat, as on a grill or in a frying pan, may create more carcinogenic compounds than cooking low and slow. It is not clear, however, whether this makes a difference in overall risk. The IARC did not evaluate whether unprocessed poultry and fish were carcinogenic, so they have nothing to say about these foods for good or ill.

In addition to cancer, red meat consumption is a risk factor for cardiovascular disease and type 2 diabetes. These problems are particularly associated with processed red meat: another good reason to cut back on bacon.

As most people are aware, raw meat products also come with a risk of foodborne illness. *Escheria coli* (*E. coli*) commonly colonize the gut of ruminant animals (like cows), and cross-contamination during butchering can lead to tainted meat. There are many different strains of *E. coli*, and many of them are harmless, but some can be very nasty and even fatal. So careful handling and cooking are called for whenever raw meat is prepared. Trichinosis and toxoplasmosis are caused by parasites that are found in raw or undercooked pork. Pregnant women are advised to avoid deli meats because of the risk of contamination with *Listeria*. But as potentially dangerous as these diseases can be, they can all be avoided by heating meat to the proper temperature. In contrast, prion diseases, like bovine spongiform encephalopathy (BSE, commonly called mad cow disease), cannot be killed by cooking. Prion diseases, which are degenerative and invariably fatal, are transmitted by meat contaminated with affected nervous tissue. For a while it was a hot topic, though it hasn't received much press lately. Notably, a cow with BSE was identified through routine surveillance in Alabama in July 2017.

In addition to the immediate personal health concerns that are tied to meat consumption, there are some secondary issues. For example, animals raised for meat are a known reservoir for novel viruses like new strains of influenza (swine flu, avian flu) and the shockingly lethal Nipah virus. Many meat animals are also dosed with antibiotics, both to prevent illness and to accelerate weight gain. This practice is one of the greatest contributors to the emergence of superbugs—strains of bacteria that are immune to one or more antibiotics.

But wait, there's more. Raising animals for food is massively inefficient compared to raising food crops in terms of both land and water usage. This makes meat very expensive and contributes to global food inequity and insecurity. Animals also produce greenhouse gases, which are, of course, implicated in global warming.

If you've been keeping track, you will have noticed that there are quite a few good reasons to cut back on your meat consumption, especially processed meats. Fortunately, our modern food supply leaves us with many good alternatives including beans, peas, nuts, seeds, quinoa, amaranth, and lots of vegetables. Try to substitute poultry, eggs, or fish for red meat, and eat smaller portion sizes when you do indulge. If you really like processed meat, save it for special occasions, and live a little.

SUMMARY

Preventability (100)

Many people (vegetarians, vegans) abstain from eating meat entirely.

Likelihood (33)

Eating red and/or processed meat slightly increases the risk of some cancers, and eating processed meat is also a risk factor for cardiovascular disease. Other risks include foodborne illness, emerging diseases, and environmental impact.

Consequence (71)

None of the potential consequences are insignificant, but they do not rise to the level of certain death.

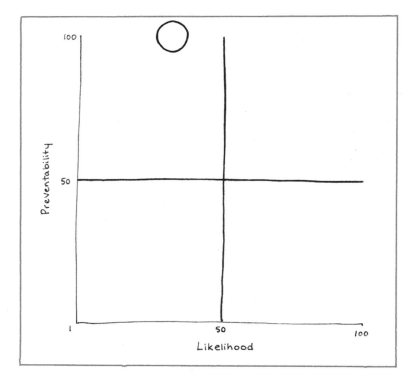

REFERENCES

Centers for Disease Control and Prevention. (2014, March 20). Nipah virus (NiV).
    Retrieved from https://www.cdc.gov/vhf/nipah/index.html
Domingo, J. L., & Nadal, M. (2017). Carcinogenicity of consumption of red meat and
    processed meat: A review of scientific news since the IARC decision. *Food and Chem-
    ical Toxicology, 105,* 256–261.
Larsson, S. C., & Orsini, N. (2014). Red meat and processed meat consumption and
    all-cause mortality: A meta-analysis. *American Journal of Epidemiology, 179,* 282–289.
Micha, R., Michas, G., & Mozaffarian, D. (2012). Unprocessed red and processed meats
    and risk of coronary artery disease and type 2 diabetes—an updated review of the
    evidence. *Current Atherosclerosis Reports, 14,* 515–524.
National Institutes of Health. (2012, March 26). Risk in red meat? NIH Research
    Matters. Retrieved from https://www.nih.gov/news-events/nih-research-matters/
    risk-red-meat
Pobiner, B. (2013). Evidence for meat-eating by early humans. *Nature Education Knowl-
    edge, 4*(6), 1.
U.S. Department of Agriculture. (2017, July 18). USDA detects a case of atypical bovine

spongiform encephalopathy in Alabama. Retrieved from https://www.aphis.usda
.gov/aphis/newsroom/stakeholder-info/sa_by_date/sa-2017/sa-07/bse-alabama

Wade, L. (2016, March 9). How sliced meat drove human evolution. *Science*. Retrieved from
http://www.sciencemag.org/news/2016/03/how-sliced-meat-drove-human-evolution

World Health Organization. (2015, October). Q&A on the carcinogenicity of the consumption of red meat and processed meat. Retrieved from http://www.who.int/
features/qa/cancer-red-meat/en/

14. FOOD SAFETY

When you sit down for a meal, you are probably thinking about how it will taste, how it will stop you from being hungry, and possibly how it will affect your waistline or your cardiovascular health. Eating is routine; unless you are getting a questionable-looking hot dog from a street vendor, you probably don't worry that the food you are about to eat may make you sick. Because surely someone has ensured that the food you are about to eat is safe. There is nothing to worry about, is there?

Food can get contaminated by pesticides, bacteria, and viruses in many steps before it arrives on your plate. First, farms must grow food, and they may use pesticides and fertilizers to improve crop yield. Factories that subsequently sort or process food may introduce pathogens and other contaminants when products are prepared and packaged. Food products are then distributed to warehouses, stores, and restaurants. If some foods are not refrigerated properly, they can become contaminated with bacteria or mold. Finally, food must be prepared so it is ready to eat. If utensils used to prepare raw meat are not cleaned properly, they can contaminate other food such as fruits and vegetables. Some products, such as chicken, pork, beef, and fish, must be cooked thoroughly to eliminate harmful pathogens. Many people handle your food on its way to you (e.g., farmers, pickers, packers, cooks, servers), and if any of them are sick, they can infect the food you eat. Indeed, some viruses that cause respiratory illnesses can survive on fruit and vegetables for several days.

Most countries have agencies to safeguard the food supply, but regulations differ from country to country, and enforcement and inspection mechanisms are not are always followed. Contamination is not only an issue for the domestic food supply because it can also affect food that is imported from other countries. In the United States, the governmental agencies primarily responsible for keeping food safe are the Food and Drug Administration (FDA) and the U.S. Department of Agriculture (USDA). The USDA is responsible for ensuring that meat, poultry, and egg products are safe and that these foods are labeled and packaged properly. Within the USDA, the Food Safety and Inspection Service (FSIS) is authorized by the U.S. Congress to inspect all meat, poultry, and egg products. To reduce the risk of foodborne illness, the FSIS inspects factories to ensure that companies follow food safety practices. The FDA regulates food products (domestic and imported) that the USDA does not cover such as seafood, fruits, vegetables, bread, cereal, dairy products, dietary supplements, bottled water, and food additives.

Even with these large governmental agencies monitoring and inspecting the food supply, the large number of manufacturers and huge quantities of food that require examination are a burden. It is impossible to inspect everything, and, therefore, foodborne illness is a serious public health concern. Knowing that in the United States one in six people gets sick, 128,000 people are hospitalized, and 3,000 people die each year from eating contaminated food, you might think twice before sinking your teeth into that juicy hamburger. The CDC lists more than 30 different microorganisms that can cause foodborne illness. In the United States, the pathogens most likely to cause trouble are norovirus, *Salmonella, Clostridium perfringens, Campylobacter,* and *Staphylococcus aureus.* Less common but more serious foodborne illnesses are caused by *Clostridium botulinum, Listeria,* Shiga toxin–producing *Escherichia coli (E. coli)* O157, and *Vibrio.* When the USDA or FDA find contaminated products or discover an outbreak of a foodborne disease, they issue recalls and alerts to notify the public.

Common symptoms of these foodborne illnesses are gastrointestinal problems such as an upset stomach, diarrhea, cramps, vomiting, and nausea. Depending on the pathogen causing the illness, symptoms may first appear from a few hours to several days after exposure. Many people experience only mild discomfort and recover, but others develop severe symptoms that require hospitalization. *E. coli* bacteria infections, for example, can produce toxic chemicals that can damage the kidneys. *Salmonella* and *Campylobacter* infections can cause chronic arthritis, and *Listeria* infections can result in neurological disorders. *Listeria* is a pathogen of particular concern to pregnant women since the bacteria can cross the placental barrier, sometimes leading to preterm birth, stillbirth, or miscarriage.

In addition to microbes that cause foodborne illness, pesticides that remain on foods may also pose health risks to consumers. Many different types of pesticides are used during food production to control insects, rodents, fungi, weeds, and bacteria. Although the U.S. Environmental Protect Agency (EPA) approves pesticides for specific uses and establishes the maximum level of pesticide that can remain on food, the FDA and FSIS are responsible for enforcing the limits on approximately 700 pesticides that may be found on products that they oversee. Foods found in violation of the guidelines can be seized or, in the case of food from outside the country, refused entry.

Pesticides can improve the yield of a crop or prevent a product from becoming infected with a pest. But people can ingest pesticides when they eat food with pesticide residues. Some pesticides used in food production are carcinogenic, neurotoxic, or endocrine disruptors. The EPA sets limits on the amount of pesticide residue that can remain on food based on what its research shows to be safe. Some critics argue that the EPA data are not complete and that the long-term effects of pesticide exposure and the effects of pesticides on developing children are not adequately known. Eating organic will not help you avoid all pesticides because organic food is not neces-sary pesticide free. Many organic farmers still use pesticides on their crops, but the chemicals are usually not synthetic.

In addition to allowing pesticides (within limits), the FDA also allows insect parts, rodent hair, and maggots into food, within limits, of course. For example, 30 or more insect fragments per 100 grams of peanut butter, two or more maggots per 500 grams of canned tomatoes, and 11 rodent hairs per 25 grams of ground paprika are necessary before the FDA will take action. These levels have been determined to be natural or unavoidable, and while eating food contaminated with these extras is disgusting, it should not pose any health problems to people.

While we have government agencies trying to protect the food supply, there are some simple steps we can all take to reduce the risk of eating contaminated food. First, wash your hands and any cutting surfaces before and after you handle any food. Also, wash all fruits and vegetables before cutting and serving them to remove microorgan-isms that might contaminate the skin. To avoid cross-contamination, make sure that raw meat, poultry, seafood, and their juices stay away from food that will not be cooked. When meat, poultry, and sea-food are cooked, ensure that they are heated to the proper internal temperature to kill pathogens. If you are unsure when food reaches the proper temperature, use a cooking thermometer to remove any guesswork. When you are finished with your delicious meal, get all of the leftovers into the refrigerator to slow the growth of bacteria.

SUMMARY

Preventability (61)

Everyone should take steps to keep their own food preparation areas clean and safe. However, if you eat out at a restaurant, you are trusting cooks and servers to provide you with uncontaminated food.

Likelihood (83)

Foodborne illnesses are very common.

Consequence (48)

The result of a foodborne illness depends on the agent causing the disorder. Symptoms range from mild gastrointestinal discomfort to infections that require a stay in the hospital.

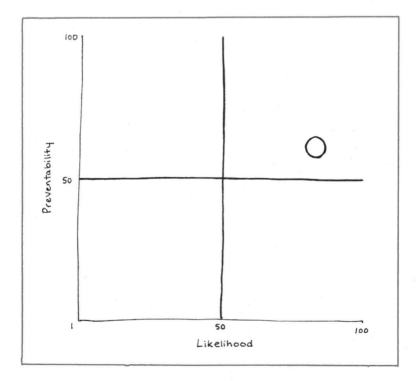

REFERENCES

CDC. (2016, July 15). Burden of foodborne illness: Findings. Retrieved from https://www.cdc.gov/foodborneburden/2011-foodborne-estimates.html

CDC. (2017, December 12). Food safety. Retrieved from https://www.cdc.gov/food safety/index.html

U.S. Food and Drug Administration. (2017). *Defect levels handbook.* Retrieved from https://www.fda.gov/Food/GuidanceRegulation/GuidanceDocumentsRegulatory Information/SanitationTransportation/ucm056174.htm

Yépiz-Gómez, M. S., Gerba, C. P., & Bright, K. R. (2013). Survival of respiratory viruses on fresh produce. *Food and Environmental Virology, 5,* 150–156.

15. FAT

Anyone who remembers the 1990s remembers low-fat diets. It was a time when fat was vilified as dietary enemy number one. Everyone was checking labels for fat content and opting for alternative low-fat or fat-free options, of which there were many. The low-fat craze made some intuitive sense, because if you want to avoid being fat, not eating it seems logical. Just look at a bucket of lard. It's not hard to imagine what that would look like under your own skin. So we were all doing what we thought was the right thing and replacing the fat in our diets with carbohydrates. We were eating bagels with fat-free cream cheese for breakfast, taking the avocado off our salads, and drinking skim milk. But the fat-free revolution didn't help us to lose weight. Quite the contrary. Even as Americans were shifting their diets away from fats and toward carbohydrates, the rates of obesity and type 2 diabetes soared.

And then, inevitably perhaps, the pendulum swung the other way. In more recent times, low-carbohydrate, high-fat diets have become all the rage. Now we are encouraged to eat fat, lots of it. It's now okay to put butter on your bacon, just as long as you don't eat it with toast. Is that really better for you?

The first thing to recognize is that not all fats are the same. Dietary fats are fatty acids—long chains of carbon and hydrogen atoms with a carboxyl group at the end. The carbons are the backbone of the chain. The hydrogens are bound to the carbons and sort of stick out to the sides. Different dietary fats have different properties corresponding to their length (how many carbons there are), the number of double bonds, and the location of those double bonds. When fatty acids are fully saturated, they are very symmetrical, and straight as an arrow. They pack together well and are solid at room temperature. But double bonds are tighter than single bonds, and this causes unsaturated fatty acid chains to have little kinks in them. These little kinks mean that the fats don't pack together as tightly. Unsaturated fatty acids are more fluid than saturated fats and therefore liquid at room temperature. Trans fats are another kind of fatty acid configuration that has been historically important, but is becoming less so. Trans fats are industrially produced by busting up some of the double bonds in a naturally polyunsaturated fat and adding hydrogens. In the process, the remaining double bonds get twisted around into what is called the trans configuration. A diagram is really necessary to show how these bonds are different than the bonds that are found in naturally derived fatty acids, but let's just say that the double bonds cause the kink to go in the opposite direction.

In terms of food, saturated fats are found in animal products (meat, dairy) and tropical oils (coconut and palm oil). Polyunsaturated fats are found in nuts, seeds, and fish. Monounsaturated fats are found in animal products as well as fatty fruits and vegetables like avocados, olives, and peanuts. Trans fats were historically found in products like margarine and shortening (partially hydrogenated vegetable oil) as well as in many processed foods and fast foods.

Biochemically speaking, fats are very important molecules. Fatty acids are integral to the cell membrane of every cell in your body. There are some fatty acids that we refer to as essential fatty acids, and we call them this because humans must consume them if they want to keep living. These fats are polyunsaturated and are found in vegetable and seed oils. You have to eat them because your body cannot make them itself. But fats are also important because they store a lot of energy. That is, they are highly caloric. They are, in fact, more caloric than carbohydrates, and this is one of the reasons that people have focused on reducing fat for weight loss. When you eat fat, your body can break it down and use it for energy, and when you consume extra energy your body stores it as fat in special cells (adipocytes) that exist just for this reason. But it is important to note that your body will store any extra energy as fat, no matter how you consume it. This is one of the reasons why low-fat diets have failed.

In the 1980s and '90s, low-fat versions of cookies, ice cream, potato chips, mayonnaise, salad dressing, and basically everything else you can think of showed up in grocery stores everywhere. But fat is a big part of what makes all of those things taste good in the first place. Fat-free products kind of taste like cardboard. So, extra sugar and salt were added to make them more palatable. For the most part, they still didn't taste great. But strangely, people tended to eat a lot more of them. This is probably partly because people thought they were eating guilt free and therefore didn't have to worry about how much they consumed, and partly because fat may help signal satiety. In any case, overall calorie consumption became a problem. This brings us to a very well-substantiated (but unpopular) rule of weight loss: if you consume fewer calories than you burn, you will lose weight.

But weight loss isn't the only issue associated with fat. Fat consumption is also related to cardiovascular disease. This is where it gets a little complicated, because different kinds of fat have different effects, and parsing exactly what these effects are is an ongoing project. But the picture that is emerging is that the type of fat you eat is more important than the quantity of fat that you eat. Decades ago it was observed that reducing saturated fat intake had positive effects on cardiovascular risk. But what we understand now is that it is equally important how you replace those saturated fats in your diet. Eating more refined carbohydrates will not provide a benefit, but replacing those calories with more mono- and polyunsaturated fats provides a clear benefit. Likewise, if you reduce the number of carbohydrates you eat, you should not replace those calories with saturated fats. You should replace them with mono- and polyunsaturated fats, vegetables, and fruits.

This is, of course, a stripped-down version of a much more complicated story. For example, not all saturated fats seem to carry the same health risks, and polyunsaturated fats may have health benefits that extend beyond the cardiovascular system. But there is one thing we know for sure, and that is you shouldn't be eating trans fats because they are clearly associated with cardiovascular disease. For this reason, they are being phased out of food production and their use will be banned entirely by 2018.

SUMMARY

Preventability (72)

It can take a lot of effort to reorganize your diet, but if you have the time and money to spend, it can be done.

Likelihood (41)

If you eat a lot of saturated fat, it does increase your risk of cardiovascular disease, although other factors (like genetics) can affect how much.

Consequence (65)

Cardiovascular disease is very common, but that doesn't mean it isn't a big deal. A heart attack or a stroke can be fatal or debilitating.

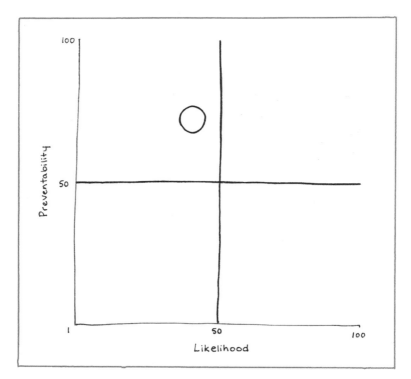

REFERENCES

Harvard Health Publishing. (2017, August 22). The truth about fats: The good, the bad, and the in-between. Retrieved from https://www.health.harvard.edu/staying-healthy/the-truth-about-fats-bad-and-good

Mozaffarian, D., & Ludwig, D. S. (2015). The 2015 US dietary guidelines: Lifting the ban on total dietary fat. *JAMA, 313*, 2421–2422.

Oregon State University. (n.d.). Essential fatty acids. Retrieved from http://lpi.oregon state.edu/mic/other-nutrients/essential-fatty-acids#metabolism-bioavailability

Wang, D. D., & Hu, F. B. (2017). Dietary fat and risk of cardiovascular disease: Recent controversies and advances. *Annual Review of Nutrition, 37*, 423–446.

16. ANTIBIOTICS IN FOOD ANIMALS

Antibiotics are great. They make diseases like leprosy, syphilis, and cholera treatable rather than life threatening. They cure ear infections and strep throat and urinary tract infections. They are the closest thing to a magic bullet that medicine has ever seen. These drugs also make animals gain weight, which is a nice bonus if you raise animals for meat. That is why ranchers around the world have been routinely dosing their healthy livestock with antibiotics since the middle of the last century. More than 33 million pounds of antibiotics were sold or distributed for food-producing animals in 2014. Of that, 62% of these antibiotics came from classes of drugs that are medically important to humans.

Animals are not a sink into which antibiotics go and do not return. On the contrary, most of the drug, up to 75% or 80%, is not metabolized. The leftovers are excreted unchanged. Because animal excrement is frequently used as a fertilizer, antibiotics contaminate soil, ground water, and crops. They are consumed by insects and birds. They are consumed by us. Antibiotics are everywhere, and for a number of reasons, this is not good.

First, antibiotics can mess with the way your body works. Animals (including humans) evolved with bacteria over millions of years, and we have developed a love-hate relationship with them. There are many different kinds of bacteria in the world, and most of them will not make you sick. You live in easy indifference with the vast majority of bacterial strains, but some will try to kill you. Some will actively help you. And, with some, you will enter into a complicated frenemy relationship. The problem with antibiotics is that they take a scorched-earth attitude. Antibiotics kill pathogenic bacteria, but they also kill beneficial bacteria. Antibiotics destabilize your microbiome—that carefully balanced network of bacteria, fungi, and archea (another kind of microorganism) living on and in your body (e.g., skin, gut, lungs, vagina). This is why some of the most common side effects of antibiotic treatment are diarrhea and vaginal yeast infections, conditions that are irritating but treatable. In some cases, however, a course of antibiotics can unleash a *Clostridium difficile* infection. This fun organism typically lives in your gut at low levels but is outcompeted by other, more benign bacteria. *C. difficile* infections, however, are difficult to kill with antibiotics. If you wipe out the friendly bacteria with a course of antibiotics, you give *C. difficile* a golden opportunity to take over. This is not something you want to happen. *C. difficile* kills thousands of people every year. This is unlikely to happen as a consequence of environmental exposure to antibiotics, but the point remains that these drugs are not innocuous. They are not without serious consequences. If you're sick, then the cost-benefit ratio may push you toward therapeutic antibiotics, but if you aren't sick, then you probably don't want to snack on penicillin. And if that doesn't motivate you, consider this: chronic doses of antibiotics are given to food animals to make them gain weight. We are also animals. All of the environmental antibiotics that we consume are quite possibly, even probably, making us well-marbled.

An even more dire consequence of giving livestock regular doses of antibiotics is that it promotes antibiotic resistance. Many of our antibiotics are no longer effective because bacteria have developed evasive maneuvers. Bacteria have been here for a long time, and they have some good tricks. Almost all the antibiotics that we currently use have a natural origin. Penicillin, for example, was distilled from a fungus. Alexander Fleming discovered penicillin in his lab in 1928, but bacteria had seen it before. In fact, a team of scientists recently discovered multi-drug-resistant bacteria in a cave in New Mexico, even though it has been isolated from the Earth's surface for 4 million years. Resistant bacteria have been out there for a long time. But these so-called superbugs are super only in the sense that they can resist antibiotics—they aren't super in terms of competing with other bacteria. As long as there is no selective pressure, there is no reason why they should thrive more than any other strain. Unfortunately, antibiotics provide that selective pressure. When we salt the earth with antibiotics, we pave the way for antibiotic-resistant bacteria. This is not to mention the reservoir that the animals themselves provide for bacterial storage and transmission as well as gene exchange and mutation.

This isn't a warning about something that is going to happen; this is a warning about something that has already happened. In the United States, the antibiotic of last resort is colistin. This is the drug that we have been saving to treat infections that are resistant to our preferred antibiotics. But in 2016, a strain of a particularly nasty colistin-resistant bacteria was identified in a woman in Pennsylvania. This last-defense antibiotic has been commonly used in livestock feed in China, where resistant strains of bacteria have been found in animals, raw meat, and humans. In early 2017, a woman in Nevada died of an infection that was resistant to all 26 antibiotics available in the United States. The post-antibiotic age isn't coming—it is already here.

So the regular use of antibiotics in healthy animals is a problem, and a scary one at that. But is there anything you can do about it? You can't avoid the issue of environmental antibiotics entirely, because you have to eat something. You don't, however, have to eat meat and dairy that is raised with antibiotics. The best way to change behavior in the food industry is to create a demand for responsibly raised meat. The good news is that more and more antibiotic-free options are available to consumers. The bad news is that these options are pricey, which may mean cutting back on your overall consumption. But look on the bright side. You should be cutting back on red meat anyway, because it probably causes cancer.

SUMMARY

Preventability (42)

You can choose animal products that were raised without antibiotics, or you can avoid them altogether, but you can't regulate the entire food livestock industry, which is what it is going to take to make a difference.

Likelihood (87)

Everyone is going to live with the consequences of antibiotic resistance, but scientists have a few antibiotic alternatives on the cooker. It remains to be seen how effective any of them will be.

Consequence (80)

There is no doubt about it: bacterial infections will kill some people. It's already happening. On the other hand, if history is any guide, they won't kill all of us.

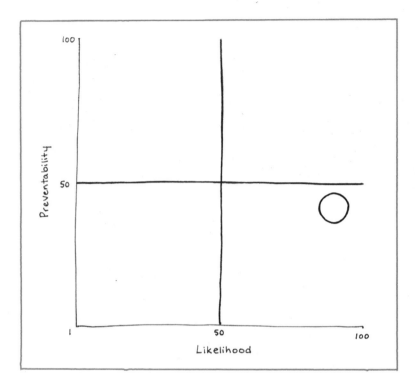

REFERENCES

Bouvard, V., Loomis, D., Guyton, K. Z., Grosse, Y., Ghissassi, F. E., Benbrahim-Tallaa, L., . . . Straif, K. (2015). Carcinogenicity of consumption of red and processed meat. *Lancet Oncology, 16*, 1599–1600.

Centers for Disease Control and Prevention. (2016, May 31). Discovery of first mcr-1 gene in E. coli bacteria found in a human in United States. Retrieved from https://www.cdc.gov/media/releases/2016/s0531-mcr-1.html

Liu, Y.-Y., Wang, Y., Walsh, T. R., Yi, L. X., Zhang, R., Spencer, J., . . . Shen, J. (2016). Emergence of plasmid-mediated colistin resistance mechanism MCR-1 in animals and human beings in China: A microbiological and molecular biological study. *Lancet Infectious Disease, 16*, 161–168.

Pawlowski, A. C., Wang, W., Koteva, K., Barton, H. A., McArthur, A. G., & Wright, G. D. (2016). A diverse intrinsic antibiotic resistome from a cave bacterium. *Nature Communication, 7*, 13803.

Raoult, D. (2008). Obesity pandemics and the modification of digestive bacterial flora. *European Journal of Clinical Microbiology and Infectious Disease, 27*, 631–634.
Rosenblatt-Farrell, N. (2009). The landscape of antibiotic resistance. *Environmental Health Perspectives, 117*, A244–A250.
U.S. Food and Drug Administration. (2016, December 22). FDA annual summary report on antimicrobials sold or distributed in 2014 for use in food-producing animals. Retrieved from https://www.fda.gov/AnimalVeterinary/NewsEvents/CVMUpdates/ucm534244.htm

Medicine

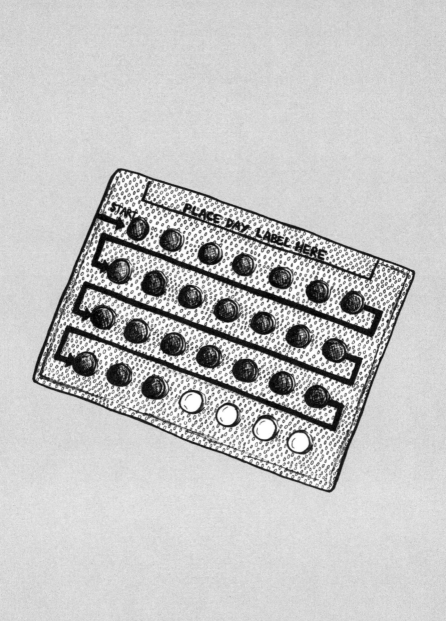

17. ORAL CONTRACEPTION

Whatever your personal feelings about oral contraception may be, debate about the pill has been historically important. Since its introduction in the 1960s, the birth control pill has become the most popular form of contraception in the United States. And, in addition to its contraceptive use, the pill is now prescribed to treat a number of other ailments including acne, irregular menstrual cycles, and polycystic ovary syndrome. But regardless of its popularity, doubts about the safety of the pill linger.

Birth control pills belong to the larger category of hormonal contraception, which also includes injectable birth control, the contraceptive patch, and the vaginal ring. In all cases, hormonal birth control is short-acting and reversible. When used correctly, these methods are very effective (failure rate: 6–12%). They work to prevent pregnancy by modulating the hormonal signaling pathways involved in fertility. In women, hormonal contraception aims to interfere with the menstrual cycle via the sex hormones estrogen and progesterone. Both estrogen and progesterone are elevated during pregnancy, and for this reason many people think of the pill as mimicking a pregnant state, but this is true only as a crude approximation. But these hormones do accomplish something that is critical during pregnancy: they suppress ovulation. They prevent eggs from being released from the ovaries. This is important in pregnancy because you don't want to simultaneously carry multiple fertilized eggs in different stages of development. Suppression of ovulation, in addition to other physical changes such as thickening of the cervical mucus and thinning of the uterine lining, provide the contraceptive benefit of hormonal birth control. No egg, no baby.

There are two basic formulations of hormonal contraception: progestin-only and combined. The progestin-only type contains (unsurprisingly) only the drug progestin—a synthetic version of the natural hormone progesterone. Progestin-only methods are effective, but may not be as effective as combined methods that include both progestin and estradiol, a form of estrogen (failure rate: 9%). In addition, women using progestin-only methods are more likely to have breakthrough bleeding. And, critically, women who take a progestin-only pill (sometimes called the minipill) must take the pill at the same time every day. Combined pills should be taken at the same time every day too. But in reality, there are a few hours of leeway.

So given that combined pills are more effective and more forgiving, why would anyone use a progestin-only formulation? Well, one reason is that estrogen interferes with breastfeeding, but progesterone does not. Actually, breastfeeding is a contraceptive measure in itself, but only as long as the baby is exclusively breastfed. Once the baby starts to eat solid foods, women need something else, and in that case the minipill fits the bill. But there are other indications for progestin-only birth control, which include being over the age of 35, smoking, or a history of blood clots or cardiovascular disease. This gets to one of the most established side effects of hormonal birth control—an increased risk of blood clots. Blood clots can be very serious, especially if they travel to the heart, lungs, or brain. This increased risk is associated with estrogen, which is an important biological molecule with (as is frequently the case in biology) more than one role. The increased risk is small, especially for newer birth control formulations that have lower doses of estrogen (relative risk: 1.93), and the overall incidence of these events is small for a young, nonsmoking demographic. But the elevated risk is significant, and the magnitude becomes greater with age. In addition, different methods (i.e., different pill formulations, the patch, and the ring) carry different relative risks, which is important to consider when choosing a birth control method. Notably, progestin-only birth control does not increase the risk of blood clots.

Another well-publicized side effect of hormonal birth control is cancer. For something like birth control, cancer risk is very difficult to assess. First of all, cancer can take years to develop, which requires a long-term study. But over time people tend to go on and off birth control and switch the type that they use, and they may do this for reasons that independently impact cancer risk (for example, giving birth or breastfeeding). The formulations that are available also change over time, as do the lifestyles of the people who are taking it. But all of that said, it does appear that hormonal contraception slightly increases the risk of breast cancer (odds ratio: 1.08) and may increase the risk for cervical cancer. On the other hand, taking these drugs decreases the risk of colon (odds ratio: 0.83), ovarian (odds ratio: 0.73), and endometrial cancers (odds ratio: 0.57). This makes the cost-benefit analysis very difficult, as every individual will have different risk factors and tolerances.

But there is one more thing to consider when thinking about the health risks of birth control, which is the risk of the alternative. Pregnancy is attended by its own health risks and benefits. This is especially true when you consider the impact of many pregnancies or unintended pregnancies, or pregnancy in women with other significant risk factors. To this end, it should also be pointed out that there are other, nonhormonal, forms of birth control. These, of course, carry their own risk factors.

One issue that has more recently come into national consciousness is how hormonal contraception affects the ground and drinking water. When people consume synthetic hormones, some percentage (approximately 50–80%) of the drug is excreted and enters the wastewater treatment system. Furthermore, depending on the wastewater treatment method, these hormones may not be entirely removed. Estrogen and estrogenic compounds are endocrine disruptors because they interact with the body's hormone signaling pathway. Indeed, as described above, that is the very mechanism that makes them useful for birth control. But this is also what makes them an environmental pollutant. Estrogenic compounds in the water may be leading to an increase in intersex fish and other aquatic species. They're not great for humans either and could be contributing to a number of reproductive problems. However, a 2011 literature review from a group at the University of California, San Francisco, concluded that oral contraception was only one of a number of sources of endocrine-modulating pollutants. Other sources include natural estrogens excreted by humans and livestock (particularly the pregnant kind), processing facilities for plants high in plant-based estrogens (like soy), pesticides, and industrial chemicals. The good news and bad news is, of these sources, oral contraception is the least significant contributor to water pollution.

In the end, hormonal contraception is like any other medical intervention: not without side effects. The overall increased risk is small, but especially for people with other risk factors, it may be important. The key is to make a decision taking into consideration the risk of treatment, but also the risk of the alternative.

SUMMARY

Preventability (80)

There are other forms of birth control, so oral contraception is not strictly necessary. However, there are some cases when alternative forms of birth control are not practical or desirable.

Likelihood (18)

The likelihood of a negative outcome changes with age, medical history, smoking history, and drug formulation. Some side effects are very common, but not very serious. The risk of serious side effects is not that high, but high enough to take into account.

Consequence (75)

Blood clots and cancer are nothing to trifle with, but not all will be fatal.

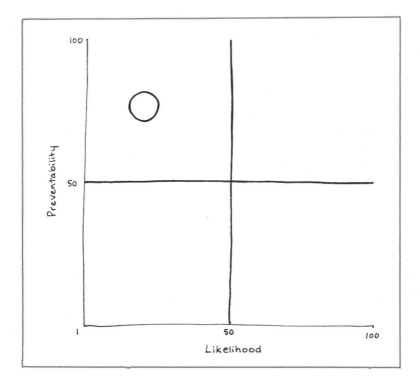

REFERENCES

Centers for Disease Control and Prevention. (2018, February 9). Contraception. Retrieved from https://www.cdc.gov/reproductivehealth/contraception/index.htm
Eunice Kennedy Shriver National Institute of Child Health and Human Development. (2017, January 31). What are the different types of contraception? Retrieved from https://www.nichd.nih.gov/health/topics/contraception/conditioninfo/Pages/types.aspx#LARC

Gierisch, J. M., Coeytaux, R. R., Urrutia, R. P., Havrilesky, L. J., Moorman, P. G., Lowery, W. J., . . . Myers, E. R. (2013). Oral contraceptive use and risk of breast, cervical, colorectal, and endometrial cancers: A systematic review. *Cancer Epidemiology, Biomarkers, and Prevention 22,* 1931–1943.

Gillum, L. A., Mamidipudi, S. K., & Johnston, S. C. (2000). Ischemic stroke risk with oral contraceptives: A meta-analysis. *JAMA, 284,* 72–78.

Havrilesky, L. J., Moorman, P. G., Lowery, W. J., Gierisch, J. M., Coeytaux, R. R., Urrutia, R. P., . . . Myers, E. R. (2013). Oral contraceptive pills as primary prevention for ovarian cancer: A systematic review and meta-analysis. *Obstetrics and Gynecology, 122,* 139.

Lidegaard, Ø., Løkkegaard, E., Jensen, A., Skovlund, C. W., & Keiding, N. (2012). Thrombotic stroke and myocardial infarction with hormonal contraception. *New England Journal of Medicine, 366,* 2257–2266.

Wise, A., O'Brien, K., & Woodruff, T. (2011). Are oral contraceptives a significant contributor to the estrogenicity of drinking water? *Environmental Science and Technology, 45,* 51–60.

18. GIVING BIRTH IN A HOSPITAL

Some people have very strong feelings about childbirth. If you think about it, you can see why. Giving birth is a life-altering event for at least two people. It is a profoundly emotional experience involving one of nature's most powerful physiological bonds. As anyone who has ever done it can tell you, giving birth is difficult. All mammals give birth to live young (you can't be a mammal if you don't), but it is especially difficult for humans because of our big brains. In addition to being painful and exhausting, having a baby can be dangerous for both the mother and the baby.

Most women in the U.S. give birth in hospitals, but a growing number are choosing to have their babies in birth centers or at home. Sometimes the reasons for this are emotional; women want to welcome their children into their own homes surrounded by the people that they love. But there are often concerns about the over-medicalization of childbirth. Some people are worried that if they go to the hospital, they will be more likely to receive medical interventions, such as assisted delivery or caesarean delivery (C-section), when they don't really need them. This perspective was championed by the 2008 documentary *The Business of Being Born*, which has been very influential in some circles.

Some physicians and scientists have expressed alarm and dismay at this trend, which they believe puts both mothers and babies at grave risk, even when the pregnancy is otherwise low risk. The problem, they claim, is that a routine birth can turn into a medical emergency in a very short time frame. In other words, having a baby isn't a medical event until it is. If you are in the hospital when this happens, you can get help within minutes. If you are at home, the extra minutes that it takes to get to the hospital can mean brain damage or even death.

The points made on both sides of this argument are correct. Therefore, when you ask whether it is safer to have a baby in the hospital or at home, a lot of the answer is going to depend on what you mean by safe.

In 1915, the infant mortality rate in the U.S. was about 10% and the maternal mortality rate was about 9%. By 1997, these rates had dropped 90% and 99% respectively, prompting the Centers for Disease Control and Prevention to name healthier mothers and babies as one of the ten great public health achievements of the 20th century. The CIA (yes, the Central Intelligence Agency) estimates that the infant mortality rate in the U.S. in 2016 was 0.0058, or 5.8 deaths per 1,000 births. So having a baby in the U.S. is fairly safe. It is true that home births are associated with more negative outcomes for the baby. According to a 2015 report by Snowden et al. ("Planned Out-of-Hospital Birth and Birth Outcomes"), the odds of perinatal death (just before or just after birth) were 2.43 times higher for births that were planned to be out of hospital (some women transfer to the hospital when they have complications). In addition, babies born at home were 3.6 times as likely to have neonatal seizures. It is important to keep in mind, however, that the absolute number of adverse events was low, corresponding to 2.1 additional perinatal deaths per 1,000 births. This corroborates the findings of other studies, although the value of the increased risk has varied between studies.

On the other hand, the study also found that women who give

birth at home were 5.63 times more likely to have an unassisted vaginal birth and women who gave birth in the hospital were 5.55 times more likely to have a C-section. These procedures are common enough now that they don't seem like a big deal, but a C-section is still a major surgery, and that implies a certain level of risk in and of itself. This is not to mention that taking care of an infant, and potentially that infant's older siblings, while recovering from surgery is the pits. Having a C-section also increases a woman's chances of delivering future children in the same way, and repeating the surgery over and over compounds the risk. In addition, scientists are just beginning to understand that children also benefit from being born naturally. Children who are born vaginally acquire a microbiome from their mothers that helps develop their immune systems. C-section deliveries are associated with an increased risk of obesity, asthma, allergies, and immune deficiencies for the child. A study published in *Nature Medicine* in 2016 suggests it may be possible to partially restore this maternal microbial contribution to children delivered by C-section, but the jury is still out on the long-term health effects for the baby.

So when it comes to choosing the safest place to have a baby, it really depends on how you weigh the absolute and relative risks. There are steps a mother can take to mitigate overall risk no matter where she chooses to have her baby. If the decision is to plan a home birth, it is imperative to make sure that a qualified, licensed midwife is in attendance. A woman needs to verify with her doctor that she is a good candidate for home delivery, and she should have a hospital transfer plan. If the decision is to deliver in a hospital, a woman should make sure to communicate with her doctor beforehand about what is important to her. Every woman, regardless of where she chooses to give birth, should make a birth plan and share it with her healthcare provider. Some physicians and some hospitals will be more accommodating than others, so before making a decision, women should do some research and examine all of their options. In many places it is possible to have a baby delivered by a midwife in the hospital. Remember that patients always have the right to decline medical interventions, even in the hospital. Women should bring someone (a spouse, friend, parent, or doula) who is designated and prepared to act as their advocate, and they should insist that they are always informed.

Ultimately, the most important part of a birth experience is that the baby and new mother are healthy. The real problems start when you get that baby home and realize you have to be a parent. No amount of planning can ever really prepare you for that.

SUMMARY

Preventability (100)

In some cases it is much safer to have a baby in the hospital, but ultimately it is up to the mother where she wants to give birth.

Likelihood (28)

The odds of having a C-section or other medical intervention are higher if you give birth in the hospital, but the health outcomes are statistically better for the baby. The rates of infant and maternal mortality are very low for both in-hospital and home births.

Consequence (35)

Having a C-section is good if you really need one, and not so good if you don't. But while painful and difficult to recover from, it is unlikely to be fatal.

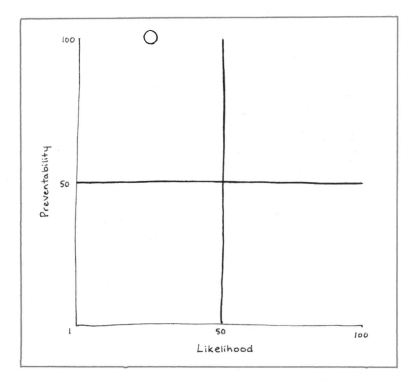

REFERENCES

Centers for Disease Control and Prevention. (1999). Ten great public health achievements—United States, 1900–1999. *MMWR*, *48*(12), 241–243. Retrieved from https://
www.cdc.gov/mmwr/preview/mmwrhtml/00056796.htm

Centers for Disease Control and Prevention. (1999). Achievements in public health,
1900–1999: Healthier mothers and babies. *MMWR*, *48*(38), 849–858. Retrieved from
https://www.cdc.gov/mmwr/preview/mmwrhtml/mm4838a2.htm

Central Intelligence Agency. (2017). *The world factbook*. Retrieved from https://www.cia
.gov/library/publications/the-world-factbook/rankorder/2091rank.html

Dominguez-Bello, M. G., De Jesus-Laboy, K. M., Shen, N., Cox, L. M., Amir, A., Gon-
zalez, A., . . . Clemente, J. C. (2016). Partial restoration of the microbiota of cesarean-
born infants via vaginal microbial transfer. *Nature Medicine*, *22*, 250–253.

Snowden, J. M., Tilden, E. L., Snyder, J., Quigley, B., Caughey, A. B., & Cheng, Y.
W. (2015). Planned Out-of-Hospital Birth and Birth Outcomes. N Engl J Med
373:2642–2653.

19. EBOLA

Ebola is a river in the Democratic Republic of Congo. It is also the name of a genus of viruses that causes highly lethal viral hemorrhagic fevers. In 1976, Ebola virus disease made its first appearance in a village near the Ebola River; hence the name. While viral hemorrhagic fevers are classified by their symptoms, they can actually be caused by several different families of viruses. Ebolaviruses are in the family Filoviridae. There is only one other member of the family, Marburgvirus (named after Marburg, Germany). This is not a family you want to associate with. Ebolavirus and Marburgvirus are a gruesome pair. Infection with either Ebolavirus or Marburgvirus has an average mortality rate of about 50%; in various different outbreaks the recorded mortality range has been from 25% to as high as 90%. Even in cases where infections aren't fatal, these diseases are very, very unpleasant. The initial symptoms are fever, headache, sore throat, and malaise. This is followed by vomiting, diarrhea, rash, and (since it is a hemorrhagic fever) internal and external bleeding.

Many Americans were introduced to Ebola virus disease (often shorthanded to Ebola) in 1995 when the best-selling book *The Hot Zone* by Richard Preston and the box-office hit *Outbreak* were released in the same year as an actual Ebola outbreak in the Democratic Republic of Congo. But while that outbreak killed 81% of the people who contracted the disease, the overall magnitude was small

(315 people total) and, while new outbreaks cropped up every few years, they were always well contained and far away, in Africa.

There are a few reasons why Ebola stayed mostly a local problem for so many years. First, it isn't highly contagious. On average, one person with Ebola infects only one or two additional people. That's obviously not great (especially for those one or two people), but it isn't nearly as contagious as measles. One person with measles infects an average of 12–18 additional people, making it one of the world's most contagious diseases (incidentally, you might want to worry about that). Ebola is spread primarily through contact with the bodily fluids of an infected person after the onset of symptoms. That means you are only likely to get the disease if you are caring for someone who is sick or touching or cleaning their corpse. The second reason Ebola didn't cause any major outbreaks for so long is that it is a very lethal disease. That means that people die too quickly to pass it on. This combination of factors meant that when Ebola surfaced, it quickly burned itself out. In the U.S., Ebola became a bit of a bogeyman.

But at the close of 2013, the specter of Ebola was raised again in earnest. On December 26 of that year, a 2-year-old boy in Guinea became ill. It isn't totally clear how he got Ebola, but it was probably through contact with an animal. The animal was likely a fruit bat, the virus's presumed natural host. (As an aside, bats serve as the reservoir for some of the world's scariest diseases.) Two days later, the boy died. The disease spread, and this time it didn't stay local: it made its way to Conakry, the capital city of Guinea. From there it spread to the neighboring countries of Liberia and Sierra Leone, then their respective capitals, and from there it took off like wildfire. It became an epidemic in West Africa. Between 2014 and 2016, more than 28,000 people in Guinea, Liberia, and Sierra Leone came down with the disease, and more than 11,000 people died. At the peak of the crisis, the disease spread to nine countries, including the United States. For many people, this brought Ebola fears back to the front burner. The epidemic is now over, but the virus isn't gone.

There are a number of ways you can choose to be worried about Ebola. You might be worried about the incredible pain, suffering, and death it caused in West Africa. That is obviously legitimate. Without the resources and infrastructure to combat an epidemic, the people who live in these countries are vulnerable. You might also be worried that you will contract Ebola yourself. This is a natural fear, but in the U.S., a major outbreak is unlikely. This is because the U.S. has the resources and infrastructure to stop the disease (at least in its current form). The 2014 epidemic proved that, even in the U.S., this was more difficult than anticipated. But there was no epidemic in the U.S. The public health system has since made improvements where Ebola is concerned, providing more guidance and support to hospitals and health care workers. Another reason you might worry about an Ebola epidemic is that it gives the virus a chance to evolve. One of the reasons this outbreak was different from prior outbreaks was that it reached capital cities—areas of high population density and mobility. But in addition, right around the time it was taking off as an epidemic, the virus may have undergone a mutation that made it more infectious to human cells. This is obviously undesirable. Finally, you might worry about a global epidemic of Ebola. There are other countries with populations that are equally vulnerable to the disease. Some of them, like India, are much more physically and economically interconnected with the rest of the world than West Africa. In addition to being horrific from a humanitarian point of view, this could also lead to a global financial crisis.

The good news is that people are now paying attention to Ebola, and the global response is mobilized. There is also a promising new vaccine. Even so, it is too early to stop worrying about

Ebola. But the really bad news is that there are other viruses poised to flare up in the same way. There are some dangerous viruses we already know about, like Zika virus, Nipah virus, Middle East respiratory syndrome coronavirus, and influenza viruses. But there are many more viruses incubating in animal populations that we have no experience with—yet. Furthermore, the rate of emerging infectious diseases has been steadily increasing over time. This is probably, at least in part, due to human development encroaching on wildlife habitat. This increases the interaction between humans and wild animals, which gives viruses the opportunity to spill over into our species.

If you live in the U.S., your chances of getting Ebola are low. But your incentive to invest in global public health measures should be high.

SUMMARY

Preventability (57)

In its present form, Ebola is not as contagious as many diseases and can be avoided by staying away from people who are exhibiting symptoms. However, short of advocating for more funds for the international public health system, there is isn't much you can do to prevent an out-of-control epidemic in another part of the world.

Likelihood (16)

In the U.S. you are very unlikely to contract Ebola, but you could be affected by an outbreak even if you don't get the disease.

Consequence (100)

Obviously, if you do get Ebola it is serious.

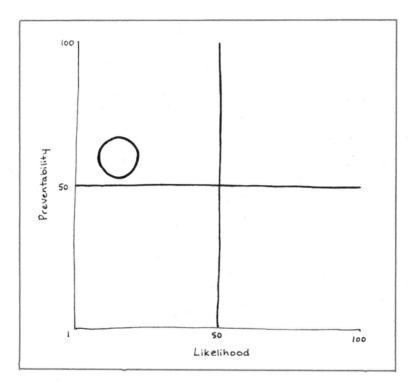

REFERENCES

Centers for Disease Control and Prevention. (2014, April 7). Filoviridae. Retrieved from
   https://www.cdc.gov/vhf/virus-families/filoviridae.html
Centers for Disease Control and Prevention. (2017, June 13). Ebola (Ebola virus disease).
   Retrieved from https://www.cdc.gov/vhf/ebola/index.html
Cohen, J. (2016, November 3). Has a new mutation in the Ebola virus made it dead-
   lier? *Science*. Retrieved from http://www.sciencemag.org/news/2016/11/has-new
   -mutation-ebola-virus-made-it-deadlier
Han, H.-J., Wen, H., Zhou, C.-M., Chen, F.-F., Luo, L.-M., Liu, J., & Yu,, X.-J. (2015).
   Bats as reservoirs of severe emerging infectious diseases. *Virus Research*, *205*, 1–6.
Jones, K. E., Patel, N. G., Levy, M. A., Storeygard, A., Balk, D., Gittleman, J. L., &
   Daszak, P. (2008). Global trends in emerging infectious diseases. *Nature*, *451*, 990.
Servick, K. (2014, August 13). What does Ebola actually do? *Science*. Retrieved from
   http://www.sciencemag.org/news/2014/08/what-does-ebola-actually-do
Shute, N. (2014, October 30). Why it's OK to worry about Ebola, and what's
   truly scary. Health News from NPR. Retrieved from http://www.npr.org/sec
   tions/health-shots/2014/10/30/359843440/why-its-ok-to-worry-about-ebola
   -and-whats-truly-scary

WHO Ebola Response Team. (2016). After Ebola in West Africa—unpredictable risks, preventable epidemics. *New England Journal of Medicine, 375*, 587–596.

World Health Organization. (2016, December 23). Final trial results confirm Ebola vaccine provides high protection against disease. Retrieved from http://www.who.int/mediacentre/news/releases/2016/ebola-vaccine-results/en/

World Health Organization. (2017, October). Marburg virus disease. Retrieved from http://www.who.int/mediacentre/factsheets/fs_marburg/en/

World Health Organization. (2018, January). Ebola virus disease. Retrieved from http://www.who.int/mediacentre/factsheets/fs103/en/

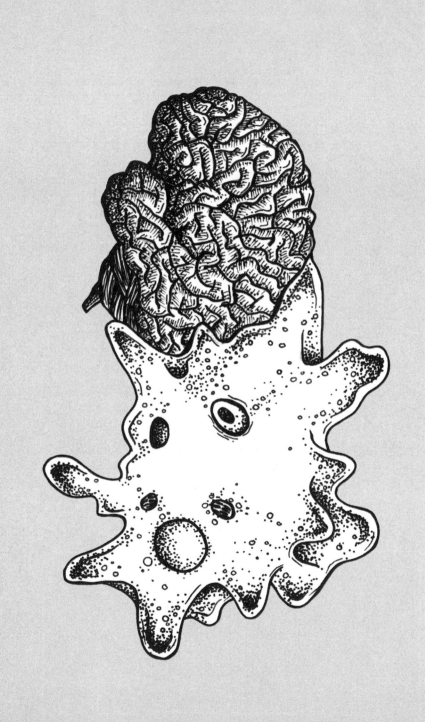

20. BRAIN-EATING AMOEBA

The zombie lurches forward with its hands outstretched, steadfast in its intent to feast on its victim's brain. Or so Hollywood would have you believe. Your brain is safe from the appetite of the undead because there is no such thing as a zombie. However, there is a much smaller, real-life creature with a fondness for brain tissue that might concern you: *Naegleria fowleri*.

Naegleria fowleri, commonly known as brain-eating amoeba, is a microscopic, single-celled organism found around the world in soil and freshwater lakes, ponds, rivers, and hot springs. Cases of *Naegleria fowleri* infection have been reported on every continent except Antarctica. The amoeba prefers warm climates and multiplies when the temperature is warmer than 30°C.

Unlike Hollywood zombies that can be seen from a distance, *Naegleria fowleri* has a much more insidious avenue to the brain; it typically affects people who swim in infected water. Infection starts when water containing the amoeba enters a swimmer's nose. The amoebas merge with the nasal mucosa, follow the olfactory nerve and tracts, and cross through the ethmoid bone that separates the nasal cavity from the brain. Once in the brain, *Naegleria fowleri* starts consuming neural tissue, causing primary amoebic meningoencephalitis (PAM). The amoeba feeds by extending food cups around cells that pull food in for digestion. The process may be aided when the amoeba releases proteases that work to dissolve proteins. Damage to the brain includes internal bleeding, inflammation, and cell death. Symptoms of PAM usually start with a change in the sense of smell, headache, fever, nausea, and vomiting and can progress to seizures, stiff neck, hallucinations, coma, and death. Death is thought to be the result of inflammation and swelling that cause increased intracranial pressure. This pressure affects brain stem areas that control breathing. Infections are fatal in approximately 97% of the cases within two weeks after exposure. But take note: the amoeba must make its way to the brain via the nose. *Naegleria fowleri* does not pose any danger when they are swallowed with contaminated water, because stomach acid kills the little vermin. So it is not a problem unless it gets high into the nasal passages.

Infections by *Naegleria fowleri* are not common. A total of only 142 cases of PAM were reported to the U.S. Centers for Disease Control and Prevention (CDC) and other databanks between 1937 and 2013. Most of the patients with PAM reported to the CDC were male (76%) and 18 years old or younger (83%). The prevalence of *Naegleria fowleri* in the environment makes it likely that many people are exposed to the amoeba but never show any symptoms of illness. It is not known why some people are affected by *Naegleria fowleri* while others are not. Administration of drugs such as amphotericin B (an antifungal medication) and miltefosine, which kills amoebas, have saved the lives of a few people with *Naegleria fowleri* infections.

Warm-water swimmers are not the only potential victims of *Naegleria fowleri*. Some people with sinus problems or allergies use neti pots to clear their nasal passages so they can breathe easier. Neti pots are also used during ritual ablution in some religious practices. Neti pots look a bit like miniature teapots or gravy boats. To use a neti pot, a saline (salt) solution made with sterile, distilled, or boiled water that has cooled is prepared in a thoroughly cleaned unit. The spout of the neti pot is placed in a nostril to flush the nasal cavity. Unboiled tap water or naturally sourced water should never be used because it may contain microbes, including *Naegleria fowleri*. A few deaths due to *Naegleria fowleri* have been traced to neti pots in Pakistan, Louisiana, and other areas (e.g., U.S. Virgin Islands). Louisiana responded to the deaths in its state by raising the minimum chlorine level in its water supply in order to kill the amoeba.

Terrifying headlines ("She loved the river. A 'brain-eating amoeba' lurking in the water ended up killing her") meant to scare people should not cause you to avoid your favorite swimming spot. The public's exposure to *Naegleria fowleri* is high and the number of infections is extremely small. Of course, the consequences of an infection by *Naegleria fowleri* are devastating, but the actual risk of contracting PAM is low.

However, to reduce the risk of *Naegleria fowleri* infection:

- Stay out of warm-water sources such as freshwater ponds, lakes, and hot springs.
- Use nose clips or hold your nose shut while in warm-water sources.
- Add appropriate chemicals (e.g., chlorine) to your pool and spa.
- Follow the directions when using a neti pot. Most importantly, use only sterile, distilled, or boiled water. Specially designed filters can also be used to screen out microorganisms.

It is unlikely that an amoeba will eat your brain. But if you are worried about brain-eating amoebas and cannot resist the urge to swim in warm water, you might stick to the ocean where *Naegleria fowleri* do not live.

SUMMARY

Preventability (88)

You can avoid contracting a brain-eating amoeba infection by staying out of freshwater lakes, ponds, rivers, and hot springs and leaving the neti pot on the shelf.

Likelihood (3)

Although *Naegleria fowleri* is common in freshwater sources, few infections occur.

Consequence (97)

Contracting a *Naegleria fowleri* infection is almost always fatal.

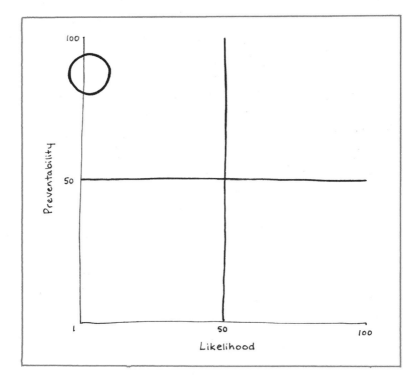

REFERENCES

Cabanes, P.-A., Wallet, F., Pringuez, E., & Pernin, P. (2001). Assessing the risk of primary amoebic meningoencephalitis from swimming in the presence of environmental Naegleria fowleri. *Applied Environmental Microbiology, 67,* 2927–2931.

Capewell, L. G., Harris, A. M., Yoder, J. S., Cope, J. R., Eddy, B. A., Roy, S. L., . . . Beach, M. J. (2015). Diagnosis, clinical course, and treatment of primary amoebic meningoencephalitis in the United States, 1937–2013. *Journal of the Pediatric Infectious Diseases Society, 4,* e68–e75.

Centers for Disease Control and Prevention. (2017, February 28). Parasites—Naegleriafowleri—primary amebic meningoencephalitis (PAM)—amebic encephalitis. Retrieved from https://www.cdc.gov/parasites/naegleria/

Hannisch, W., & Hallagan, L. F. (1997). Primary amebic meningoencephalitis: A review of the clinical literature. *Wilderness and Environmental Medicine, 8,* 211–213.

Heggie, T. W. (2010). Swimming with death: Naegleria fowleri infections in recreational waters. *Travel Medicine and Infectious Disease, 8,* 201–206.

Hunte, T., Morris, T., da Silva, A., Nuriddin, A., Visvesvara, G., Hill, V., . . . Morris, J. (2013). Notes from the field: Primary amebic meningoencephalitis associated with ritual nasal rinsing—St. Thomas, U.S. Virgin Islands, 2012. *Morbidity and Mortality Weekly Report (MMWR), 62,* 903–903.

Linam, W. M., Ahmed, M., Cope, J. R., Chu, C., Visvesvara, G. S., da Silva, A. J., Qvarnstrom, Y., & Green, J. (2015). Successful treatment of an adolescent with Naegleria fowleri primary amebic meningoencephalitis. *Pediatrics, 135,* e744–e748.

Serrano-Luna, J., Cervantes-Sandoval, I., Tsutsumi, V., & Shibayama, M. (2007). A biochemical comparison of proteases from pathogenic Naegleria fowleri and nonpathogenic Naegleria gruberi. *Journal of Eukaryotic Microbiology, 54,* 411–417.

Shakoor, S., Beg, M. A., Mahmood, S. F., Bandea, R., Sriram, R., Noman, F., . . . Zafar, A. (2011). Primary amebic meningoencephalitis caused by Naegleria fowleri, Karachi, Pakistan. *Emerging Infectious Diseases, 17,* 258–261.

Wootson, Jr., C. R. (2016, August 8). She loved the river. A "brain-eating amoeba" lurking in the water ended up killing her. *Washington Post.* Retrieved from https://www.washingtonpost.com/news/morning-mix/wp/2016/08/08/she-loved-the-river-a-brain-eating-amoeba-lurking-in-the-water-ended-up-killing-her/

Yoder, J. S., Strait-Bourgeois, S., Roy, S. L., Moore, T. A., Visvesvara, G. S., Ratard, R. C., . . . Beach, M. J. (2012). Primary amebic meningoencephalitis deaths associated with sinus irrigation using contaminated tap water. *Clinical Infectious Diseases, 55,* e79–e85.

21. MEDICAL ERRORS

If you are like most people, when you consider how you are likely to die, medical error doesn't jump to mind. But it probably should. Medical errors are far more common than you might think, and while most of them are not serious, some can be fatal.

When most of us think of medical errors, we think of people like Willie King, a diabetic patient who famously had the wrong leg amputated in 1995. But as complex as health care has become, there are many other, less dramatic, kinds of errors that can be made. For example, failing to order tests, ordering the wrong tests, misinterpreting test results, ordering the wrong medication, filling the wrong medication, administering the medication in the wrong dose, failing to take into account possible drug interactions, not properly setting up equipment, and not having the proper equipment and resources on hand. Simply failing to wash hands is a medical error that can lead to an adverse event.

In 1999 the Institute of Medicine (now the National Academy of Medicine) dropped a bombshell of a report (*To Err Is Human: Building a Safer Healthcare System*) about medical errors in the United States. Extrapolating from two contemporary studies, the authors of the report estimated that between 44,000 and 98,000 people died every year from medical errors in hospitals. Presumably even more deaths occurred in outpatient, nursing home, in-home, and ambulatory care settings. The seriousness of the problem comes into perspective when you consider that 41,826 people died in motor vehicle accidents in 1998. The number of deaths caused by medical errors is large; it's a big problem. The committee that wrote the report made a number of suggestions for improving the safety of the system that focused on creating national leadership, enforcing mandatory reporting, changing practitioner and administrative attitudes, and implementing safeguards.

Of course, 1999 was a long time ago. So how are we doing now? Unfortunately, not so great. In 2016, a group at Johns Hopkins University published an article in which they analyzed results previously published by other research groups after 1999 (Makary & Daniel, 2016). Extrapolating from this meta-analysis, the researchers estimated that 251,454 hospital patients died per year from causes related to medical errors. If this estimate is valid, then medical error is the third leading cause of death in the U.S., following heart disease and cancer. Again, this estimate only accounts for hospital patients, so it is likely an underestimate. And while the estimate is controversial and somewhat misleading (because most patients are seeking medical care for some underlying problem), it is not a heartening result. One of the major issues pointed out by the authors of the study is that we can only make rough estimates of the actual number of medical errors leading to death because this information is not collected. Death certificates list the immediate cause of death based on the International Classification of Disease. But they do not record any information about contributing factors. So if you go into cardiac arrest because you are given an incorrect dose of medication, the death certificate will record the cause of death as cardiovascular. Unfortunately, this means we don't know how big the problem is, but we know medical error is a problem.

Why are there so many medical errors? Because doctors, nurses, and other health care professionals are people, and people make mistakes. Certainly, there are some cases of gross negligence or incompetence, but many medical errors are just slip-ups. People get tired, especially at the end of a long shift. People get distracted. People make math errors, or grab the wrong bottle, or misread someone else's handwriting. Consider how many small mistakes you make during the course of any given day. Now imagine that any one of those mistakes has the potential to do real harm to someone. That is the situation health care providers find themselves in, and that is why experts believe that in order to make an impact, the problem needs to be addressed at the system level. People will always make mistakes. The key is to expect that this will be the case and set up safeguards so that the mistakes are caught.

One of the most fundamental ways to do this is to use a checklist, an idea that is commonly used in other complex industries such as aviation. The use of checklists is gaining some traction in the medical community. Studies show that this very low-tech tool is effective in reducing the death rate after inpatient surgery and bloodstream infections related to venous catheterization. Other more high-tech tools are also proving useful. Computerized medical records make it easier for health care providers to have complete information, and computerized prescriptions reduce handwriting errors and can catch potential drug interactions or dosing errors. Automated medical devices can also help as long as personnel are appropriately trained to use them. In many ways, one of the most important changes is cultural. When medical professionals commit to prioritizing procedures and when medical administrators commit to an environment of open communication and nonpunitive reporting, things are far more likely to change for the better.

But if the burden of change is on the medical system, where does that leave the rest of us? One of the best strategies is to be an informed consumer. If you have the choice, choose health care providers and facilities that have expertise in the condition for which you are seeking treatment. This is especially important for children, who are the most vulnerable to medical errors. Always take children to pediatric emergency rooms, urgent care clinics, and primary care providers when you have the option. Ask a lot of questions before, during, and after interventions, even if your provider seems busy. Don't be intimidated or assume that people know what they are doing. If something seems wrong or unclear, speak up. Insist that people wash their hands. Make sure you know what medications are being prescribed to you and how you should take them, and verify your doctor's instructions with the pharmacist. If you are giving medication to children, double check that you are giving the right dose at the right time. Don't assume that your doctor knows about your medical history, allergies, or other medications you are taking. Always provide more information rather than less. Do not withhold information because it is embarrassing. If you are seeing multiple providers or have a complex condition, make sure that one of your doctors (for example, your primary care physician) is coordinating your care. Finally, if you are being hospitalized, it is always a good idea to designate a friend or family member who can advocate for you when you are unconscious or otherwise impaired.

When it comes down to it, you don't have the power to prevent all medical errors. But take heart—modern medicine is still more likely to cure you than kill you.

SUMMARY

Preventability (17)

Unfortunately, you don't have a lot of control over medical errors. The best you can do is try to pick a good doctor and medical treatment facility.

Likelihood (79)

Reporting gaps make it difficult to know how common they are, but it is certain that medical errors are far more common than we would like to think.

Consequence (92)

Not all medical errors will end badly, but some certainly do.

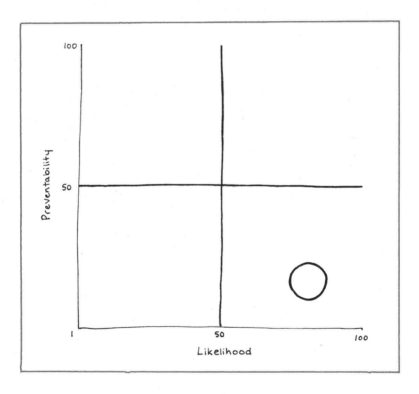

REFERENCES

Haynes, A. B., Edmondson, L., Lipsitz, S. R., Molina, G., Neville, B. A., Singer, S. J., . . . Berry, W. R. (2017). Mortality trends after a voluntary checklist-based surgical safety collaborative. *Annals of Surgery, 266,* 923.

Kohn, L. T., Corrigan, J. M., & Donaldson, M. S. (Eds.). (2000). *To err is human: Building a safer health system*. Washington, DC: National Academies Press Retrieved from http://www.ncbi.nlm.nih.gov/books/NBK225182/

Makary, M. A., & Daniel, M. (2016). Medical error—the third leading cause of death in the US. *BMJ, 353*, i2139.

Martin, J. A., Smith, B. L., Mathews, T. J., & Ventura, S. J. (1999). Births and deaths: Preliminary data for 1998. *National Vital Statistics Report, 47*, 1–45.

Pronovost, P., Needham, D., Berenholtz, S., Sinopoli, D., Chu, H., Cosgrove, S., . . . Goeschel, C. (2006). An intervention to decrease catheter-related bloodstream infections in the ICU. *New England Journal of Medicine, 355*, 2725–2732.

22. ACETAMINOPHEN

Acetaminophen (paracetamol) is an extremely popular over-the-counter pain reliever and fever reducer. By some accounts, it is the most widely used drug in the world. You have almost certainly taken it in some form. In the United States, the most popular brand name is Tylenol. However, there is no patent on the drug, and it is manufactured and sold by many different companies. One of the reasons acetaminophen is so popular is because it has long been considered very safe.

Originally discovered in the late 1800s, acetaminophen has been available in the U.S. since the 1950s. Acetaminophen is different from most over-the-counter pain medications in that it is not a nonsteroidal anti-inflammatory (NSAID) drug—it's in the aniline family. Ibuprofen (Advil), naproxen (Aleve), and aspirin are all NSAIDs, which are more effective than acetaminophen at reducing pain but can have some nasty side effects such as gastric bleeding, heart attack, and stroke. Ibuprofen has been linked to birth defects, premature birth, and miscarriage. Aspirin should not be given to children because of the risk of Reye syndrome, a potentially fatal brain disease. Acetaminophen is superior to NSAIDs in all of these respects. In fact, acetaminophen was long considered to have virtually no side effects when used as recommended. This is why it is considered to be such a safe drug and why it is frequently prescribed and recommended as a first-line treatment.

Many people were surprised, therefore, when a panel of experts convened by the FDA in 2009 recommended that the maximum daily dose, as well as the maximum single adult dose, be lowered. The FDA later proposed that all products containing acetaminophen carry stronger warning labels. In 2013, the radio program *This American Life* produced an episode titled "Use Only as Directed" in collaboration with the nonprofit group ProPublica. The show drew attention to the fact that although many, if not most, consumers were unaware of it, taking a little more than the recommended dose of acetaminophen could cause acute liver failure. In fact, as the show pointed out, at least a few hundred Americans die of acetaminophen overdoses every year. Many people started to feel like acetaminophen was maybe not so safe after all.

This is probably a good thing, because it turns out there is a difference between "safe when used as directed" and "safe." Acetaminophen is quite safe, as long as you don't take too much of it (and as long as you aren't allergic to it). But if you take too much of it, it will kill you. Acetaminophen is metabolized by the liver, so it can be eliminated in urine. This is just one of the important things your liver is quietly doing for you. There are a few different ways metabolism can happen. Acetaminophen is broken down into harmless by-products in two primary pathways. However, these pathways have a limited capacity, and when they are saturated, the drug is metabolized increasingly via a third pathway. Unfortunately, one of the by-products of this pathway is hepatotoxic—it binds to and kills liver cells. You might not spend a lot of time thinking about your liver, but you really need it. If your liver fails, you need to get a new one, or you'll die.

So the biggest problem with acetaminophen is that people take too much of it. People have a tendency to take too much of other

pain relievers too, which is also a problem. But taking too much acetaminophen is a much more immediate problem. The reason is that
acetaminophen has a narrow therapeutic window. The difference
between a safe dose and a lethal dose is small. This is not the case for
ibuprofen, for example. Unfortunately, acetaminophen doesn't work
as well as ibuprofen, so people might be more inclined to take more
of it. In addition, it is often included as a component of cough and
cold medicines, allergy medicines, sleep aids, aspirin-based headache
medicines, and opioid pain killers. The drug is so common that many
people take it without even knowing it. That's a problem, because
all those sources can add up to a toxic dose. Liver damage can occur
after a single large dose, or after sustained doses that moderately
exceed the recommended limits. Contrary to what you might think,
if prompt medical attention is sought, the prognosis for acute overdose is actually better than for a chronic overdose. This is because
there is an antidote (N-acetylcysteine). So if you accidentally take too
much acetaminophen, get to a doctor right away, even if you don't
have any symptoms.

As it turns out, even when taken as directed, acetaminophen is
not as free of side effects as we once thought, especially when it is
taken over a long time. Although it is considered safe during pregnancy, maternal consumption of acetaminophen has been tied to an
increased incidence of asthma, ADHD, neurodevelopmental problems, and problems with the development of sexual organs in babies.
But this evidence has not been strong enough to warrant a change in
the established clinical recommendations.

If it surprises you that there are side effects, it shouldn't. Acetaminophen is a drug. The only reason to take it at all is because it is
biologically active. It is interacting with your body's chemistry and,
like most pharmaceuticals, it is doing so in a nonspecific way. There
is no such thing as a perfectly safe drug. That doesn't mean there is
never a situation where acetaminophen use is warranted.

When you consider the safety of acetaminophen, you have to take into account not only the potential positive and negative effects of the drug but also the positive and negative effects of the alternatives. If you don't take acetaminophen, you're either going to take something else or live with the pain. In some cases, it might be worth trying to stick it out. Take a walk, or a bath, or a nap, or have a really good laugh. If your child is teething, you could try a cold washcloth and a little distraction. But in reality, this is not always going to cut it. Pain can be debilitating and fevers can be dangerous. Fevers can be especially problematic in some of the most vulnerable populations: young children and pregnant women—the very same populations for which the risk of NSAIDS is well established. There are many situations in which acetaminophen may be the most appropriate treatment; the key is to use it carefully.

Keep track of how much you're using (write it down). Measure liquid doses carefully. Don't use even a little bit more than the recommended amount. Pay attention to what's in different products, and don't take more than one acetaminophen-containing product at a time. Use as little as you can and don't use it with alcohol. And, whatever you do, keep acetaminophen (and all other drugs) out of the reach of children.

SUMMARY

Preventability (60)

Sometimes you can choose to use another pain reliever or to use a product that does not have acetaminophen as an ingredient, but for some populations, acetaminophen is the safest choice.

Likelihood (22)

If you aren't allergic to it, and if you use acetaminophen as directed, you are unlikely to experience a negative outcome. However, due to the narrow therapeutic range, it is surprisingly easy to take too much.

Consequence (86)

Too much acetaminophen can kill your liver, leading to a liver transplant or death.

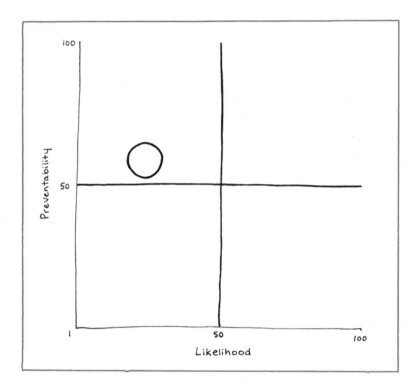

REFERENCES

Aminoshariae, A., & Khan, A. (2015). Acetaminophen: Old drug, new issues. *Journal of Endodontics, 41,* 588–593.

Brune, K., Renner, B., & Tiegs, G. (2015). Acetaminophen/paracetamol: A history of errors, failures and false decisions. *European Journal of Pain, 19,* 953–965.

Gavura, S. (2011, August 4). Tylenol: Safe painkiller, or drug of hepatic destruction? Science-Based Medicine. Retrieved from https://sciencebasedmedicine.org/tylenol-safe-painkiller-or-drug-of-hepatic-destruction/

Gavura, S. (2013, October 10). Acetaminophen: Still the pain reliever you should trust? Science-Based Medicine. Retrieved from https://www.sciencebasedmedicine.org/acetaminophen-still-the-pain-reliever-you-should-trust/

Hall, H. (2014, February 18). Tylenol may not be as safe and effective as we thought. Science-Based Medicine. Retrieved from https://sciencebasedmedicine.org/tylenol-may-not-be-as-safe-and-effective-as-we-thought/

Kress, H. G., & Untersteiner, G. (2017). Clinical update on benefit versus risks of oral paracetamol alone or with codeine: Still a good option? *Current Medical Research Opinion*, *33*, 289–304.

Prescott, L. F. (2000). Paracetamol: Past, present, and future. *American Journal of Therapy*, *7*, 143–147.

U.S. National Library of Medicine. (2017, April 15). Acetaminophen. Retrieved from https://medlineplus.gov/druginfo/meds/a681004.html

23. GENERAL ANESTHESIA

The development of effective anesthesia to permit pain-free surgery must go down in the history books as one of the greatest achievements in medicine. Up until the mid-1800s, some physicians administered opiates or alcohol to patients to dull the pain of a surgical procedure. Other physicians tried hypnosis or distraction to divert a patient's attention from the impending operation. Amputations, tumor removals, hernia operations, tooth extractions, and other surgical procedures were all performed when the patient was awake. This gruesome aspect of operations stopped with the development of drugs that could stop the sensation of pain and cause reversible unconsciousness.

None of us wants to feel a surgeon's blade as it cuts through our skin. That's where anesthesia comes to the rescue. Anesthetics are used to relax patients, eliminate their pain, and cause unconsciousness. Local anesthetics block pain to a small part of the body, but do not lead to loss of consciousness. These drugs can be used during minor surgical procedures such as stitching a small wound or having a tooth cavity filled. Regional anesthetics are used when a larger part of the body must remain pain free, for example, during surgery on the kidney or bladder or when a woman has a Cesarean section. Patients may either be awake or sedated during procedures using regional anesthetics. General anesthesia affects the entire body. It causes unconsciousness and is used during major operations, especially when the procedure will take a long time, when breathing is affected, or when there is a chance of significant blood loss.

Since the first use of ether in patients in the mid-1840s, anesthetic agents have been significantly improved such that pain-free surgeries are now routine. Nevertheless, being diagnosed with a condition or disease that requires a major operation is a source of anxiety for most people. Being anxious about an impending surgical operation is understandable when a person's health depends on the outcome of the procedure. But in addition to surgeons and nurses in the operating room, anesthesiologists are present to monitor a patient's vital signs (e.g., breathing, heart function, fluids, level of consciousness) as well as administer drugs to help a patient drift off to sleep and wake up after the surgery is completed. The dread of going under the knife is often heightened by the uncertainties associated with general anesthesia. In fact, a 2013 study found that preoperative anxiety was experienced by 81% of all surgical patients. Of those patients, 64.8% of the patients were afraid of not waking up after surgery, 42.8% were afraid that they would be aware during surgery, 41.8% were afraid that they would wake up during surgery, and 33.5% of the patients were concerned that anesthesia would paralyze them.

Statistically speaking, in the United States, approximately one person dies for every 100,000 people who receive general anesthesia. Almost half (46.6%) of the anesthesia-related deaths are caused by an overdose of anesthetics. The risk of dying from general anesthesia increases as people get older, with the elderly having the highest mortality risk.

Waking up in the middle of an operation has happened, and it is a particularly horrifying experience. Imagine being able to hear the sounds in the operating room. Even more terrifying is the thought of being paralyzed by drugs used during surgery that prevent a patient from crying out or moving. While under general anesthesia, a patient is monitored by an anesthesiologist who adjusts the drug regimen to prevent awareness and keep the patient sufficiently unconscious. Instruments to monitor brain function can also assist anesthesiologists in assessing the depth of anesthesia. Fortunately, the incidence of awareness or recall in patients who have had general anesthetics is extremely low. One study reported that only six of 87,361 (0.0068%) patients who received general anesthetics were classified as having awareness or recall of the surgery. The six patients who had some awareness or recall tended to be older and were under general anesthesia longer than patients who did not have any awareness or recall.

General anesthetics also have some less shocking potential side effects. Dizziness, nausea, and vomiting are not uncommon in patients who wake up after general anesthesia. Some people have a sore throat if a breathing tube was used or may have minor pain around the site of an injection. Some temporary confusion and memory loss, especially in elderly patients, may also occur. In rare cases, especially in elderly patients, the combination of surgery and anesthetics may cause a stroke and result in brain damage.

Patients can take several steps to reduce the risk of a poor surgical outcome that involves general anesthesia. Being in good physical shape can help reduce complications related to anesthesia. A history of smoking, obstructive sleep apnea, obesity, high blood pressure, alcoholism, and other conditions increases the risk of complications during surgery. Patients should consult with their doctors well in advance of the day of surgery and get all of their questions answered. For example, patients should ask their doctors if a local or regional anesthetic could be used instead of a general anesthetic. Some patients may have genetic factors that make them susceptible to the side effects of anesthesia. Therefore, patients should talk to family members who have had general anesthesia and ask about their experiences. If a relative has had a bad experience with general anesthesia, this information should be given to the patient's doctors. Doctors will also ask questions and provide patients with important instructions about how to prepare for surgery. For example, doctors will want to know about a patient's allergies to medicines and whether the patient is taking any drugs (including recreational drugs), medications, vitamins, or supplements. This information will be used to avoid chemical interactions with anesthetics that will be given. Patients will likely be told not to eat anything the night before surgery. This is to prevent patients from vomiting food that could block oxygen from getting to the lungs or that could be inhaled into the lungs and cause pneumonia.

Anesthesia will always have some risks, but consider the alternative. There are few people who would refuse the benefits and comfort of a pain-free surgery.

SUMMARY

Preventability (41)

If you must have major surgery, you will want general anesthesia, and there is not much you can do to avoid it. However, patients should provide a full medical history and can ask their doctors questions about anesthetic choices to avoid potential problems.

Likelihood (5)

General anesthesia is safe for most people, most of the time.

Consequence (88)

The prospect of waking up during surgery is fairly terrifying, and the side effects of general anesthesia vary in degree. In rare instances, general anesthesia can kill.

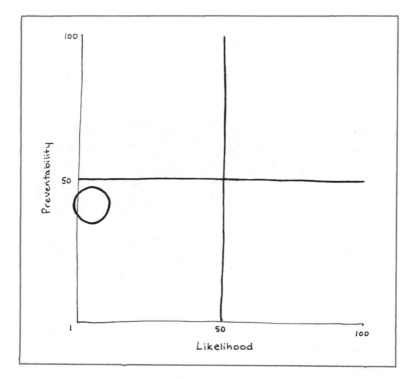

REFERENCES

Li, G., Warner, M., Lang, B. H., Huang, L., & Sun, L. S. (2009). Epidemiology of anesthesia-related mortality in the United States, 1999–2005. *Anesthesiology, 110,* 759–765.

Mavridou, P., Dimitriou, V., Manataki, A., Arnaoutoglou, E., & Papadopoulos, G. (2013). Patient's anxiety and fear of anesthesia: Effect of gender, age, education, and previous experience of anesthesia. A survey of 400 patients. *Journal of Anesthesia 27,* 104–108.

Pollard, R. J., Coyle, J. P., Gilbert, R. L., & Beck, J. E. (2007). Intraoperative awareness in a regional medical system: A review of 3 years' data. *Anesthesiology, 106,* 269–274.

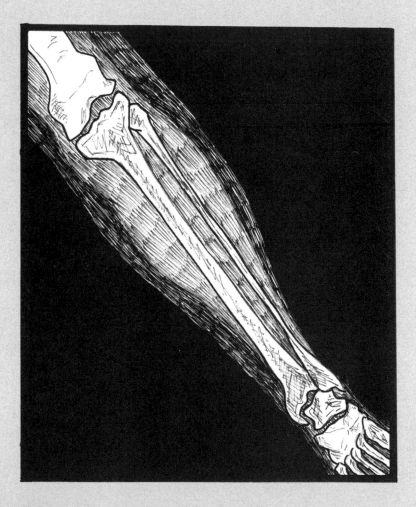

24. MEDICAL IMAGING

Skin is opaque, concealing from view all of the inner workings of our bodies. So for most of human history, there was only one way to know what was going on inside the human body: open it up and have a look. Medically, this is what we would refer to as exploratory surgery. Obviously, this method has a number of undesirable side effects. This all changed when Wilhelm Roentgen, a German physicist, made the first X-ray of his wife's hand in 1895. This ushered in the age of medical imaging, when doctors could visualize internal structures without ever using a scalpel. Our current medical imaging technology is far more advanced than those first blurry images. It is now possible to record high-resolution three-dimensional images of the body and even to create movies of physiological processes like the heart beating. It is now standard to capture the first pictures of our children before they are born.

The pioneers of X-rays used them with wild abandon. They quickly found that too high a dose could cause burns, but it wasn't until later that the more insidious, long-term effects of X-ray imaging were discovered. As most people are already aware, X-rays, like gamma rays, can cause cancer. This is because X-rays are a form of ionizing radiation. They are energetic enough to knock electrons off atoms or molecules, including the molecules that make up your DNA. Your body has a mechanism for recovering from these insults, but it is imperfect. The higher the dose of radiation, the more damage there is, and the more likely it is that there will be a mistake that ends in cancer. This makes X-rays somewhat less appealing, and it might put you off medical imaging in general. But not all imaging was created equal, in terms of either risks or diagnostic value.

X-ray imaging is used in a few different contexts, and the way it is used changes the overall risk it presents. A plain X-ray, for example, uses much less radiation than a computed tomography (CT) scan. A chest CT scan exposes a patient to an effective dose that is 3,500 times higher than a standard posterior-anterior chest X-ray. On the other hand, a CT scan provides much higher resolution and three-dimensional spatial localization. The risks of exposure to ionizing radiation are usually estimated based on the health outcomes of the survivors of the two atomic bomb explosions in Japan at the end of World War II. These survivors showed a small but significant increase in radiation-attributable cancer risk. They were exposed to between 5 and 20 mSv of radiation (a millisievert is a unit of effective dose), which is not so much greater than the effective dose from a single CT procedure, which ranges from 1 to 10 mSv. The mention of atomic bombs might scare your pants off, but remember that the increase in probability, estimated to be about 0.05% for a single CT scan, is much less than the odds that you would get cancer anyway, which are about one in five. You'll have to decide for yourself whether that is good news or bad news. In any case, the risk from radiation is not negligible, so it pays to think about it and discuss your options with your doctor. As you consider these options, you might want to bear the following points in mind. First, exposures add up. Second, some populations are more sensitive to radiation damage, like women and, especially, children. Finally, there are situations when a CT scan is medically necessary and might even safe your life.

Positron emission tomography (PET), like CT, relies on ionizing radiation to produce images. In this test you actually ingest a radioactive molecule—a sugar that is absorbed into cells when they require energy. The radioactivity that is emitted from these molecules acts like a beacon, effectively marking the location of the cells that absorbed them. PET is primarily used for cancer imaging. Rapidly dividing cancer cells require more metabolic energy than other cells in the body and therefore absorb more of the radioactive sugar. The effective dose of a PET scan is about 14 mSv, which exceeds the range of CT.

Like CT, magnetic resonance imaging (MRI) can create detailed three-dimensional images of your insides. Unlike CT, MRI does not use ionizing radiation and is not known to cause cancer. MRI relies on a combination of applied magnetic fields and radio waves. In order to get this type of imaging you have to lie in the bore of a magnet, which is usually a small tube. MRI also takes much longer than CT, which means you need to keep very still for a long time in a small space. This can be difficult for people who are claustrophobic as well as for children. Because very strong magnetic fields are involved, it is very important not to have any metal on or in your body, or even in the room with you when the magnet is on. This means people with artificial joints, bone plates or screws, pacemakers, deep brain stimulators, and other metallic devices should not get MRI scans. Metal implants can heat up and move, which is obviously not great when they are inside your body. Metallic objects can also cause distortions in the field that destroy the images. In addition, it is worth noting that just because magnetic fields do not alter DNA, it doesn't mean that they have no biological effect. Our bodies, and especially our brains, rely heavily on electrical potentials to carry out business. Applying a strong magnetic field may throw this ongoing business out of whack. Nevertheless, MRI is considered a very safe procedure for people who don't have any metal implants. There isn't a lot known about how magnetic fields might impact a fetus, so MRIs are not recommended for pregnant women unless there is a strong medical indication, for either the woman or her unborn child.

Many people associate ultrasound with babies because at least one ultrasound is now part of the standard of care for most pregnancies. It can reveal structural abnormalities in the fetus, show a breech presentation, and expose other problems, like placenta previa. Ultrasound produces images based on the reflection of mechanical waves, or pressure waves. These waves are similar to sound waves but are out of the auditory perceptible range (which is why they are called ultrasound). Ultrasound does not involve any ionizing radiation and is considered very safe, which is why it is used during pregnancy. However, it does have some effects on tissue. Notably, it produces heat, which is generally bad, especially for a developing fetus. For this reason, ultrasound is recommended only when it is medically necessary. One study has linked the severity of autism in autistic children (*not* the incidence of autism in the general population) to the number of first-trimester ultrasound scans, but this connection is controversial. Nevertheless, getting a high-resolution fetal ultrasound image at the mall for souvenir purposes is discouraged. Ultrasound has many applications beyond fetal ultrasound. Because it is especially useful for capturing movement, cardiac ultrasound is very common.

Medical imaging represents a huge diagnostic benefit, and there is no question that it has saved many lives as well as relieved a great deal of pain and suffering. At the same time, as with almost everything in life, it is wise to proceed with caution, consideration, and information.

SUMMARY

Preventability (51)

You can be cognizant of the risks of medical imaging and try to minimize the number of imaging procedures you have, and you certainly can avoid souvenir ultrasounds. But medical imaging is often necessary and appropriate.

Likelihood (25)

For adults, and especially men, medical imaging does not increase the risk of cancer or other negative health outcomes much. In children, the risks associated with exposure to ionizing radiation are a greater concern.

Consequence (97)

Ionizing radiation is known to cause cancer, so the potential consequences of too many head CTs can be grim.

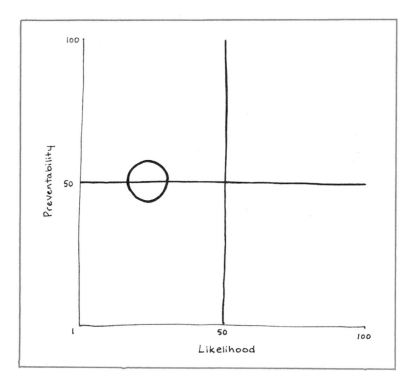

REFERENCES

American Cancer Society. (2015, February 24). Do x-rays and gamma rays cause cancer? Retrieved from https://www.cancer.org/cancer/cancer-causes/radiation-exposure/x-rays-gamma-rays/do-xrays-and-gamma-rays-cause-cancer.html

Health Physics Society. (2010, January). Radiation exposure from medical exams and procedures. Retrieved from http://hps.org/documents/Medical_Exposures_Fact_Sheet.pdf

Mayo Clinic. (2017, December 30). MRI. Retrieved from https://www.mayoclinic.org/tests-procedures/mri/home/ovc-20235698

McLennan, A. (2016). Ultrasound and autism spectrum disorder. *Australian Journal of Ultrasound Medicine, 19*, 131–132.

National Cancer Institute. (2013, July 16). Computed tomography (CT) scans and cancer. Retrieved from https://www.cancer.gov/about-cancer/diagnosis-staging/ct-scans-fact-sheet

National Institute of Biomedical Imaging and Bioengineering. (2016, July). Ultrasound. Retrieved from https://www.nibib.nih.gov/science-education/science-topics/ultrasound

Nikolić, L., Bataveljić, D., Andjus, P. R., Nedeljković, M., Todorović, D., & Janać, B. (2013). Changes in the expression and current of the Na+/K+ pump in the snail nervous system after exposure to a static magnetic field. *Journal of Experimental Biology, 216*, 3531–3541.

U.S. Food and Drug Administration. (2017, December 5). Computed tomography (CT). Retrieved from https://www.fda.gov/Radiation-EmittingProducts/RadiationEmittingProductsandProcedures/MedicalImaging/MedicalX-Rays/ucm115317.htm

U.S. Food and Drug Administration. (2017, December 5). What are the radiation risks from CT? Retrieved from https://www.fda.gov/Radiation-EmittingProducts/RadiationEmittingProductsandProcedures/MedicalImaging/MedicalX-Rays/ucm115329.htm

Webb, S. J., Garrison, M. M., Bernier, R., McClintic, A. M., King, B. H., & Mourad, P. D. (2017). Severity of ASD symptoms and their correlation with the presence of copy number variations and exposure to first trimester ultrasound. *Autism Research, 10*, 472–484.

25. FLESH-EATING INFECTION

Hearing the words "flesh-eating infection" might make you head for the hills in fear of a zombie apocalypse, but it is not undead walkers that should cause you anxiety. Rather, this flesh eating is done by bacteria such as group A *Streptococcus, Klebsiella, Clostridium, Escherichia coli, Staphylococcus aureus,* and *Aeromonas hydrophila.* Flesh-eating infections, also called necrotizing fasciitis, occur when these bacteria enter the body through a break in the skin and multiply. The bacteria damage and destroy connective tissue (fascia) around muscles, nerves, fat, and blood vessels. If the bacteria cannot be contained, the infection can lead to amputations and/or death.

Blisters, cuts, scrapes, scratches, insect bites, and puncture wounds can all provide bacteria with a path into the body. Group A *Streptococcus,* the same bacteria that cause strep throat, is responsible for most cases of flesh-eating infections. Although many healthy people host group A *Streptococcus* in or on their bodies, infections usually do not occur. In this case, the immune system likely is able to fend off an attack by the invading bacteria to prevent damage. However, in 500 to 1,500 people in the U.S. each year, the bacteria turn into hungry microscopic beasts that gobble up the skin, muscle, and fat. The bacteria can also release toxic chemicals capable of destroying tissue. Most of the people who develop flesh-eating infections have conditions or illnesses (e.g., cancer, kidney disease, diabetes) that weaken their immune systems, but healthy people can be affected too.

Symptoms of necrotizing fasciitis can come on within just a few hours after an injury. The first signs of an infection usually include pain or soreness that is out of proportion to the visible injury. The skin around the injury may swell, feel warm, and turn red. Other signs of an infection include fever, nausea, weakness, and vomiting. Blisters and spots may also appear, and the area may be tender to the touch. The infection can spread to other parts of the body at a rate up to 1 in (2.5 cm) per hour. To help diagnose an infection and to see the extent of damage, doctors may order a body scan such as a CT scan or an MRI. Untreated, the infection can lead to a drop in blood pressure, sepsis, toxic shock, organ failure, and death.

Unfortunately, the early symptoms of necrotizing fasciitis look similar to the flu or a minor injury. This makes diagnosis difficult. Therefore, a person may not seek immediate medical attention. This can be a fatal mistake because necrotizing fasciitis spreads so quickly. Any delay in treatment reduces a person's chance of survival. Without treatment, flesh-eating infections are often fatal. Even with treatment, about 25% of the people who contract these infections die.

Treating necrotizing fasciitis usually starts with intravenous antibiotics, often several different types, to fight the offending bacteria. Doctors may also perform surgery to remove damaged tissue and to stop an infection from spreading. In severe cases, an entire arm or leg or other body part must be amputated to save the patient. Hyperbaric oxygen therapy (HBO) has been used to treat necrotizing fasciitis but has not been the subject of rigorous testing for its effectiveness. HBO involves placing patients in a special container where high concentrations of oxygen can be delivered. The high concentration of oxygen slows the growth of anaerobic bacteria to improve healing and preserve healthy tissue.

The best way to prevent an infection is to have good hygiene practices. Open wounds should be washed completely with soap and water. Anyone with an open cut should also stay out of swimming pools, rivers, lakes, and oceans to avoid an infection. The injured site should be kept clean and checked until it is healed. Medical assistance should be sought immediately if the pain from an injury is much greater than expected for the size of the wound. Luckily, necrotizing fasciitis is not usually spread from person to person because bacteria must get into the body through the skin to cause an infection, but it's a good idea to avoid touching other people's infected wounds. The odds are good that you wouldn't want to anyway.

SUMMARY

Preventability (82)

Good personal hygiene practices and prompt medical attention will prevent many flesh-eating infections.

Likelihood (4)

The chance of contracting necrotizing fasciitis is low.

Consequence (94)

Without prompt, effective medical treatment, necrotizing fasciitis is often fatal.

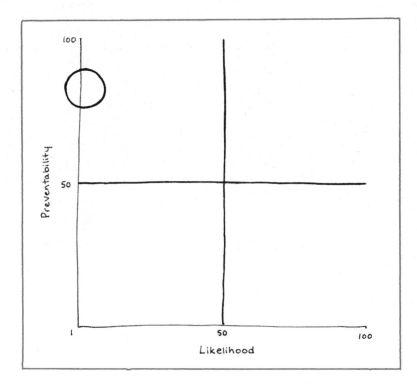

REFERENCES

Harbrecht, B. G., & Nash, N. A. (2016). Necrotizing soft tissue infections: A review. *Surgical Infections, 17*, 503–509.
Tunovic, E., Gawaziuk, J., Bzura, T., Embil, J., Esmail, A., & Logsetty, S. (2012). Necrotizing fasciitis: A six-year experience. *Journal of Burn Care Research, 33*, 93–100.

26. HEALTH CARE–ASSOCIATED INFECTIONS

When you are ill or injured, you may need to go to a hospital for treatment. While in the hospital, you expect that your health problem will be effectively addressed; you don't expect that you will end up sicker than when you were admitted. Unfortunately, this isn't always the case. Every year thousands of people contract new infections while they are in a health care facility (hospital, dialysis center, outpatient clinic, long-term care facility). In the United States, 5–10% of patients (1.7 million patients) who are hospitalized acquire a health care–associated infection (HAI) annually, and 99,000 people die as a result. HAIs also contribute to the high cost of health care, estimated to be $20 billion. There are a few procedures (e.g., surgery) and treatment devices (e.g., catheters, ventilators) that are commonly involved in these infections.

The major types of HAIs are (1) central line–associated bloodstream infections (CLABSIs), (2) catheter-associated urinary tract infections, (3) surgical site infections, (4) ventilator-associated pneumonia, and (5) *Clostridium difficile* infections. Central line–associated bloodstream infections are the result of contamination following placement of a central venous catheter. Central lines are small tubes that are inserted into large veins to provide medications, drugs, or fluids or to collect blood for testing. If a catheter is not sterile or microorganisms are present on the skin before the catheter is placed, bacteria or viruses can enter the bloodstream. Each year in the United States, there are approximately 30,100 CLABSIs. Common symptoms of CLABSIs are redness, swelling, warmth at the site of the central line, pain, and fever. Of course, medical personnel take precautions to prevent CLABSIs by washing their hands, using sterile gloves and barriers when the central line is inserted, cleaning a patient's skin properly, and removing the central line when it is no longer needed. Patients can also reduce the risk of contracting a CLABSI by keeping the area around the central line clear and clean. Even with these safety measures, infections can happen. Treatment involves the identification of the offending pathogen and the administration of medication (e.g., appropriate antibiotic) to eliminate the infection.

Urinary catheters are tubes that are inserted through the urethra into the bladder to drain urine. These catheters are used when a person cannot empty his or her bladder unassisted, for example, during some types of surgery, after a spinal cord injury, or when kidney stones block urine flow. Bacteria can enter the urinary tract through the catheter, causing a catheter-associated urinary tract infection (CAUTI). The infection can be caused by a contaminated catheter, backward flow of urine from the catheter bag into the bladder, or catheter contamination from a bowel movement. The longer a catheter is used, the more likely an infection will develop. Typical symptoms of a CAUTI are cloudy urine, bloody urine, pain in the lower back or abdomen, fever, chills, fatigue, and vomiting. CAUTIs are usually treated with antibiotics. If left untreated, CAUTIs can cause serious kidney problems.

Surgical site infections (SSIs) are a risk whenever someone has an operation. They are fairly common: each year in the United States, 2–5% of the people who have inpatient surgery get an SSI, and there are 160,000–300,000 cases of SSI. These infections can occur in the skin, in underlying tissue such as muscles or organs, or on implanted materials such as a pacemaker or an artificial joint. Common symptoms of an SSI include pain, swelling, or redness at the surgical site, fluid drainage near the wound, and fever. As with CLABSIs and CAUTIs, SSIs are treated by first identifying the bacteria causing the infection and then providing the appropriate antibiotic. Proper surgical hygiene to keep the surgical area clean and, when indicated, receiving antibiotics before surgery are among the recommendations to help prevent SSIs.

Sometimes patients must be placed on a ventilator to help them breathe. Ventilators are used during and after some surgeries and when people are too weak to breathe for themselves. The ventilator pumps oxygenated air into a patient's lung and removes carbon dioxide from the body. Because the air flows through a tube that is inserted into the patient's mouth or nose or through a hole in the neck, bacteria can travel down this path and into the lungs, causing ventilator-associated pneumonia (VAP), which is especially dangerous because it affects people who are already very ill. Health care professionals should monitor patients' ability to breathe on their own so that the ventilator can be removed as soon as possible to reduce the risk of VAP.

A particularly nasty HAI is a *Clostridium difficile* infection. In the United States in 2011, there were approximately 500,000 *C. difficile* infections, and 29,000 people died within 30 days after being diagnosed with it. *C. difficile* is a bacterium found in feces that can cause colitis (inflammation of the colon). The infection is spread when contaminated feces come in contact with objects such as bathroom surfaces, tables, and utensils. If other people touch these contaminated items, they can ingest the bacteria and transmit it to themselves. People with *C. difficile* infections may have diarrhea, fever, nausea, abdominal pain, and loss of appetite. *C. difficile* infections are notoriously difficult to treat with antibiotics, and infections often return.

Most HAIs can be treated with antibiotics, but more and more of these infections are caused by resistant bacteria. These infections are particularly dangerous because they may require antibiotics with more negative side effects, or they may not be treatable at all.

The reduction of HAIs starts by preventing them in the first place. This involves efforts to stop infections moving through catheters and ventilation tubes, eliminating the spread of bacteria from person to person, and using antibiotics appropriately. All patients should leave the hospital in better shape than they entered.

SUMMARY

Preventability (55)

Personal hygiene and asking health care providers questions when something just doesn't seem right can help reduce the risk of HAIs.

Likelihood (54)

If you must undergo surgery or have a medical procedure involving a central line, urinary catheter, or ventilator, you are at risk of developing an HAI.

Consequence (65)

An HAI can cause serious health consequences, but most can be treated with medication.

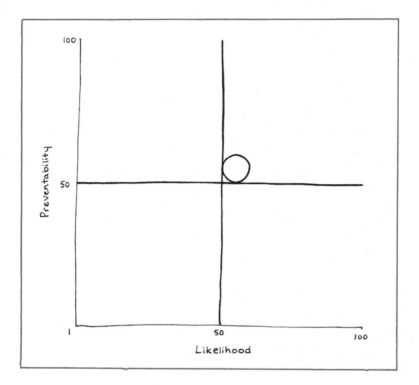

REFERENCES

Anderson, D. J., Podgorny, K., Berríos-Torres, S. I., Bratzler, D. W., Dellinger, E. P., Greene, L., . . . Kaye, K. S. (2014). Strategies to prevent surgical site infections in acute care hospitals: 2014 update. *Infection Control and Hospital Epidemiology, 35*, 605–627.

Centers for Disease Control and Prevention. (2016, October 25). HAI Data and Statistics. Retrieved from https://www.cdc.gov/hai/surveillance/index.html

Centers for Disease Control and Prevention. (2018, January). Bloodstream infection event. Retrieved from https://www.cdc.gov/nhsn/pdfs/pscmanual/4psc_clabscurrent.pdf

Centers for Disease Control and Prevention. (n.d.). Preventing healthcare-associated infections. Retrieved from https://www.cdc.gov/washington/~cdcatwork/pdf/infections.pdf

Lessa, F. C., Mu, Y., Bamberg, W. M., Beldavs, Z. G., Dumyati, G. K., Dunn, J. R., . . . McDonald, L. C. (2015). Burden of Clostridium difficile infection in the United States. *New England Journal of Medicine, 372*, 825–834.

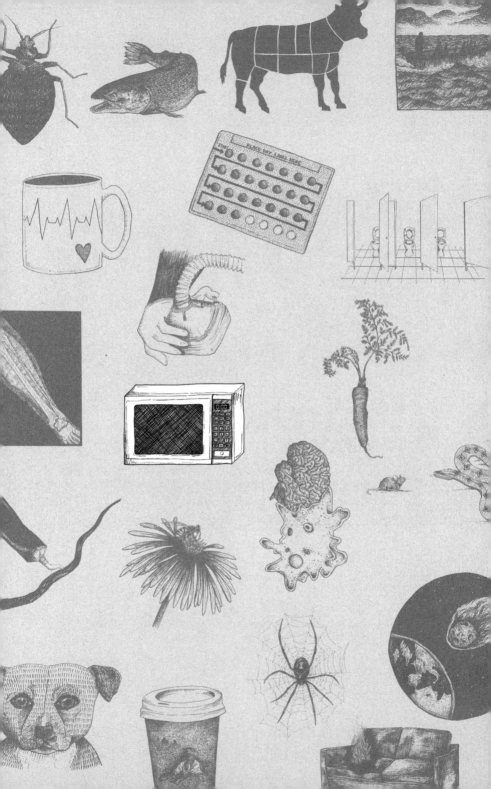

Environment

27. MOBILE PHONES

In just about 20 years, mobile phones have gone from being a novelty to a necessity and from rarity to ubiquity. Almost everyone in the world has a mobile phone. They're really not even properly described as phones anymore. Smartphones are a combination of computer, audio and video player, text messenger, and personal navigation system. It's almost incidental that they make phone calls. They have been adopted by all segments of society, including young children and the elderly. There are even special phones designed for these demographics. But for all of their popularity, mobile phones have created a lingering fear that they might give us brain tumors. That would make them significantly less desirable.

Mobile phones communicate via radio frequency, a form of electromagnetic radiation. If the word "radiation" makes you think of gamma rays, then that immediately sounds terrifying. But visible light is also a form of electromagnetic radiation. So not all radiation is the same. In terms of understanding radiation, energy is a really important quantity. Higher energy radiation is more likely to cause damage to biological tissues because it can knock electrons off the atoms or molecules in your body, making them into ions. Gamma rays, X-rays, and ultraviolet rays are all ionizing, and exposure to these types of radiation is known to cause cancer. Radio waves, however, are lower energy and are not ionizing.

This is an essential quality in a device that is meant to be held up to your head. But while radio waves are nonionizing, that doesn't mean they are inherently safe. Like microwaves, radio waves are in the thermal range. You may have noticed that if you talk on your mobile phone for a long time, your ear starts to get hot. The word "heat" is shorthand for "energy transfer," and some serious questions have been raised about the biological effects of chronic exposure to that level of energy.

As you might expect, scientific studies have investigated this issue. Unfortunately, the results have been inconclusive and sometimes conflicting. This is compounded by the fact that different studies use different methods, different populations, and different outcome measures. It is also the case that mobile phone technology has changed rapidly, and results that apply to earlier phone models may not be relevant to later phone models. Furthermore, because mobile phones are also relatively new, the long-term consequences, especially for children, are not yet manifest. In the United States, several regulatory and scientific agencies have reviewed the available data, including the Federal Communications Commission, the Occupational Safety and Health Administration, the CDC, the National Institute of Environmental Health Sciences, and the National Cancer Institute. The official opinion of these agencies is similar and can be summarized as follows: there is no conclusive evidence that mobile phones cause cancer, but more research is needed. The World Health Organization has classified radio frequency fields, including those generated by mobile phones, as "possibly carcinogenic to humans." That may not feel very comforting, but according to the FDA, "If there is a risk from being exposed to radiofrequency energy (RF) from cell phones—and at this point we do not know that there is—it is probably very small."

More research is needed and is currently underway. In 2016, the National Toxicology Program released some preliminary results from a large rodent study concerning exposure to mobile phone radiation. These results showed a small but significant increase in malignant brain tumors and noncancerous heart tumors in male rats. Notably, these are the same kind of tumors that were reported in some human studies. But as always, there are a few caveats worth noting about these data. First, they are preliminary and have not yet undergone full peer review. Second, the animals in the study were exposed to about 9 hours of radiation a day for two years, which is more time than most people spend on the phone. Finally, the incidence of tumors only increased for male rats, which is a bit odd and not yet explained. Nevertheless, these results highlight that the book on mobile phone safety is not yet closed.

Even if mobile phones do cause health problems (which is still unclear), they are so integrated into our modern lives that it's going to be hard to go back. Just try finding a pay phone these days. Fortunately, there are some simple things you can do to reduce your exposure. Primarily, you should just try to keep your phone away from your head in particular and away from your body in general. Use a headset when you're talking on your phone, and don't keep your phone in your pocket. Electromagnetic power decays exponentially as you move away from the source, so moving your phone away from your ear has a dramatic effect on the dosage. Keep in mind that while wired headsets communicate with wires (an old-fashioned but effective alternative), Bluetooth headsets also use radio frequencies to communicate (although these fields are lower power because the distance is smaller).

Mobile phones are not the only source of radio frequency fields that you are likely to encounter in a given day. Just about everything that operates wirelessly uses radio waves, for example, wireless internet, baby monitors, and, well, radios.

Finally, while the data are inconclusive when it comes to mobile phones and cancer, there is another deadly side effect of mobile phone use that is very well documented and frequently ignored. Using a mobile phone while driving (either to talk or to text) is extremely dangerous. You might think that you are good at multitasking, but if you're human, you aren't. Talking on a mobile phone, even if you're wearing a headset, can distract you from the road. Even walking is less safe when you're talking or texting or web browsing on your phone. So, while it's unclear how worried you should be about the association between mobile phone radiation and cancer, you should probably be more worried than you are about being distracted by your mobile device.

SUMMARY

Preventability (63)

You don't have to carry a mobile phone, and you don't have to have wireless internet in your home. But these devices are so integrated into modern Western society that it would take some serious lifestyle accommodation to limit usage. Even then, you can't avoid radio frequency fields.

Likelihood (16)

It is unlikely that your mobile phone will give you cancer, but it isn't clear how unlikely.

Consequence (50)

If your phone gave you brain cancer, that would be bad, but it isn't clear that there is a causal relationship between the two. For this reason, we have assigned a middling-level consequence score.

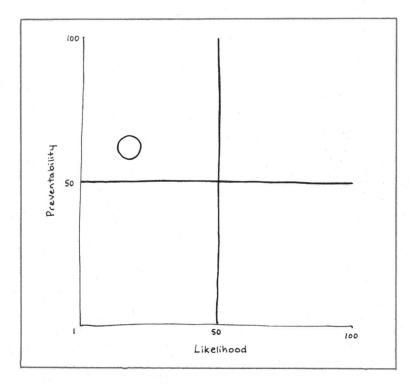

REFERENCES

American Cancer Society. (2018, February 5). Cellular phones. Retrieved from https://www.cancer.org/cancer/cancer-causes/radiation-exposure/cellular-phones.html

Federal Communications Commission. (2017, September 8). Wireless devices and health concerns. Retrieved from https://www.fcc.gov/consumers/guides/wireless-devices-and-health-concerns

National Toxicology Program. (2018, February 7). Cell phones. Retrieved from https://ntp.niehs.nih.gov/results/areas/cellphones/index.html

Portier, C. J., & Leonard, W. L. (2016, June 13). Do cell phones cause cancer? Probably, but it's complicated. *Scientific American Blog*. Retrieved from https://blogs.scientificamerican.com/guest-blog/do-cell-phones-cause-cancer-probably-but-it-s-complicated/

U.S. Food and Drug Administration. (2017, December 4). Reducing exposure: Hands-free kits and other accessories. Retrieved from https://www.fda.gov/Radiation-EmittingProducts/RadiationEmittingProductsandProcedures/HomeBusinessand Entertainment/CellPhones/ucm116293.htm

Wyde, M., Cesta, M., Blystone, C., Elmore, S., Foster, P., Hooth, M., . . . Bucher, J. (2016). Report of partial findings from the National Toxicology Program carcinogenesis studies of cell phone radiofrequency radiation in Hsd: Sprague Dawley® SD rats (whole body exposure). *bioRxiv*, 055699.

28. MOLD

I f you are like most people, you don't have especially warm feelings about mold. We tend to think of these fuzzy microbes as irritants. They spoil our food, give us athlete's foot, and discolor our shower grout. However, they also give us cheese, soy sauce, and penicillin. And, of course, they play a critical role in the ecosystem, decomposing organic matter and effectively keeping dead plants and animals from piling up everywhere. So, it's a bit of a mixed bag.

Molds are neither plants nor animals; like mushrooms and yeast, they are fungi. They reproduce by releasing millions of tiny spores that can be dispersed in air or water. Molds are everywhere; you cannot avoid them. There are many, many different kinds of mold, but one thing they all have in common is that they need moisture. This is why molds are notorious for growing in damp places, like basements, bathrooms, and Florida. Molds also need some organic matter to consume, because unlike plants they cannot photosynthesize sunlight. Some molds grow well on oranges, some on wood, and some on the dirt that collects on your windowsills.

Some molds cause infections in humans, typically on the skin. For example, ringworm, nail fungus, and thrush are all caused by mold. More serious infections include valley fever (coccidioidomycosis) and histoplasmosis, which are associated with inhalation of mold spores. People with compromised immune systems are more susceptible to invasive lung infections like aspergillosis, and these types of infections can be difficult to treat. In addition, mold is well known to be allergenic and can exacerbate asthma and other respiratory conditions.

Some molds produce mycotoxins, which, as the name would imply, are poisonous to humans and other animals when they are ingested. These compounds can be neurotoxic, carcinogenic, and teratogenic—all features that you don't want associated with your food supply. Possibly the most famous mycotoxins are the ergot alkaloids, which are produced by a mold that grows on rye. Consuming contaminated grains causes ergotism, known in the Middle Ages as St. Anthony's fire. This unpleasant disease is characterized by seizures, abnormal sensations, vomiting, diarrhea, psychosis, and gangrene. In addition to being responsible for a number of historical plagues, ergot poisoning is hypothesized by some to have played a role in the Salem witch trials. In more modern times, ergot alkaloids are used to treat migraine headaches. Some mycotoxins are antibiotics. Some mycotoxins, called trichothecenes, have been developed for chemical warfare. Trichothecenes were discovered to be pathogenic in Russia after an outbreak of serious disease in humans and horses in the 1930s. The culpable fungus was eventually determined to be *Stachybotrys chartarum* (also known as *Stachybotrys atra*)—now popularly known as toxic black mold.

Cases of mold-contaminated food still come up from time to time. But if you're worried about mold, it's probably because you have heard of toxic mold syndrome (TMS), a controversial and poorly defined condition that is associated with exposure to mold-contaminated environments. Symptoms include headache, eye irritation, stuffy nose and sinuses, bloody nose, fatigue, gastrointestinal problems, and neurological complaints (like difficulty concentrating). Most frighteningly, in the mid-1990s, the CDC identified an association between pulmonary hemorrhage in infants and mold growth in their homes. The report called out *Stachybotrys chartarum* as a potential causative agent in the cluster of cases they examined in Cleveland, Ohio. This added fuel to the fire of mold-related angst, which would lead to building demolitions, insurance claims, multimillion-dollar lawsuits, and an entire industry specializing in mold removal.

But the connection between environmental mold exposure and human illness is complicated, and TMS remains controversial. A follow-up by the CDC revealed errors in the initial reports on infant pulmonary hemorrhage, and the agency concluded that the connection with mold exposure was unproven. The symptoms of TMS are vague, and the studies that have shown effects have been methodologically flawed. It is not out of the question or even unreasonable to believe that there could be some health effects of living, working, or going to school in a damp building. However, it is difficult to know what to attribute to mycotoxins, mold spores, bacteria (like *Legionella*, which also lives in damp environments), and chemicals like formaldehyde that may be released from damp building materials. And there is almost certainly a psychological component. There is currently no solid scientific evidence that inhalation exposure to toxic black mold poses a serious threat to human health.

That being said, it is still recommended that you avoid hosting mold in your home. Mold needs water and humidity, so the best thing you can do is keep things dry. Use ventilation fans, air conditioners, and dehumidifiers. Fix water leaks and properly dry any parts of your home that get flooded. Wipe up the condensation on your windowsills. Take care of small patches of mold before they can spread, and, if you have a major mold problem, get a professional to do remediation. Of course, if you get a fungal infection on your skin or in your lungs, you should have it treated. And you shouldn't eat moldy food. Really, mold is most likely to make you sick if you eat it.

SUMMARY

Preventability (53)

You can do your best to reduce mold, but if you live in a damp environment, you should prepare for a long-term war with fungus.

Likelihood (45)

If you eat mold, it will very likely make you sick. If you live in a moldy building, you may have allergies or respiratory problems, especially if are already prone to them.

Consequence (66)

Inhaling mold spores can make you sick, but it probably won't kill you. Eating toxic mold can make you very sick, but in modern times it is rare for otherwise healthy people to die from mold poisoning.

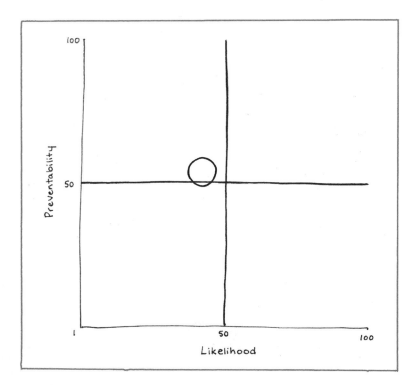

REFERENCES

Bennett, J. W., & Klich, M. (2003). Mycotoxins. *Clinical Microbiology Reviews, 16,* 497 516.

Centers for Disease Control and Prevention. (1997). Update: Pulmonary hemorrhage/hemosiderosis among infants—Cleveland, Ohio, 1993–1996. *MMWR Morbidity and Mortality Weekly Report, 46,* 33–35.

Centers for Disease Control and Prevention. (2000). Update: Pulmonary hemorrhage/hemosiderosis among infants—Cleveland, Ohio, 1993–1996. *MMWR Morbidity and Mortality Weekly Report, 49,* 180–184.

Centers for Disease Control and Prevention. (2017, December 20). Facts about Stachybotrys chartarum and other molds. Retrieved from https://www.cdc.gov/mold/stachy.htm

Edmondson, D. A., Nordness, M. E., Zacharisen, M. C., Kurup, V. P., & Fink, J. N. (2005). Allergy and "toxic mold syndrome." *Annals of Allergy, Asthma and Immunology, 94,* 234–239.

Fung, F., & Clark, R. F. (2004). Health effects of mycotoxins: A toxicological overview. *Journal of Toxicology: Clinical Toxicology, 42,* 217–234.

Kuhn, D. M., & Ghannoum, M. A. (2003). Indoor mold, toxigenic fungi, and Stachybotrys chartarum: Infectious disease perspective. *Clinical Microbiology Review, 16,* 144–172.

National Institute of Environmental Health Sciences. (2017, September 1). Mold. Retrieved from https://www.niehs.nih.gov/health/topics/agents/mold/index.cfm

Pettigrew, H. D., Selmi, C. F., Teuber, S. S., & Gershwin, M. E. (2010). Mold and human health: Separating the wheat from the chaff. *Clinical Reviews of Allergy and Immunology, 38,* 148–155.

Richard, J. L. (2007). Some major mycotoxins and their mycotoxicoses—an overview. *International Journal of Food Microbiology, 119,* 3–10.

29. MICROWAVE OVENS

Pop in some food or drink, push a button, wait a minute or two, and voilà, out comes a hot meal or beverage. You can't beat the convenience of a microwave oven. The first commercial microwave ovens were built for restaurants by Raytheon in 1946, followed by the introduction of a wall-mounted consumer microwave oven by Tappan in 1955, and then the Amana home countertop microwave in 1967. Since the late 1960s, the microwave oven has been a ubiquitous appliance with a place in more than 90% of all homes in the United States. The increasing use of microwave ovens has been accompanied by some concerns about their safety and possible effects on health.

Microwave ovens use nonionizing electromagnetic radiation to transfer energy to food. This form of energy travels in waves with frequencies around 2,450 megahertz, which means that microwaves fall between radio waves and infrared rays on the electromagnetic spectrum. Unlike metallic materials that reflect microwaves, items that contain water absorb their energy. To heat, microwaves bounce off the oven walls and hit the food or beverage spinning on a central turntable. Food gets hot because microwaves vibrate water molecules: the faster the water molecules vibrate, the hotter the food.

Since 1971, the U.S. Food and Drug Administration (FDA)

has set standards for microwave ovens to ensure that they do not pose a risk to the public. Microwave ovens must not leak more than 5 milliwatts of radiation per square centimeter at a distance of 5 centimeters from the oven surface. This amount of microwave radiation is far below the amount known to cause damage to people. In addition, the amplitude of radiation drops quickly as the distance from the source increases. So, to minimize exposure, people just need to step back from the microwave. The FDA also requires that microwave ovens have a double lock system to prevent microwaves from escaping if the door is opened. Microwave ovens that have damaged seals, doors, or outer casing should not be used.

Zapping food with microwaves does not appear to reduce the nutritional value of the item significantly. On the contrary, microwaves cook food quickly and may even help maintain the color and beneficial chemicals of cooked vegetables. Pork and chicken retain higher levels of vitamin B_6 and thiamine after microwave cooking compared to cooking in conventional ovens. There is no need to worry about food becoming radioactive, because after a microwave oven is turned off, the emission of microwaves stops, and none of the microwave energy is left in the food.

Some people are concerned that microwaved food is somehow toxic because molecules are changed by microwave radiation. Cooking, regardless of the way food is heated, does change how proteins are shaped. These denatured proteins allow food to be absorbed by the digestive system. There is nothing inherently toxic about denatured proteins.

Some potential dangers associated with microwave ovens have to do with underestimating the temperature of cooked food. For example, water heated in a microwave oven can exceed its boiling point without any visible bubbles. This may happen when water is placed in a clean glass container with smooth walls. The superheated water can explode and cause serious scalding and burns when a spoon or other material is inserted into the container. To minimize the chance of injury caused by superheated water, a nonmetallic object can be placed in the container with the water before the microwave oven is turned on.

It is a good idea to use containers labeled "microwave safe" in the microwave. Many plastic containers contain chemicals that help them maintain their shape. The FDA tests plastic containers to measure the quantity of these chemicals, such as bisphenol-A and phthalates, that might leach into microwaved food. If measured levels are in a range that has been shown to be safe for lab animals, then a container can be labeled "microwave safe."

The low level of exposure to radiation produced by microwave ovens makes "zapping" and "nuking" food a relatively safe way to cook, as long as microwave-safe containers are used. Incidentally, you should never put metal in the microwave. You'll get an interesting light show, but you'll ruin your machine and might burn down your house.

SUMMARY

Preventability (89)

You do not need a microwave oven to cook or warm up food. Care should be used to ensure food is not too hot to eat after it comes out of a microwave oven.

Likelihood (8)

Exposure to dangerous levels of microwave radiation is not likely.

Consequence (17)

Normal use of microwave ovens should not cause any health-related problems. Superheated food may cause burns.

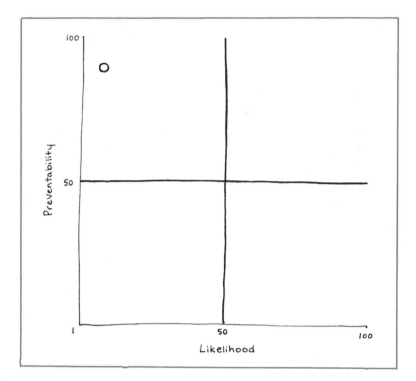

REFERENCES

Pellegrini, N., Chiavaro, E., Gardana, C., Mazzeo, T., Contino, D., Gallo, M., . . . Por-
rini, M. (2010). Effect of different cooking methods on color, phytochemical concentration, and antioxidant capacity of raw and frozen brassica vegetables. *Journal of
Agricultural and Food Chemistry, 58*, 4310–4321.

Siebens, J. (2013). Extended measures of well-being: Living conditions in the United
States: 2011. U.S. Census Bureau. Retrieved from https://www.census.gov/history/
pdf/sipp-data-appliances.pdf

Uherová, R., Hozová, B., & Smirnov, V. (1993). The effect of microwave heating on
retention of some B vitamins. *Food Chemistry, 46*, 293–295.

30. ASBESTOS

Asbestos is the name given to a group of natural minerals including chrysotile, amosite, crocidolite, tremolite, anthophyllite, and actinolite. Since the late 1800s, builders have capitalized on the versatile properties of asbestos to make materials that are strong, light, chemical resistant, and heat resistant. When buildings in the United States were constructed in the 1900s, asbestos was used for insulation, fireproofing, and soundproofing. Roof, floor, and wall materials all commonly incorporated asbestos. Unfortunately, this wonder material has a nasty side effect: inhaled asbestos fibers can cause lung disease that is often fatal.

In the United States, several regulations (e.g., National Emission Standards for Hazardous Air Pollutants, Toxic Substances Control Act, Clean Air Act) issued by the Environmental Protection Agency, Consumer Product Safety Commission, and Occupational Safety and Health Administration banned or restricted the use of asbestos-containing products. Yet asbestos has not been eliminated completely, and it can still be imported and used in many products such as clothing, roofing materials, brake pads and linings, cement sheets and pipes, and gaskets. In fact, in 2016, 340 tons of asbestos were imported into the United States. Additionally, a lot of legacy asbestos is still out there. Any home, office, school, or other building constructed before 1980 likely contains some form of asbestos. Outside the U.S., the United Kingdom, Japan, and the European Union have developed measures to restrict the use of asbestos and protect the public from asbestos-related health problems, but other countries such as India and China have no such restrictions.

The World Health Organization estimates that 125 million people around the world are exposed to asbestos in the workplace. Asbestos poses a problem to health when its microscopic fibers are released into the air. When inhaled, the asbestos fibers can become lodged in the lungs or other parts of the body where they can cause lung cancer, asbestosis, and mesothelioma. The symptoms of these diseases may not appear for decades after the exposure to asbestos. At least 107,000 people worldwide die each year from asbestos-related lung cancer, mesothelioma, and asbestosis.

Most people know that smoking increases the risk of developing lung cancer, but exposure to asbestos can also increase the chance of getting a lung cancer that is very similar to that caused by smoking. A second form of cancer associated with asbestos exposure is mesothelioma. Mesothelioma is a cancer of the linings of the lungs, chest, or abdomen. Most people who develop mesothelioma have worked in places where asbestos was used, or they lived with people who worked in those places. Between 1999 and 2015, 45,221 people in the United States died of mesothelioma. The majority (51.7%) of those people were 75 years old or older, but the number of younger people who died of mesothelioma indicates that asbestos exposure is still a health risk. Depending on the location and stage of cancer and the age and overall health of a patient, doctors may recommend surgery to remove tumors, chemotherapy, or radiation to treat mesothelioma.

The third major disease related to asbestos is asbestosis, a non-cancerous lung disease caused when prolonged exposure to asbestos fibers scars lung tissue. People with asbestosis may have shortness of breath, a cough, and chest pain. The disease also makes it more likely that a person will develop lung cancer. Because there is no cure for asbestosis, doctors focus on managing the symptoms of the disease and may recommend a lung transplant to relieve suffering in people with severe symptoms.

Exposure to asbestos was much more common in the past than it is today. Decades ago, workers in shipyards, asbestos factories, and mines often worked in areas where asbestos fibers could be inhaled. These workers could bring home asbestos fibers on their clothing and on their skin and hair that then posed a danger to their families. Unfortunately, the dangers of asbestos are still with us, especially for people who work on structures containing asbestos that were built before 1980. A tragic example of the dangers associated with asbestos exposure occurred when the World Trade Center buildings fell during the September 11, 2001, attack in New York City. First responders, construction workers, and others were exposed to high concentrations of asbestos when the towers collapsed. As a consequence, these people are at risk of developing mesothelioma or other lung problems in the future.

Today, construction workers face the greatest risks of being exposed to asbestos. But everyone should remain on guard, because asbestos still lurks in many buildings and houses. Common places for asbestos-containing materials are pipes and ducts wrapped with asbestos tape, floor tiles and adhesives, insulation around furnaces and stoves, soundproofing on walls and ceilings, and cement roofing, shingles, and siding. Asbestos poses little risk if it remains bonded or embedded in solid materials. However, when asbestos-containing materials are disturbed, for example, during home remodeling, asbestos fibers can be released into the air. Never touch or move materials that might contain asbestos. Instead, contact professionals trained to handle asbestos whenever an older building is demolished, repaired, or remodeled to minimize asbestos exposure.

Most everyone will be exposed to low levels of asbestos because it is found naturally in the environment. Laws, standards, and regulations help reduce the risks associated with prolonged exposure to asbestos, and knowledge about asbestos and how to deal with it will help reduce the risks even further.

SUMMARY

Preventability (66)

Steps to reduce exposure to asbestos can be taken by home owners, construction workers, and building managers.

Likelihood (52)

Homes, offices, and schools, especially those in older buildings, may contain materials with asbestos. In many instances, if the asbestos-containing materials are left undisturbed, then exposure to asbestos fibers is less likely.

Consequence (86)

Asbestos exposure can cause significant health consequences, including lung disease and cancer, leading to death.

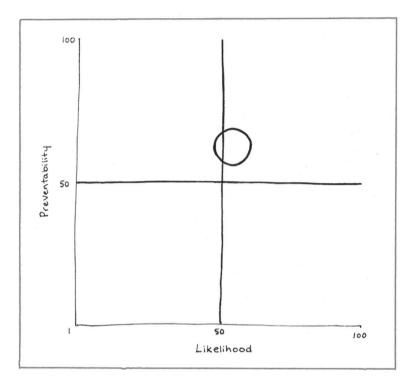

REFERENCES

Landrigan, P. J., Lioy, P. J., Thurston, G., Berkowitz, G., Chen, L. C., Chillrud, S. N., . . . Small, C., NIEHS World Trade Center Working Group. (2004). Health and environmental consequences of the World Trade Center disaster. *Environmental Health Perspectives, 112,* 731–739.

Mazurek, J. M., Syamlal, G., Wood, J. M., Hendricks, S. A., & Weston, A. (2017). Malignant mesothelioma mortality—United States, 1999–2015. *MMWR Morbidity and Mortality Weekly Report, 66,* 214–218.

U.S. Geological Survey. (2017). *Mineral commodity summaries 2017.* Retrieved from https://doi.org/10.3133/70180197

World Health Organization. (2014, March). Elimination of asbestos-related diseases. Retrieved from http://www.who.int/entity/ipcs/assessment/public_health/Elimination _asbestos-related_diseases_EN.pdf

Chemicals

31. ALUMINUM

Aluminum is the most abundant metal in Earth's crust. It follows oxygen and silicon as the third most abundant element on Earth's surface. Although oxygen is still almost six times more common than aluminum, there is a lot of aluminum on Earth. Aluminum doesn't seem to have any biological role, but that's okay because we use it to do plenty of other things. It's handy because it is lightweight, easy to shape, and resistant to corrosion. Aluminum is used to make a positively dizzying number of things including pots and pans, cans, foil, weatherproof siding and roofing, ductwork, toys, and airplanes. But it is also used in many ways you might not expect. For example, it is an ingredient in over-the-counter antacids, baking powder, vaccines, buffered aspirins, cosmetics, antiperspirants, and fireworks. Perhaps most surprisingly, aluminum sulfate is widely used in water treatment. To repeat: there's a lot of it around. According to the Agency for Toxic Substances and Disease Registry (a division of the Centers for Disease Control and Prevention), "virtually all food, water, air, and soil contain some aluminum." According to the same source, adults in the United States eat about 7–9 mg of it every day in their food. Unless you plan to stop breathing, eating, and drinking water, you can't avoid aluminum. This being the case, if aluminum were toxic, it would be a big deal.

The good news is, contrary to what many people think, aluminum is not especially toxic. Regardless of whether you inhale it, ingest it, or get it on your skin, aluminum is poorly absorbed by the body. And as long as your kidneys are working properly, the aluminum that is absorbed does not tend to accumulate, either in humans or in other animals (like the ones we eat). It doesn't really accumulate in plants either, with the notable exceptions of tea and some ferns.

Not surprisingly, in large quantities aluminum is not great for you. The nervous system and the lungs are the organ systems that are most sensitive to aluminum toxicity. The neurotoxic effects of aluminum are demonstrated by dialysis dementia, a neurodegenerative syndrome that can occur in people with kidney disease. It results from a combination of a reduced capacity of the kidneys to clear aluminum and an increase in aluminum exposure through dialysis fluid. This leads to an accumulation of aluminum in the brain and symptoms that include the loss of motor, speech, and cognitive functions.

Scientists have also postulated a link between aluminum exposure and Alzheimer's disease. This connection was proposed decades ago, but it remains a controversial hypothesis. Some studies have found a correlation between aluminum consumption and Alzheimer's disease, but others have not. The mixed data make it impossible to make a definitive statement, but scientific interest in the subject seems to have drifted. The Alzheimer's Association states, "Experts today focus on other areas of research, and few believe that everyday sources of aluminum pose any threat." We confirmed this with a neurologist specializing in dementia. This isn't very satisfying, but Alzheimer's disease is complicated. There probably isn't just one thing that is responsible.

Aluminum does not appear to cause cancer either. According to an internet rumor that has been circulating for some time, the use of underarm antiperspirant can cause breast cancer. But everyone who has felt guilty for valuing dry armpits over breast health can breathe a sigh of relief. Both the National Cancer Institute and the American Cancer Society say there is no truth to this claim.

An examination of the literature suggests that aluminum is not the metal you should be most concerned about (lead is really at the top of that list). If you still want to limit your exposure to aluminum, unfortunately, it might be difficult to do. A small amount of aluminum is absorbed into food via cooking utensils, especially when you are cooking acidic food. The same is true for antiperspirants: only a small percentage of the aluminum that makes contact with your skin is actually absorbed. There is very little aluminum in vaccines, and only in some of them (hepatitis A and B, DTaP/Tdap, Hib, HPV, pneumococcus). The aluminum is added because it increases the effectiveness of the vaccine, and skipping a vaccine because of the aluminum is a bad trade-off. For people who don't have workplace or industrial waste exposure, the major sources of aluminum exposure are treated water and some processed foods (for example, bread, cereal, and processed cheese). You can certainly cut back on the number of processed foods that you eat; this is in fact a healthy choice for a number of reasons. But it is not a good idea to drink water that has not been treated. If you use antacids frequently or drink a lot of tea, you might also be consuming more than a normal dose of aluminum, and you can reduce your exposure by cutting back on these products.

In some cases, aluminum is the least troubling part of the equation. For example, if you're thinking about opening up a can of chicken noodle soup for lunch, you should worry less about the aluminum that may have leached into your food than you should about the BPA it may have picked up from the can lining, or the whopping dose of salt you're about to consume, or the potential for botulism contamination.

SUMMARY

Preventability (10)

Most people are exposed to aluminum primarily through their food and drinking water. So there isn't much you can do to avoid it.

Likelihood (1)

Unless you are undergoing dialysis or are exposed to much higher doses of aluminum than most people, you are unlikely to suffer any adverse outcomes from aluminum exposure.

Consequence (12)

The typical level of aluminum exposure has not been shown to cause any serious health outcomes. The mixed results of studies on aluminum and dementia make the potential consequence score higher than zero.

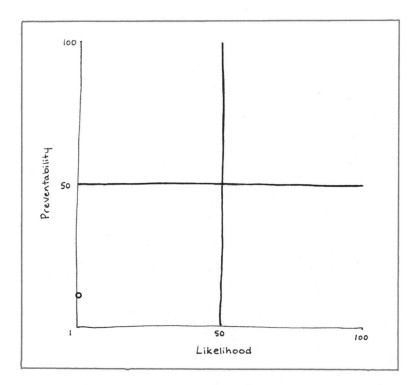

REFERENCES

Agency for Toxic Substances and Disease Registry, Toxic Substances Portal. (2008, September). Aluminum. Retrieved from https://www.atsdr.cdc.gov/toxfaqs/tf.asp?id=190&tid=34

Alzheimer's Association. (2018). Alzheimer's myths. Retrieved from http://www.alz.org/alzheimers_disease_myths_about_alzheimers.asp

American Cancer Society (2014). Antiperspirants and breast cancer risk. Retrieved from https://www.cancer.org/cancer/cancer-causes/antiperspirants-and-breast-cancer-risk.html

Centers for Disease Control and Prevention. (2016, September 12). Vaccine adjuvants. Retrieved from https://www.cdc.gov/vaccinesafety/concerns/adjuvants.html

Fleischer, M. (1953). Recent estimates of the abundances of the elements in the earth's crust. U.S. Geological Survey. Retrieved from http://pubs.er.usgs.gov/publication/cir285

National Cancer Institute. (2016, August 9). Antiperspirants/deodorants and breast cancer. Retrieved from https://www.cancer.gov/about-cancer/causes-prevention/risk/myths/antiperspirants-fact-sheet

Syracuse Research Corporation. (2018). Priority data needs for aluminum. Retrieved from https://www.atsdr.cdc.gov/pdns/pdfs/pdn_doc_22.pdf

U.S. Food and Drug Administration (2014, May 1). Common ingredients in U.S. licensed vaccines. Retrieved from https://www.fda.gov/biologicsbloodvaccines/safetyavailability/vaccinesafety/ucm187810.htm

32. FLAME RETARDANTS

Humans developed a dependency on fire in prehistoric times, and since that time, fire has been an ever-present danger in our lives. It's a bit of a double-edged sword in that fire has facilitated the rise of our species but has also consumed our homes, crops, cities, and lives. In modern times we are more removed from the everyday use of fire, as we typically don't rely on it to heat and light our homes or to cook our food (unless we're looking for ambiance). But the danger of fire is still with us. Open flames from fireplaces, candles, outdoor grills, and gas stoves can accidentally ignite fires. Add to that electrical fires, chemical fires, grease fires, toaster fires, dryer fires, forest fires, industrial fires, and on and on. If you have ever experienced a structure fire, you know that they are terrifying and can be lethal. But the news gets worse because some of the synthetic materials we use to build and furnish our homes make fires even more dangerous. Polyurethane foam, for example, catches fire quickly, burns hot, and produces copious quantities of toxic smoke. But foam is such a useful material that it is nearly ubiquitous in consumer products with padding. If you are sitting on a couch or an upholstered chair right now, you are almost certainly sitting on polyurethane foam. This can be a problem, especially if you like to smoke while you're sitting on your highly flammable couch or bed.

People igniting their furniture with cigarettes was a bigger problem in 1975 when more people smoked. And 1975 was the year that the state of California created a rule (technical bulletin 117, or TB117) which mandated that all furniture sold in the state had to be filled with materials that could withstand an open flame for 12 seconds. Manufacturers achieved this standard by adding chemical flame retardants to their products. Although this rule applied only to furniture sold in California, most manufacturers just started adding flame retardants to all their stock to avoid having to sell different products in different markets. Over the years, flame retardants have been routinely added to many different categories of products, including baby products (bouncers, nap mats, strollers, toys, etc.), carpets, car and plane interiors, clothing, building materials, packaging materials, and electronics. These chemicals are now so abundant that you couldn't avoid them if you wanted to. So, do you want to? Probably.

Chemical flame retardants, particularly brominated flame retardants, have been associated with obesity, endocrine disruption, thyroid problems, damage to the developing nervous system, decreased IQ, hyperactivity, infertility, and, yes, cancer. Hundreds of different chemical compounds are used as flame retardants, and little is known about the health effects of most of them. Many are persistent environmental pollutants, which means they hang around for a long time before decomposing. Many flame retardants are bioaccumulative, which means they build up in our bodies, primarily in fatty tissues. On top of all of that, it's not even clear that these chemicals are achieving their intended objective. According to a 2009 test by the Consumer Product Safety Commission, flame retardant foam chairs go up in flames just about as hot and as fast as regular foam. In 2017 the CSPC recommended that manufacturers refrain from adding organohalogen flame retardants to their products because the risks outweighed the benefits. They concluded that chemical flame retardants pose a threat to human health, especially for children and pregnant women. They further recommended that consumers avoid purchasing products that contain these chemicals.

In 2013 the state of California revised TB117. The new rule (TB117-2013) replaces the open-flame test with a smolder test, making it possible for manufacturers to meet the standard with flame-retardant fabric linings rather than flame-retardant chemicals. Finally, you can buy furniture and baby products that are not burdened with these extra chemicals. It is probably worth it to pay attention and try to choose products that don't come with an extra helping of flame retardants. This is especially important with baby products. But the new rule doesn't forbid added chemical flame retardants, so you're going to have to do some homework and ask some questions.

But even if you can afford to replace all the furniture in your home with new, flame retardant–free versions (and who can?), you're likely still going to be surrounded by flame retardants. Remember, they are environmentally persistent, and they are found in all sorts of places, including soil, water, and food. Flame retardants have even been found in the fatty tissues of arctic polar bears. Pretty much everyone in the United States has some concentration of these chemicals in their bodies, and unfortunately the concentration is highest in small children. One of the reasons for this is that so many children's products are treated with flame retardants. Another reason is that flame retardants collect in breast milk and are off-loaded into infants when they nurse. Yet another reason is that these chemicals are concentrated in the dust in our homes. Dust can be seriously toxic, and children who have more hand-to-mouth behaviors end up eating a lot of it.

When it comes to reducing your exposure to chemical flame retardants, controlling the dust in your home and washing your hands frequently are your best defense. Vacuum frequently and with a high-efficiency particulate air (HEPA) filter. Dust with a wet cloth. Open the windows and go outside.

SUMMARY

Preventability (22)

If you are willing to put in a lot of work, you can find furniture and baby items that don't have chemical flame retardants. But you can't find a car or a car seat that doesn't have flame retardants, and you can't live in a world where there are no flame retardants. Even polar bears can't avoid them.

Likelihood (50)

Because so many different chemicals are used as flame retardants, it is difficult to estimate what the actual risk of harm might be. Therefore, we have gone with a middle-of-the-road value.

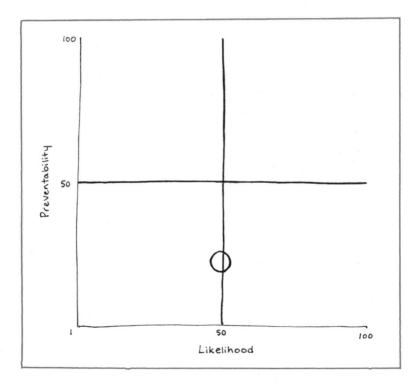

Consequence (50)

Again, because there are so many different chemicals in play, it is difficult to say how severe the consequences of exposure might be.

REFERENCES

Consumer Product Safety Commission. (2017). Guidance document on hazardous additive, non-polymeric organohalogen flame retardants in certain consumer products. *Federal Register, 82*(187). Retrieved from https://www.gpo.gov/fdsys/pkg/FR-2017-09-28/pdf/2017-20733.pdf

Environmental Protection Agency. (2016, March). Reducing your child's exposure to flame retardant chemicals. Retrieved from https://www.epa.gov/sites/production/files/2016-05/documents/flame_retardant_fact_sheet_3-22-16.pdf

McKinney, M. A., Letcher, R. J., Aars, J., Born, E. W., Branigan, M., Dietz, R., . . . Sonne, C. (2011). Flame retardants and legacy contaminants in polar bears from Alaska, Canada, East Greenland and Svalbard, 2005–2008. *Environment International, 37*, 365–374.

Mehta, S. (2012, May 9). Upholstered furniture full scale chair tests—open flame ignition results and analysis [memorandum]. United States Consumer Product Safety Commission. Retrieved from https://www.cpsc.gov/s3fs-public/openflame.pdf

National Institute of Environmental Health Sciences. (2016, July). Flame retardants. Retrieved from https://www.nichs.nih.gov/hcalth/matcrials/flame_retardants_508.pdf

State of California Department of Consumer Affairs. (2013, June). Requirements, test procedure and apparatus for testing the smolder resistance of materials used in upholstered furniture. Retrieved from http://www.bearhfti.ca.gov/about_us/tb117_2013.pdf

Tox Town. (2017, August 23). Polybrominated diphenyl ethers (PBDEs). Retrieved from https://toxtown.nlm.nih.gov/text_version/chemicals.php?id=79

33. FLUORIDE

In small doses, fluoride is good for your teeth. It protects against tooth decay by binding to the enamel (the hard, outer shell of the tooth) and remineralizing the enamel with calcium and phosphate. This makes the enamel harder and more resistant to bacteria. For this reason, most toothpastes contain fluoride, and dentists apply topical fluoride treatments to their patients' teeth, and many communities add fluoride to their water supplies.

Grand Rapids, Michigan, was the first city in the world to add fluoride to community drinking water as part of a pilot program to see if it would reduce the incidence of tooth decay. It did, by up to 50% compared to control communities where fluoride was not added to the water. This result has been replicated many times in different studies and in different parts of the world. The evidence is clear: fluoride protects against dental caries (cavities). Because of this, community water fluoridation is common all over the world, although some cities, like Portland, Oregon, have consistently refused to participate. The Centers for Disease Control and Prevention (CDC) lists water fluoridation as one of the top 10 public health achievements of the 20th century. Several pages of the CDC's website are devoted to reassuring the public that fluoridation is safe and healthy.

But some people are not reassured. Water fluoridation was controversial when it was introduced and remains controversial today. Critics claim that fluoride in drinking water causes myriad health problems including cancer, Alzheimer's disease, lowered IQ, thyroid problems, digestive complaints, and bone fractures. In the more than 70 years since water fluoridation was introduced, these concerns have waxed, waned, and changed, but never disappeared.

Fluoride is an inorganic anion, which means that it doesn't contain carbon and it has a negative charge (calcium and phosphate are also inorganic ions, although they carry a positive charge). Fluoride occurs naturally in the environment, including rocks, dirt, and seawater. In many places, high concentrations of fluoride exist naturally in the water. This is, in fact, how the dental protective effect of fluoride was discovered. In the early 1900s, a Colorado dentist noticed that the children in Colorado Springs had some really ugly teeth. Specifically, children that were born in the area, or who moved there when they were young, developed permanent teeth that were pitted and stained dark brown (like chocolate). But in addition to being unattractive, these teeth were curiously resistant to decay. The culprit turned out to be (surprise!) fluoride, which was present in high concentrations in the local water supply. The condition, originally called Colorado brown stain, was subsequently renamed fluorosis. Consumption of very high levels of fluoride can lead to skeletal fluorosis, a painful and debilitating joint condition. Fluoride can also be acutely toxic in high doses, which is why you should call poison control if your kid eats a tube of fluoride toothpaste.

Debilitating disease and acute toxicity are clearly undesirable, which is why the Environmental Protection Agency (EPA) has set the upper limit for how much fluoride can be in drinking water at 4 parts per million (ppm). But the existence of an upper limit is not in itself cause for alarm. Dosage is an important factor. Many things that are good for us in small doses are bad for us in large doses. Iron is a good example of this. If you don't get enough iron, you will be anemic; if you take too much, it will kill you. The same is true of vitamins A, D, E, C, and K. Even too much water is lethal. The fact that fluoride has negative consequences in large doses is not unusual and shouldn't disqualify its use in any form.

One notable difference between fluoride and the vitamins and minerals listed above is that fluoride is not known to be necessary for human health. It is, however, helpful (again, like a lot of things). Low doses of fluoride reduce the incidence of tooth decay without causing fluorosis. Artificial fluoridation of water is targeted at the sweet spot where there is an observable benefit but minimal (ideally zero) side effects (slight cosmetic fluorosis is considered acceptable).

Many people don't believe that such a sweet spot exists, but scientific consensus says that it does. This does not mean that there has been no legitimate dissent. Because fluoridation has been around for a long time, there is a fair bit of epidemiological data to look at, which is good in terms of assessing health outcomes. Numerous studies in animals have also tested the effects of fluoride. However, care is required when evaluating this scientific literature because there is a fair bit of pseudoscience (or straight-up bad science) mixed in with the real thing. Some studies link fluoride consumption to bone cancers, lowered IQ, ADHD, and hypothyroidism. However, these studies have suffered from methodological concerns such as small sample sizes and improper controls. These critiques may sound trivial, but these issues can lead to false conclusions. For example, if the water that has high fluoride concentrations also has high lead concentrations, you might misidentify the problem. Therefore, it is important to interpret these studies as part of the entire corpus of scientific evidence.

The National Academy of Sciences has conducted several reviews of fluoride. In a 2006 report on the EPA's standards for fluoride in drinking water ("Fluoride in Drinking Water: A Scientific Review of

EPA's Standards"), the reviewing committee identified severe dental fluorosis as the critical end point of concern (the problem that will develop at the lowest dose that is likely to cause a problem). The committee found that the EPA's upper bound of 4 ppm was too high to prevent this problem and, further, it was probably too high to protect against bone fractures. In other words, their opinion was that the maximum allowed concentration should be lower. For reference, this upper limit was (and still is) 4 ppm, and the recommended range for artificial fluoridation is only 0.7 ppm. The committee did not address artificial water fluoridation because that is not within the purview of the EPA. The committee also reviewed the effects of fluoride on other body systems including reproduction and development, neurotoxicity and behavior, the endocrine system, genotoxicity, and cancer. They identified cancer and endocrine effects as potential areas of concern and recommended that the EPA keep an eye on them.

The EPA published a 6-year review ("Six-Year Review 3—Health Effects Assessment for Existing Chemical and Radionuclide National Primary Drinking Water Regulations—Summary Report") in December 2016. The report covered all of the chemicals (and radionuclides) that are found in water supplies, but included an entire appendix about fluoride. The EPA did review the emerging literature on cancer effects; follow-up studies showed that there weren't any effects (in bone cancers). They also reviewed the study linking fluoride to hypothyroidism, but concluded that it did not properly control for several variables. The EPA also studied the data for other health concerns, but did not find anything alarming enough to suggest a revision to the existing upper limit for fluoride concentrations in water. The EPA acknowledges that lowering the limit has the potential to improve health, but fluoride is a low priority compared to other issues, and they do not want to divide their resources. In other words, there are bigger problems with drinking water that you should probably be worried about instead.

For its part, the U. S. Public Health Service, which sets the recommendation for artificial fluoridation levels, revised its fluoride numbers down from 0.7–1.2 ppm to 0.7 ppm in 2015. This is because people are exposed to more fluoride now than they were in the mid-20th century when the original recommendation was made.

If you're on the fence about fluoride, it is worth pointing out that while we tend to think of cavities as unpleasant, we don't usually think of them as such a big deal. This might be because, as a society, we do not get as many cavities as we used to. But cavities can be incredibly painful. Left untreated, they can even kill you. Most of us wouldn't leave cavities untreated if we could afford to do something about it. And that's the crux of the issue. Not everyone can afford to do something about it, and those who can't are also less likely to have access to healthy food and other preventative measures. Your kids aren't the only ones who are affected by fluoride in the water.

SUMMARY

Preventability (5)

You can choose not to use fluoride-containing toothpaste or mouthwash, but if you live in a community with fluoridated water, you're going to be exposed.

Likelihood (7)

Exposure within the normal range is very unlikely to cause any problems.

Consequence (2)

The most likely effect of excessive fluoride is mild dental fluorosis, which can be unattractive but isn't dangerous.

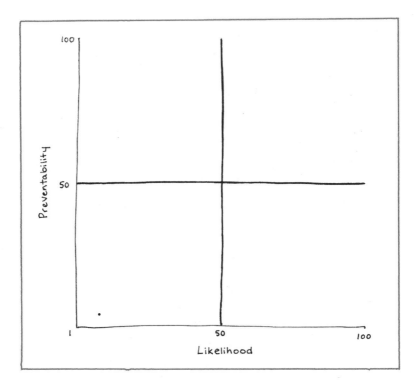

REFERENCES

Fagin, D. (2008). Second thoughts about fluoride. *Scientific American, 298,* 74–81.

Grimes, D. R. (2015). Commentary on "Are fluoride levels in drinking water associated with hypothyroidism prevalence in England? A large observational study of GP practice data and fluoride levels in drinking water." *Journal of Epidemiology and Community Health, 69,* 616.

Mullen, J. (2005). History of water fluoridation. *British Dental Journal, 199,* 1.

National Institute of Dental and Craniofacial Research. (2018, February). The story of fluoridation. Retrieved from https://www.nidcr.nih.gov/OralHealth/Topics/Flu oride/TheStoryofFluoridation.htm

National Research Council. (2006). *Fluoride in drinking water: A scientific review of EPA's standards.* Washington, DC: National Academies Press. https://doi.org/10 .17226/11571

Peckham, S., Lowery, D., & Spencer, S. (2015). Are fluoride levels in drinking water associated with hypothyroidism prevalence in England? A large observational study of GP practice data and fluoride levels in drinking water. *Journal of Epidemiology and Community Health, 69,* 619–624.

United States Environmental Protection Agency. (2016, December). Six-year review 3—health effects assessment for existing chemical and radionuclide national primary drinking water regulations—summary report. Retrieved from https://www.epa.gov/sites/production/files/2016-12/documents/822r16008.pdf

United States Environmental Protection Agency. (2017, January 24). Review of the fluoride drinking water regulation. Retrieved from https://www.epa.gov/dwsixyearreview/review-fluoride-drinking-water-regulation

34. FORMALDEHYDE

ormaldehyde is classified as a fixative because it prevents decomposition and putrefaction of tissue, provides structural stability through cross-linking of proteins, and preserves the spatial relationship of biological molecules so that you can study them. That is why it is commonly used by scientists and morticians. If you have ever been in a cadaver lab, the smell of formaldehyde will take you right back. The strong odor of formaldehyde is enough to make some people nauseated. It smells like it must be bad for you. It is. But it's complicated.

Formaldehyde is an organic (in the chemical sense) molecule; it is the simplest compound in a larger group called the aldehydes. It is a colorless, flammable gas that is soluble in water. When it is dissolved in water, it is called formalin. Formaldehyde occurs naturally and would be present in your bloodstream even if you were never exposed to external sources. This is because it is formed as part of ongoing metabolic processes. Your body doesn't need formaldehyde, but making it is a necessary intermediate step in the creation of chemicals that your body does need. This is true not just in humans, but also in other animals and plants. A solid block of wood will, in fact, emit a measurable quantity of formaldehyde.

So, a little bit of formaldehyde is clearly okay. But at high enough concentrations, inhalation of formaldehyde fumes irritates the eyes, nose, and throat, and causes respiratory problems and nausea. Skin contact can also cause irritation or allergic reactions. Furthermore, in 2011, the National Toxicology Program classified formaldehyde as a known human carcinogen. Specifically, occupational exposure has been associated with sinonasal cancer (cancer of the nasal cavity and nearby sinuses) as well as leukemia and lymphoma.

This being the case, it makes sense to try to limit your exposure to formaldehyde. And you may be thinking that should be pretty easy to do—just don't spend a lot of time around preserved tissues, which most of us don't anyway. But if that's what you're thinking, you're wrong. There is a lot more formaldehyde out there than can be accounted for by the embalming industry.

For one thing, formaldehyde is a by-product of combustion. That includes wood fires, gas stoves, automobile exhaust, and cigarette smoke. But it is also used in building materials, permanent press fabrics, paints, glues, paper products, cosmetics, dishwashing and laundry detergents, fertilizers, and pesticides. The largest share of formaldehyde production is devoted to the manufacture of industrial resins used in composite wood products such as plywood, particle board, and medium-density fiberboard—materials found in most new furniture and cabinetry. Formaldehyde off-gases from these materials over time, which is one of the reasons that concentrations of formaldehyde can be much higher indoors, and much higher in new construction, especially trailers and manufactured homes.

This issue made news after Hurricanes Katrina and Rita when the Federal Emergency Management Agency (FEMA) resettled some people displaced by the storms into travel trailers and manufactured homes. After occupying these temporary homes, some residents developed respiratory problems, headaches, and nosebleeds. When the CDC tested the air inside these shelters, they found formaldehyde concentrations up to 0.59 ppm. For reference, average outdoor air usually has a concentration less than 0.1 ppm. Since most of the homes that were tested were more than two years old, it is likely that the initial concentrations of formaldehyde were even higher.

There are some reasons to be concerned about formaldehyde exposure, but there are also some things you can do to reduce your exposure. Formaldehyde is easy to smell, even in small concentrations. So, if your home, office, or furniture smells noxious, it's a good bet that it is off-gassing formaldehyde. One of the easiest things to do is open a window or turn on a ventilation fan. If you have the option to let your furniture air out in a garage for a while, by all means, let it air out until it doesn't smell. Be picky about the furniture and cabinets you buy. Ask what they are made of and whether they contain formaldehyde. Wash permanent press fabrics before you wear them or hang them up as curtains. Don't smoke cigarettes, or, at the very least, don't smoke inside your home. Keep your home as cool and dry as possible because heat and humidity increase off-gassing. Read labels and be conscious of what preservatives are in the cosmetics and cleaners you buy. Formaldehyde can masquerade under different names and can be listed in product ingredients as formalin, formic aldehyde, methanediol, methanal, methyl aldehyde, methylene glycol, and methylene oxide. You can check the Household Products Database (maintained by the Department of Health and Human Services) for specific products containing formaldehyde. In addition, be on the lookout for these eight formaldehyde-releasing preservatives: benzylhemiformal, 5-bromo-5-nitro-1,3-dioxane, 2-bromo-2-nitropropane-1,3-diol, diazolidinyl urea, 1,3-dimethylol-5,5-dimethylhydantoin, imidazolidinyl urea, quaternium-15, and sodium hydroxymethylglycinate. Until 2014, Johnson and Johnson's iconic baby shampoo contained quaternium-15, and these preservatives can still show up in some familiar products.

If you have an old house, an old couch, and an old kitchen, pat yourself on the back. The formaldehyde is probably long gone. Of course, if your house is really old, you'll still need to watch out for lead paint.

SUMMARY

Preventability (65)

With some effort, you can reduce your exposure to formaldehyde at home. But if you work or go to school in a nice new building, you might still be exposed to it.

Likelihood (35)

Unless you are more sensitive than most, small exposures to formaldehyde are unlikely to cause problems. But if you have asthma or other respiratory problems, or if you get a whopping dose, you could get sick.

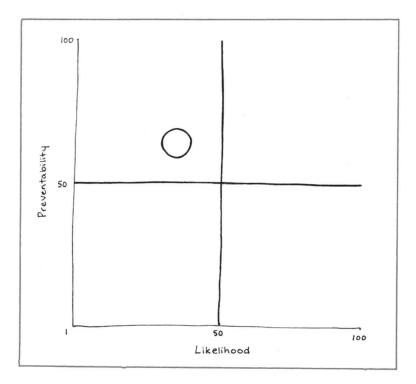

Consequence (72)

Long-term exposure to high levels of formaldehyde is linked to respiratory issues and cancer.

REFERENCES

Agency for Toxic Substances and Disease Registry. (2016, February 10). Formaldehyde in your home: What you need to know. Retrieved from https://www.atsdr.cdc.gov/formaldehyde/home/index.html

Centers for Disease Control and Prevention. (n.d.). What you should know about formaldehyde. Retrieved February 26, 2018, from https://www.cdc.gov/nceh/drywall/docs/whatyoushouldknowaboutformaldehyde.pdf

National Cancer Institute. (2011, June 10). Formaldehyde and cancer risk. Retrieved from https://www.cancer.gov/about-cancer/causes-prevention/risk/substances/formaldehyde/formaldehyde-fact-sheet

National Institute of Environmental Health Sciences. (2017, August 28). Formaldehyde. Retrieved from https://www.niehs.nih.gov/health/topics/agents/formaldehyde/index.cfm

National Toxicology Program, Department of Health and Human Services. (2016). Formaldehyde. Retrieved from https://ntp.niehs.nih.gov/ntp/roc/content/profiles/formaldehyde.pdf

Thavarajah, R., Mudimbaimannar, V. K., Elizabeth, J., Rao, U. K., & Ranganathan, K. (2012). Chemical and physical basics of routine formaldehyde fixation. *Journal of Oral and Maxillofacial Pathology, 16*, 400–405.

United States Environmental Protection Agency. (2017, June 15). Facts about formaldehyde. Retrieved from https://www.epa.gov/formaldehyde/facts-about-formaldehyde

35. LEAD

I f you don't already know that lead is toxic, you haven't been paying attention. Lead is notoriously poisonous. Lead poisoning can be acute or chronic, both of which are very serious. Lead has detrimental effects on all of the organ systems in your body, but it hits the nervous system especially hard. This is because lead mimics calcium, an important player in the brain. Lead easily crosses the blood-brain barrier, where it builds up in nervous tissue; it also accumulates in bone, another organ system heavily dependent on calcium. It is toxic both when it is ingested and when it is inhaled as lead vapor or dust. Children are more vulnerable to lead because they are smaller, and their brains are still developing.

Since at least the late 1800s, it has been known that lead is poisonous. But toxicity aside, lead has some very desirable properties. It is a dense, malleable, abundant, easily mined metal that is resistant to decay, is impenetrable to radioactive particles, and has a low melting point. And it tastes sweet. The Romans used it to sweeten wine—an exceptionally bad idea in retrospect.

The overwhelming harm caused by lead has resulted in heavy regulations in the United States since 1980. And these regulations have significantly reduced the public's exposure to lead. Average blood lead levels decreased by a factor of 10 between children studied in 1976–1980 and 2007–2008. This is great. Unfortunately, there is still a lot of lead out there. Some of it is legal (e.g., in car batteries, solder, hair dye, dental aprons), and some of it is illegal (e.g., in children's toys, ceramic glazes), and a lot of it is legacy (e.g., in paint, pipes, dirt, crystal, jewelry). The list of things that historically contained lead is so long that it is difficult to compile and impractical to print. Lead is in seemingly everything (except pencils, which are filled with graphite).

The question then is not whether lead is bad for you, but how bad it really is. Most people who were born before regulations were passed in 1980, and those born in the next decade after, were exposed to lead as children. Leaded gasoline was sold until the late 1990s, and many people lived in houses that were built before lead paint was banned in 1978. Lead water pipes and fixtures were commonly installed in homes and schools before 1986, and many students learned to solder in high school with lead-based solder. And we're fine, right? That's difficult to say, because many of us may be suffering the adverse effects of lead exposure without attributing them to lead. Lead is associated with loss of IQ points, behavioral problems, tremor, cognitive decline, hearing problems, allergies, cardiovascular problems, kidney disease, and reproductive issues. Concerningly, a 2012 report by the National Toxicology Program ("NTP monograph on health effects of low-level lead") found evidence for some of these health effects even at low blood concentrations (less than 10 micrograms per deciliter and in some cases less than 5 micrograms per deciliter). The CDC has revised the high blood lead level down from 25 micrograms per deciliter in 1985 to 10 in 1991 to 5 (the current level) in 2012. They emphasize that "no safe blood level in children has been identified," but it is important to remember that the health effects of lead are not limited to children.

If a blood test reveals high lead concentrations, chelating agents can be used to reduce the burden of lead. However, after the body is damaged by lead, especially if this damage affects the nervous system, it is irreversible. So it's worth trying to prevent lead exposure in the first place. According to the National Institute of Environmental Health Sciences, the most common sources of lead in the U.S. are lead-based paint, contaminated soil, household dust, drinking water, lead crystal, and lead-glazed pottery. Of these potential sources, it is easiest to avoid lead crystal and lead-glazed pottery. Don't eat off it and don't drink out of it.

Drinking water is trickier, because as individuals we don't have the authority or resources to rip up and replace the city pipes (think Flint, Michigan). Most of us don't even have the resources to rip out the lead pipes from our own homes. You can buy water filters that will remove lead and other heavy metals, but you need to make sure that the filter you are using is certified for that use.

Lead contamination in dirt is usually the result of either decaying lead paint or historical exposure to leaded gasoline fumes. Dirt around older homes or close to high-traffic areas is most likely to be contaminated. Exposure to lead in soil can be either direct (like children putting dirty fingers in their mouths) or through produce grown in the soil. Soil that is potentially contaminated can, and should, be tested.

The biggest problem in terms of lead exposure is paint. Old lead paint cracks, chips, and flakes. This poses a risk to children, who may eat paint chips (remember, it's sweet), but it also produces a fine dust that can be ingested or inhaled by children, adults, and pets. This is a huge problem because there are so many residences painted with old lead paint. You should just assume that any older paint you find in your home has lead in it, but you can also buy lead paint test kits at the hardware store. The problem is, what do you do if you have a positive test? The best (but most expensive) option is to call in a lead abatement professional. If you are considering renting or buying a home or planning a remodel, have it tested for lead first.

Lead tends to accumulate in household dust because of decaying paint, contaminated soil, or both. So try to keep the dust levels in your home down (this is a good idea anyway). Make sure everyone in your family washes their hands frequently, and teach your children not to put nonfood items in their mouths (easier said than done). Also, buy high-quality children's toys and pay attention to the Consumer Product Safety Commission recall list. Be aware that your home isn't the only place you can be exposed to lead. You also need to think about workplaces, schools, day care centers, and playgrounds. Finally, if you're worried about lead exposure, get a blood test.

If you grew up with lead paint, your IQ may have taken a permanent hit from lead. But if you take precautions, you may end up with kids that are smarter than you are. That might be its own kind of problem.

SUMMARY

Preventability (74)

There is a lot of legacy lead in buildings, water pipes, and even dirt. But if you take precautions, you can reduce your lead exposure.

Likelihood (80)

Even very small quantities of lead can have measurable negative outcomes.

Consequence (79)

Lead can have negative consequences for all of your organ systems, but it is especially bad for your brain.

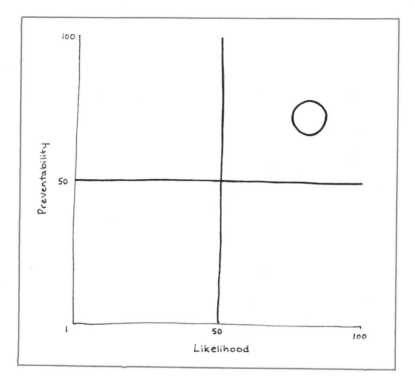

REFERENCES

Centers for Disease Control and Prevention. (2017, May 17). What do parents need to know to protect their children? Retrieved from https://www.cdc.gov/nceh/lead/acclpp/blood_lead_levels.htm

Consumer Product Safety Commission. (n.d.) Recall list. Retrieved from http://www.cpsc.gov/Recalls

Eisinger, J. (1982). Lead and wine: Eberhard Gockel and the Colica Pictonum. *Medical History, 26*, 279–302.

Flora, G., Gupta, D., & Tiwari, A. (2012). Toxicity of lead: A review with recent updates. *Interdisciplinary Toxicology, 5*, 47–58.

National Toxicology Program. (2012). NTP monograph on health effects of low-level lead. Washington, DC: U.S. Department of Health and Human Services.

PennState Extension. (n.d.). Lead in residential soils: Sources, testing, and reducing exposure. Retrieved from http://extension.psu.edu/plants/crops/esi/lead-in-soil

Sanders, T., Liu, Y., Buchner, V., & Tchounwou, P. B. (2009). Neurotoxic effects and biomarkers of lead exposure: A review. *Reviews of Environmental Health, 24*, 15–45.

World Health Organization, International Programme on Chemical Safety. (n.d.). Lead. Retrieved from http://www.who.int/ipcs/assessment/public_health/lead/en/

36. MERCURY

Mercury is the 80th element in the periodic table and is abbreviated Hg, from a Greek word meaning "water-silver." It is also commonly known as quicksilver because, although it is a metal, it has the unique property of being a liquid at room temperature (and standard atmospheric pressure). It has been used by humans since ancient times, and pretty much everyone in history has been able to agree that it is super cool. Mercury has long been used for both magical and medicinal purposes. It was once a popular, if ultimately unsuccessful, treatment for syphilis. It also has some legitimately useful properties. For instance, it can dissolve gold and silver in amalgams, which is helpful in both mining and dentistry. It has been used in thermometers and fluorescent lamps and dental fillings and antiseptic ointments and skin-lightening creams and fishing lures and (famously) hat making. Really, it is tremendously useful. Unfortunately, it is also incredibly toxic, which is why the Mad Hatter was mad (crazy, not angry).

Mercury exists in a variety of forms. Elemental, or pure, mercury is the silvery liquid that we think of when we think of mercury. Divalent mercury tends to exist as a compound or mercury salt. Organic mercury has carbon attached, often as a methyl group (carbon and three hydrogen atoms). But no matter what form it comes in, mercury is bad for your health.

The most dangerous thing about elemental mercury is the

vapors, or fumes. This might sound strange, because we don't think of metals as being particularly vaporous. But we've already established that mercury is weird stuff, and part of its weirdness is extreme volatility, or tendency to evaporate. Inhaling high concentrations of mercury vapor causes acute lung damage, pneumonia, and possibly death. Even at lower concentrations, inhaled mercury is easily absorbed into the blood, crosses the blood-brain barrier, and causes permanent brain damage. Over time, the body converts elemental mercury into divalent mercury, which accumulates in the kidneys, where it causes additional damage. As is generally the case, children and fetuses are more susceptible to mercury toxicity.

The extreme toxicity of mercury wasn't generally known until the middle of the 20th century. But now that we know how nasty it is, we tend not to use it. Thermometers are now commonly made with alcohol, and it is illegal to sell mercury-filled fishing lures. Unfortunately, there is still a lot of legacy mercury floating around. People keep old thermometers or they have jars of mercury in their garages. Most unfortunately, a lot of mercury still exists in schools, both in thermometers and just sitting around in supply closets. Historically, many schoolchildren were given blobs of mercury to hold in their hands and play with. It made science fun (but toxic). Although this practice has been discontinued, the mercury might still be around, waiting to be spilled or misappropriated by curious children. This is bad, because mercury is difficult (and expensive) to clean up. Just sweeping it up or washing it down the drain isn't good enough. It lingers, it spreads, and it causes brain damage. A *Scientific American* article ominously titled "Dangerous Mercury Spills Still Trouble Schoolchildren" (Knoblauch, 2009) reports that a mercury thermometer broken in a home bathroom caused significant levels of mercury vapor twenty years after it was broken. So, while we can all agree that it looks cool, elemental mercury is not something to mess around with. This is something that should be communicated to all children.

Elemental mercury is still used in gold mining around the world, and poses a major threat to the miners and their communities. But it is rarely used for this purpose in the United States. The other common First World exposure to elemental mercury is through dental amalgams, which contain about 50% elemental mercury. Given the previous paragraph, this might sound scary. However, these fillings have been used for about a hundred years, and extensive research from around the world has failed to show any association between amalgam fillings and health problems, except in a small number of hypersensitive people. If it still makes you nervous, there are other types of fillings you can get. But the Food and Drug Administration (FDA) does not recommend removing any amalgam fillings you already have. This would, among other things, expose you to more mercury vapor.

Most of the talk of mercury these days has to do with fish. That's because fish are a known source of an organic form of mercury, methylmercury. Awareness of methylmercury as a public health issue followed a mass poisoning event in Minamata, Japan, in 1956. A chemical company dumped industrial wastewater containing high concentrations of methylmercury into Minamata Bay, where it accumulated in fish and shellfish—dietary staples for the local population. Unlike other forms of mercury, methylmercury is easily absorbed by the digestive tract and doesn't clear from the body quickly. It accumulates in humans, just as it does in fish. As a result, thousands of people acquired what would later be called Minamata disease, a syndrome characterized by a constellation of neurological symptoms, leading to death in severe cases.

Obviously, very high concentrations of methylmercury are toxic and, thankfully, Minamata is a special case in this regard. But there is a fair bit of mercury kicking around in both fresh and saltwater sources around the world. This is partly due to human causes, like industrial pollution and coal-burning emissions, and also partly due to natural sources, like erosion of mercury ore. All of this means that virtually all fish and shellfish will contain some mercury, and this is concerning, especially when it comes to children and pregnant women. On the other hand, fish is really good for you, especially during neurocognitive development. Scientists and public health authorities have struggled to balance these two truths.

Part of the problem is that the data about the health effects of mercury in fish are incomplete and often contradictory. There are several reasons why this might be true. First, the effects may be small. In addition, fish with high concentrations of methylmercury may also have high concentrations of other contaminants like PCBs, arsenic, and lead. There are also other dietary and environmental sources of mercury that may be difficult to control. There may be some nutritional components of fish that counterbalance or even out-weigh the effects of mercury, or some people may consume other foods that have a protective effect. Finally, genetic and epigenetic factors mean that people react differently to similar quantities of mercury, making it difficult to generalize results. Ongoing research is directed at untangling some of these issues.

Taking all of this into account, the FDA recommends that pregnant women and children eat fish, but not too much. It also matters what kind of fish you eat. Because methylmercury accumulates, fish higher up in the food chain will have more mercury than fish closer to the bottom. So, no shark. At the same time, it's better to eat fish with higher omega-3 fatty acid content, like salmon or sardines.

In the good news column, an international treaty called the Minamata Convention was adopted in 2013 that should decrease the global level of mercury pollution. The bad news is that mercury is not going to stop being a problem any time soon.

SUMMARY

Preventability (58)

You can reduce your exposure to methylmercury by choosing sea-food wisely. But fish is still considered a health food, and all fish will have some methylmercury. You can reduce your exposure to elemental mercury by staying away from it and by teaching your children to do the same. But it's hard to know if someone broke a mercury thermometer in your apartment two decades ago.

Likelihood (68)

Exposure to elemental mercury is quite likely to produce negative health outcomes. It is more difficult to know how moderate exposure to methylmercury might impact health, and the answer could be "it depends."

Consequence (89)

They called them "mad hatters" for a reason.

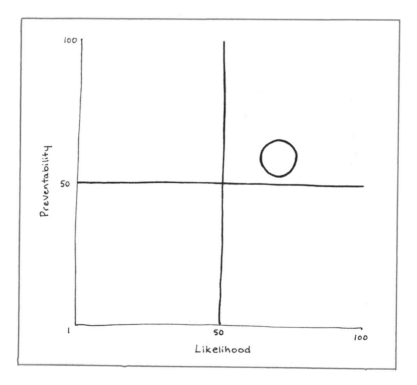

REFERENCES

Ekino, S., Susa, M., Ninomiya, T., Imamura, K., & Kitamura, T. (2007). Minamata disease revisited: An update on the acute and chronic manifestations of methyl mercury poisoning. *Journal of Neurological Science, 262,* 131–144.

Ha, E., Basu, N., Bose-O'Reilly, S., Dórea, J. G., McSorley, E., Sakamoto, M., & Chan, H. M. (2017). Current progress on understanding the impact of mercury on human health. *Environmental Research, 152,* 419–433.

Knoblauch, J. (2009, May 5). Dangerous mercury spills still trouble schoolchildren. *Scientific American, Environmental Health News.* Retrieved from https://www.scientificamerican.com/article/mercury-spills-trouble-schoolchildren/.

National Institute of Environmental Health Sciences. (2017, September 28). Mercury. Retrieved from https://www.niehs.nih.gov/health/topics/agents/mercury/index.cfm

U.S. Food and Drug Administration. (2017, December 5). About dental amalgam fillings. Retrieved from https://www.fda.gov/MedicalDevices/ProductsandMedical-Procedures/DentalProducts/DentalAmalgam/ucm171094.htm

U.S. Food and Drug Administration. (2004, March). What you need to know about mercury in fish and shellfish. Retrieved from https://www.fda.gov/food/foodborneillnesscontaminants/metals/ucm351781.htm

World Health Organization. (2017, March). Mercury and health. Retrieved from http://www.who.int/mediacentre/factsheets/fs361/en/

37. BPA

Even if you don't know what BPA is, you probably have a vague notion that it is bad. This is because many consumer products are labeled "BPA free." If this is an advertising point, you can reasonably conclude that there is some reason that people want to avoid it. But is there a good reason?

BPA is an abbreviation for bisphenol-A. It is an industrial chemical that is commonly used in the production of plastics and epoxy resins. It can be found in a large and diverse array of products, including food packaging, water bottles, and baby bottles. BPA has one of the highest production volumes of any chemical. With more than 6 billion tons produced annually, BPA is found just about everywhere. There is a lot of it around. This means that we all have some level of exposure. BPA has been detected in human urine and blood as well as in amniotic fluid, placental tissue, and umbilical cord blood. It is ubiquitous. This is potentially problematic because BPA binds to estrogen receptors. That is to say, it is an endocrine modulator.

The endocrine system produces hormones, molecules that your internal organs use to send signals to each other. Physiologically, this method of inter-organ communication is very important. It regulates many different functions including growth and development, sleep-wake cycles, metabolism, and reproduction. Estrogen is a sex hormone that is involved in the development of secondary sex characteristics and the regulation of ovulation, puberty, and menopause. It also has effects on other organ systems and plays an important role in both men and women. When BPA binds to estrogen receptors, it triggers the same response as estrogen. This inappropriate response can cause health problems such as cancer, obesity, diabetes, miscarriage, developmental disorders, cardiovascular disease, polycystic ovary syndrome, and male infertility.

Although BPA was discovered in the late 1800s and was investigated as an artificial estrogen in the 1930s, concerns about the endocrine-modulating properties of the compound didn't surface until the 1990s. It was at this time that BPA was found to be much more strongly estrogenic than previously thought. This caused many scientists to reevaluate whether BPA was safe at the doses to which we are commonly exposed. But this has turned out to be controversial. Specifically, people have questioned whether the exposure that people typically have is likely to cause any real health problems. Although the National Toxicology Program has found cause for concern, especially for fetuses, infants, and children, the FDA maintains that the levels currently found in foods are safe. More research is clearly needed, but prudence would suggest a cautious approach.

For most people, the main route of exposure to BPA is through food and drink. BPA leeches out of plastic containers and epoxy resins and into the foods they contain. Canned foods are a notoriously large source of BPA, as are plastic drink bottles. If you need another reason not to drink soda, most soda cans are lined with BPA. Plastics that have the recycling codes 3 or 7 are more likely to contain BPA. Plastic food storage containers can also be a source of exposure. This is especially the case when the plastic is exposed to high heat or when it is older. BPA can also be absorbed through skin exposure. The prime culprit here is thermal paper, usually used for receipts and tickets, which can be coated with very large quantities of the chemical.

However, BPA is not bioaccumulative, and you can reduce your exposure by avoiding the things listed above. In addition, enough people are concerned about BPA that many manufacturers are now producing BPA-free plastics, canned foods, and thermal paper.

That might seem like good news, but remember, BPA was originally included because it served a purpose. If you remove BPA, you need to find an alternative. Many manufacturers have replaced bisphenol-A with bisphenol-S (BPS) or bisphenol-F (BPF). BPS and BPF make good substitutes for BPA because they are very similar and have many of the same properties. But because they are so similar to BPA, they have a similar effect on human physiology. Not as much is known about BPS and BPF, but the studies that have been done suggest that these replacement chemicals are just as bad, if not worse, than BPA. As the authors of one review put it, "when evaluating the safety of compounds for consumer use, it may be prudent to consider entire classes instead of individual compounds" (Rochester & Bolden, 2015). Unfortunately, BPS and BPF have been measured in human urine at the same levels as BPA and have become equally ubiquitous in the environment. Remember, products made with BPS and BPF can be labeled "BPA free." You shouldn't assume that these products are any safer than their regular counterparts.

SUMMARY

Preventability (50)

Although you can take steps to reduce your exposure to BPA, the ubiquity of this chemical means you can only do so much.

Likelihood (50)

This is extremely difficult to estimate, partly because it is very controversial. For this reason, we've assigned a value right in the middle of the road.

Consequence (50)

The consequences run a broad range of severity. But while almost everyone will be exposed, not everyone will suffer a highly negative outcome as a result.

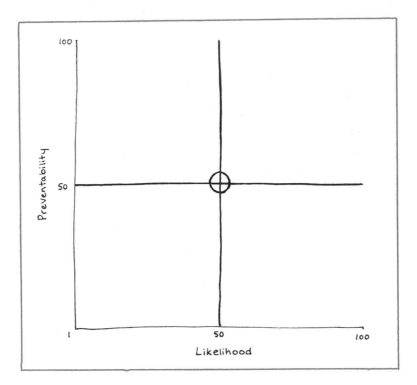

REFERENCES

National Institute of Environmental Health Sciences. (2017, May 24). Bisphenol A (BPA). Retrieved from https://www.niehs.nih.gov/health/topics/agents/sya-bpa/index.cfm

Rochester, J. R., & Bolden, A. L. (2015). Bisphenol S and F: A systematic review and comparison of the hormonal activity of bisphenol A substitutes. *Environmental Health Perspectives, 123*, 643–650.

Shelby, M. D. (2008). NTP-CERHR monograph on the potential human reproductive and developmental effects of bisphenol A. *NTP CERHR Monographs*, no. 22.

U.S. Food and Drug Administration. (2018, February 6). Bisphenol A (BPA): Use in food contact application. Retrieved from https://www.fda.gov/newsevents/publichealthfo cus/ucm064437.htm

Vandenberg, L. N., Hauser, R., Marcus, M., Olea, N., & Welshons, W. V. (2007). Human exposure to bisphenol A (BPA). *Reproductive Toxicology, 24*, 139–177.

Vogel, S. A. (2009). The politics of plastics: The making and unmaking of Bisphenol A "safety." *American Journal of Public Health, 99*, S559–S566.

38. DEET

Being outside and enjoying nature are usually pleasant experiences. But being attacked by hordes of bloodthirsty mosquitoes and ticks can make it less pleasant. That's why insect repellents have been developed: so people can enjoy all that nature has to offer without ending up as a blood meal for bugs.

Insect repellents have been used for centuries to ward off and kill biting pests. These tiny vermin can be more than irritating. Mosquitoes pose significant health risks and can transmit diseases such as malaria, West Nile disease, Zika, chikungunya disease, dengue fever, yellow fever, and encephalitis. Ticks are also vectors for diseases (e.g., Lyme disease, Rocky Mountain spotted fever). Effective, inexpensive, and safe insect repellents have the potential to reduce the economic and health burden of these diseases.

Early insect repellents were made by burning certain plants to create smoke. Botanical oils such as those distilled from citronella, cedarwood, eucalyptus, lemon grass, lavender, and peppermint have also been used for this purpose, but have met with mixed success. Later, the military developed synthetic chemicals for use in World War II, but these did not provide adequate protection either. Soon after World War II, the U.S. Department of Agriculture and the military screened thousands of chemicals for their effectiveness as mosquito repellents. *N,N*- diethyl-3-methylbenzamide (i.e., *N*,N-diethyl-*m*-toluamide) applied to the skin or on clothes proved to be an effective repellent with low toxicity and by 1957 it was available for use by the public. Because people thought the word "diethyltoluamide" was too long and not easily remembered, the Committee on Insecticide Terminology changed the name of the chemical to DEET. Today, more than a hundred different products with concentrations of DEET ranging from 4% to 100% are available to consumers.

Mosquitoes find their meals (you and other mammals) using their sense of smell. Carbon dioxide and lactic acid in our breath and sweat, for example, are especially attractive to these and other insects. These chemicals float in the air until they meet odor receptors on the mosquito. As a mosquito approaches a potential target, it uses thermoreceptors to detect body heat and its eyes to guide it to a potential host.

Although DEET does not kill mosquitoes or other insects, it stops them from biting. Some data suggest that DEET binds to mosquito odor receptors, causing the insect olfactory system to malfunction and preventing a mosquito from finding you. Other data show that mosquitoes detect DEET and avoid it. Thus, DEET may work to block or mask odors or as a chemical that mosquitoes just don't like, or both.

But what impact does DEET have on us when we apply it to our skin? DEET is absorbed through the skin and digestive system, metabolized in the liver, and excreted through urine. The chemical is not stored in any organs within the body. The safety of DEET has been a topic of concern for decades because of occasional reports pointing to DEET as the cause of significant health problems. However, the published literature contains few examples of disorders associated with DEET compared to the widespread use of the chemical. For example, there is little evidence that DEET causes cancer, and the U.S. Environmental Protection Agency does not classify DEET as a human carcinogen. Also, women who are pregnant and apply DEET daily during the second and third trimesters of pregnancy do not appear to suffer any significant neurological, gastrointestinal, or dermatological effects. Babies born to these women also appear healthy as they grow and develop at a pace similar to that of babies not exposed to DEET.

A review of data from the National Registry of Human Exposure to DEET uncovered 242 cases in which DEET reportedly caused moderate and major symptoms. Of these 242 cases, 59 seizures were reported and 58 cases of other neurological symptoms ranging in severity from moderate to high. This sounds bad, but because more than 75 million people use DEET each year, the percentage of neurological problems associated with the insect repellent is very low. Rashes, itching, hives, and other nonneurological problems are more common. The EPA concludes that most incidents associated with DEET are minor and that any symptoms resolved quickly. The CDC also concluded that the number of negative health effects caused by DEET is low and cites reports that the majority of incidents reported to poison control centers were for minor problems.

The soothing words of the EPA and CDC about the safety of DEET do not satisfy everyone. If DEET can liquefy plastic, do you really want to put it on your skin? Although the EPA regards DEET as safe when it is applied properly, it still requires a long set of precautions on every product that contains DEET. These precautions include warnings and safety procedures about where the product should be used, how the product should be applied, the concentration of DEET, and how to report an adverse reaction.

Furthermore, DEET should be used with caution on children. The American Academy of Pediatrics and the National Capital Poison Center recommend that children should not use products with more than 30% DEET and that children younger than two months old should not use any insect repellents.

There are other options for people who do not want to use products containing DEET. For example, insect repellents with picaridin provide protection similar to some products with DEET. Pyrethrins, a chemical found in chrysanthemum flower, and synthetic pyrethroids can kill some insects on contact. Some essential oils provide moderate protection for a shorter period of time than DEET or picaridin. It should be pointed out, however, that just because these alternatives are natural does not mean they are necessarily safer than DEET. For a nonchemical insect repellent, there is always a fly swatter, which is definitely safe for everyone but the fly.

SUMMARY

Preventability (98)

You have the choice to use products with or without DEET.

Likelihood (6)

Adverse reactions to DEET are rare.

Consequence (52)

Application of DEET can cause skin irritation or, more rarely, neurological symptoms.

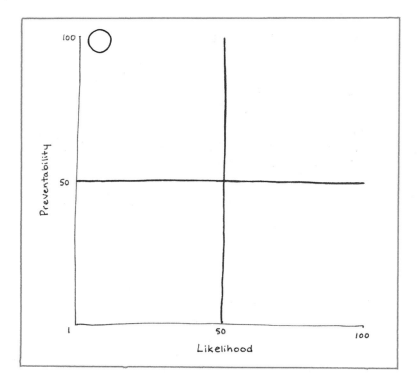

REFERENCES

Ditzen, M., Pellegrino, M., & Vosshall, L. B. (2008). Insect odorant receptors are molecular targets of the insect repellent DEET. *Science, 319,* 1838–1842.

Fradin, M. S., & Day, J. F. (2002). Comparative efficacy of insect repellents against mosquito bites. *New England Journal of Medicine, 347,* 13–18.

McGready, R., Hamilton, K. A., Simpson, J. A., Cho, T., Luxemburger, C., Edwards, R., . . . Lindsay, S. W. (2001). Safety of the insect repellent N,N-diethyl-M-toluamide (DEET) in pregnancy. *American Journal of Tropical Medicine and Hygiene, 65,* 285–289.

Osimitz, T. G., Murphy, J. V., Fell, L. A., & Page, B. (2010). Adverse events associated with the use of insect repellents containing N,N-diethyl-m-toluamide (DEET). *Regulatory Toxicology and Pharmacology, RTP, 56,* 93–99.

Smith, C. N. (1960). New approved common names of insecticides. *Journal of Economic Entomology, 53,* 677–677.

Syed, Z., & Leal, W. S. (2008). Mosquitoes smell and avoid the insect repellent DEET. *Proceedings of the National Academy of Sciences, 105,* 13598–13603.

Animals

39. SNAKES

Snakes are not at the top of the cute and cuddly pet list, even though some people consider these reptiles to be good companion animals. At the sight of a snake, many people recoil in terror. Although there is some debate whether this reaction is a product of learning or our genetics, it is clear that snakes are something that worry many of us.

The more than 3,000 extant species of snake range in size from the small thread snake, with a length of about 3.9 inches (10 cm), to the reticulated python, which can grow to 30 feet (9 meters) long. Snakes can live just about anywhere and are found on all continents except Antarctica. Different snakes have adapted to different habitats and environments, including forests, deserts, oceans, rivers, and swamps. Because they are cold-blooded, snakes need external sources of heat to keep their bodies warm. Humans often heat their homes, and this sometimes results in humans sharing their homes with snakes.

The majority of snake species are not venomous and pose no danger to people. In fact, snakes play a beneficial role in reducing harmful pests by preying on rodents, insects, and other animals that destroy crops. The reputation of snakes as dangerous creatures is mostly undeserved, but venomous snakes do have the ability to cause serious injury and death. On the other hand, snake venom has the potential to provide new medications for diseases of the cardiovascular and nervous systems.

The four major families of venomous snakes are Atractaspididae (burrowing asps, mole vipers, stiletto snakes), Colubridae (boomslang), Elapidae (sea snakes, taipans, brown snakes, coral snakes, kraits, death adders, tiger snakes, mambas, cobras), and Viperidae (Russell's viper, puff adders, rattlesnakes, copperheads, and cottonmouths). Snakes inject their venom into their victims through fangs connected to glands located in the snake's head. The constituent chemistry of snake venom is a cocktail of proteins that differs among snake species. Some venoms attack the nervous system (neurotoxins), while others destroy cell membranes (cytotoxins). Neurotoxins inhibit the transmission of electrical signals sent by nerve cells and can cause paralysis or numbness. Some cytotoxins target cardiac muscle cells to cause heart irregularities while other cytotoxins destroy red blood cells and disrupt blood clotting. The primary purpose of venom is to allow a snake to capture its prey and make it easier to digest. Humans are not on a snake's menu, and snakes do not actively hunt or chase people. Generally, snakes are shy and will take steps to avoid humans or warn people about their presence before they get too close. Snakes will bite in self-defense when they are threatened, startled, or harassed.

The World Health Organization estimates that up to 5 million people are bitten by snakes every year. Approximately half of these bites (2.4 million) are from venomous snakes, resulting in 94,000–125,000 deaths and 400,000 amputations and other health consequences. Globally, South Asia, Southeast Asia, and sub-Saharan Africa have the largest number of venomous snake bites and human deaths caused by venomous snakes; snakes in India alone kill approximately 11,000 people each year. In the United States, 7,000–8,000 people are bitten by venomous snakes each year, but only about five people die as a result.

Many snake bites occur when people accidentally step on a snake or place their hands in places occupied by snakes. People are also bitten when they mishandle snakes, provoke them, or try to harm them. Even dead venomous snakes are capable of biting, so a snake corpse demands respect. Many venomous snakes can also deliver dry bites when no venom is released.

The best defense against a snake bite is preparation. This means being able to identify the snakes in your area and recognizing when and where they are most active. If you are walking through areas frequented by snakes, wear long pants and boots. If you are clearing brush or moving wood, be careful where you put your hands or use a tool to move material from place to place. When you encounter a snake, do not try to pick it up or capture it; just give it space and leave it alone.

In the event that someone is bitten by a snake, the victim should be kept calm. As soon as possible, victims should get to a doctor for evaluation. To reduce the spread of venom through the body, snake bite victims should not exert themselves. Swelling, pain, weakness, numbness, and nausea are common symptoms of snake bites and, depending on the type and amount of venom injected, bleeding, respiratory problems, necrosis, and paralysis may result. Jewelry and tight-fitting clothing near the bite should be removed before swelling starts. Health care providers who are familiar with the species of snakes in the area will determine if antivenom is needed. A tetanus booster shot may also be recommended. Forget about those old tales with remedies for snake bites; they don't work and may exacerbate the problem. For example, never cut into the bite wound, never try to suck out the venom, and never use a tourniquet. Also, people bitten by snakes should not drink caffeinated or alcoholic beverages. The best course of action is to seek immediate medical care.

Snakes are equipped with the anatomy and physiology to do

great harm, but they are essential inhabitants of a healthy ecosystem. They may provide benefits to human health in the future, and they do not attack people unprovoked. It is not difficult to avoid unpleasant encounters with snakes. Just give them plenty of respect—from a distance.

SUMMARY

Preventability (85)

Many steps can be taken to avoid an unpleasant encounter with a snake. For example, if you don't venture out in the wilderness and stay inside cities, you probably will not come across a snake. However, some people like to hike and others live in areas shared by snakes. In these cases, watch where you step and put your hands.

Likelihood (12)

For most people, the likelihood of encountering a dangerous snake is low.

Consequence (47)

The consequence of a snake bite is highly dependent on the type of snake doing the biting. Small, nonvenomous snakes pose little risk, but venomous snakes can cause serious injury or death. Access to medical care and antivenom reduce the danger of snake bites.

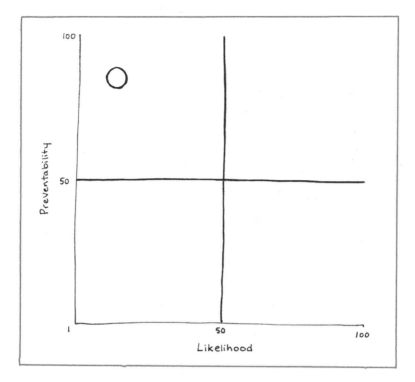

REFERENCES

Centers for Disease Control and Prevention. (2016, July 1). Venomous snakes. Retrieved from https://www.cdc.gov/niosh/topics/snakes/default.html
Kasturiratne, A., Wickremasinghe, A. R., de Silva, N., Gunawardena, N. K., Pathmeswaran, A., Premaratna, R., . . . de Silva, H. J. (2008). The global burden of snakebite: A literature analysis and modelling based on regional estimates of envenoming and deaths. *PLOS Medicine, 5*, e218.
Polák, J., Sedláčková, K., Nácar, D., Landová, E., & Frynta, D. (2016). Fear the serpent: A psychometric study of snake phobia. *Psychiatry Research, 242*, 163–168.
Suchard, J. R., & LoVecchio, F. (1999). Envenomations by rattlesnakes thought to be dead. *New England Journal of Medicine, 340*, 1930.
World Health Organization. (2013, February). Animal bites. Fact sheet no. 375. Retrieved from http://www.who.int/mediacentre/factsheets/fs373/en/

40. CATS

Your furry feline friend likely brings you joy and companionship in addition to the occasional dead bird or mouse. Sure, your cat might shed on your furniture or spray urine on your belongings to mark them as territory, but you love your pet. Having a cat might even lower your blood pressure and improve your mental health. But although Tiger and Fluffy are good hunters, and you know they are smart, cats may pose some risks to your health.

When it comes to animal bites, dogs get most of the attention. In the United States, approximately 1–2% of all emergency department visits are due to animal bites, and dogs are responsible for 60–90% of these bites. But cats are responsible for 10–15% of the emergency room visits due to animal bites, and 30% of people who visited a doctor for a cat bite have to be hospitalized. There are significant differences in the wounds caused by cat bites and dog bites. Dogs use their teeth and jaws to tear and rip. The resulting gash can be large and open. Cats have sharp teeth that can penetrate deep into tissue and leave pathogens in closed wounds beneath the skin. The mouths of both dogs and cats are teeming with different types of bacteria, but the bacteria that most commonly causes infections after a cat bite is *Pasteurella multocida*. When *P. multocida* gets trapped under the skin, it can multiply and spread to surrounding tissue. Such infections look red and swollen and are painful. Left untreated, *P. multocida* infections can cause cellulitis and septicemia. In rare cases, especially in children, the elderly, and people with suppressed immune systems, these disorders can be lethal.

People who are bitten by a cat should wash their wounds with warm water as soon as possible and control any excessive bleeding. A visit to a health care provider is also in order to ensure that the wound does not get infected. A prescription of antibiotics and a tetanus booster may be recommended, and a decision whether to leave the wound open or closed will be made. The possibility that the cat carries the rabies virus will also be assessed.

Bites are not the only way cats can transmit disease to people. A scratch or simple lick from a cat can spread a bacterium called *Bartonella henselae* that causes cat-scratch disease (CSD). Approximately 40% of all cats are infected by *B. henselae* sometime during their lives, but they may not show any signs of illness. Cats get infected with *B. henselae* when they are bitten by fleas or when flea droppings get into their mouths or under claws. Bacteria are transmitted to people when cats bite, scratch the skin, or lick a person's wound or scab. Approximately 12,500 people are diagnosed with CSD each year in the United States. People with CSD may develop a fever, headaches, enlarged lymph nodes, and fluid-filled blisters around the wound. On rare occasions, CSD can cause serious illness affecting the brain (encephalopathy), eyes (neuroretinitis), bones (osteomyelitis), lungs (pneumonia), and other organs. The infection often clears up on its own, but sometimes antibiotics are recommended. Eliminating fleas is a good way to reduce the risk of CSD and, as with other animal bites, a scratch should be washed immediately.

Cats also transmit toxoplasmosis, an illness caused by a single-celled parasite called *Toxoplasma gondii*. The parasite is very common, with approximately 33% of all people on earth having been infected with it. People can become infected with the *Toxoplasma* parasite if they eat undercooked, contaminated meat or drink contaminated water. Cats sometimes carry the *Toxoplasma* parasite and excrete it in their feces. People may ingest the parasite accidentally when they clean a cat litter box or touch anything that had contact with cat feces. Most people don't know they have the *Toxoplasma* parasite because they have a strong enough immune system to keep it from causing illness. Some people may have flu-like symptoms, swollen glands, and general aches and pains. However, *Toxoplasma* infections can cause serious health problems, especially in people with compromised immune systems. Concerningly, *Toxoplasma* can be passed from pregnant mothers to their unborn children. Although most newborns infected with *Toxoplasma* will not show symptoms at birth, they can develop eye or brain damage later in life.

Toxoplasma gondii may also affect the brain in peculiar ways. Rodents infected with the *Toxoplasma* parasite become slower and less cautious and display less fear. In fact, they may even be attracted to the smell of cat urine. This change in behavior makes a rat an easy target for cats hunting for a meal. Although the underlying brain mechanisms involved with these new behaviors are not well understood, it appears that neural circuits responsible for fear and anxiety are rewired. Some data suggest that *Toxoplasma gondii* may have a role in changing human behavior, resulting in psychiatric problems such as schizophrenia, obsessive-compulsive disorder, and bipolar disorder.

Several other diseases can be transmitted from cats to humans, including rabies (a viral infection affecting the nervous system), campylobacter infections (a bacterial skin infection), cryptosporidiosis and giardiasis (parasitic diseases causing gastrointestinal discomfort), echinococcosis (tapeworms), hookworms, roundworms, salmonella poisoning (bacterial infections causing gastrointestinal problems), cat roundworm, and ringworm (fungal skin infection). People, especially women who are pregnant, who have cats should be careful when playing with their felines and gardening in places visited by their pets. Women who are pregnant should not change their cat's litter box. Children's sandboxes should be kept covered when they are not in use to prevent cats from using these areas as litter boxes.

There is no need to abandon your cat: feel free to snuggle with your pet, but make sure you wash up afterward to keep yourself healthy.

SUMMARY

Preventability (83)

If you own a cat, maintaining good hygiene practices will prevent most cat-to-human transmission of disease. Of course, you can further limit your exposure to any pathogens hosted by cats if you stay away from cats altogether.

Likelihood (12)

If you own a cat, it is likely that you will be exposed to some of the pathogens hosted by your pet, but these are unlikely to be of major concern.

Consequence (32)

The severity of the illness depends on the pathogen; some cases will cause minor symptoms while others can cause significant health problems.

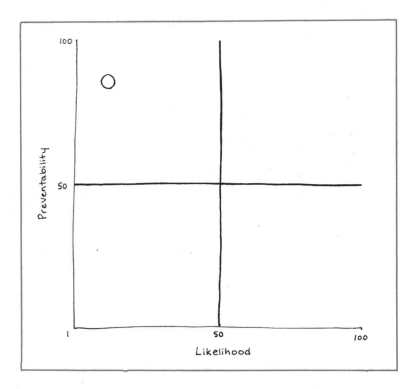

REFERENCES

Babovic, N., Cayci, C., & Carlsen, B. T. (2014). Cat bite infections of the hand: Assessment of morbidity and predictors of severe infection. *Journal Hand Surgery, 39*, 286–290.

Bregman, B., & Slavinski, S. (2012). Using emergency department data to conduct dog and animal bite surveillance in New York City, 2003–2006. *Public Health Reports, 127*, 195–201.

Centers for Disease Control. (2014, April 30). Cat-scratch disease. Retrieved from https://www.cdc.gov/healthypets/diseases/cat-scratch.html

Moncada, P. A., & Montoya, J. G. (2012). Toxoplasmosis in the fetus and newborn: An update on prevalence, diagnosis and treatment. *Expert Review of Anti-Infective Therapy, 10*, 815–828.

Nelson, C. A., Saha, S., & Mead, P. S. (2016). Cat-scratch disease in the United States, 2005–2013. *Emerging Infectious Diseases, 22*, 1741–1746.

Sutterland, A. L., Fond, G., Kuin, A., Koeter, M. W. J., Lutter, R., van Gool, T., . . . de Haan, L. (2015). Beyond the association. Toxoplasma gondii in schizophrenia, bipolar disorder, and addiction: Systematic review and meta-analysis. *Acta Psychiatrica Scandinavica, 132*, 161–179.

41. BEARS

Getting back to nature with a hike in the wilderness is a great way to relax. The smell of fresh air, the sights of brightly colored mountain wildflowers, and the sounds of bluebirds chirping in the trees are experiences enjoyed by millions of people each year. Confronting a 600-pound grizzly bear with its two-inch-long teeth and six-inch claws while on the trail? Not so relaxing.

All bears belong to the family Ursidae. Within Ursidae, there eight species of bears. Brown bears (*Ursus arctos*), which include the grizzly bear (*Ursus arctos horribilis*) and the Kodiak bear (*Ursus arctos middendorffi*), are found in Europe, Asia, and North America. Black bears such as the Asian black bear (*Ursus thibetanus*) and American black bear (*Ursus americanus*) are also found in Asia and North America. Confrontations between humans and all types of bears, including sloth bears (*Melursus ursinus*), polar bears (*Ursus maritimus*), and panda bears (*Ailuropoda melanoleuca*), have been documented. These confrontations are especially likely to take place when a bear is protecting its young or is approached unexpectedly.

Meeting a bear in the wild can be a harrowing experience for the human and likely for the bear. Humans are not part of the standard bear diet, so there should be no concern about being hunted down by one of these large animals. However, people do not always dispose of and secure their food properly. Therefore, bears can acquire a fondness for human food and lose their fear of people, increasing the likelihood of bear-human interactions.

The best defense against a bear attack is to avoid a bear in the first place. The National Park Service has these tips to stay safe in bear country:

- Be aware of your surroundings.
- Hike in groups of people.
- Hike during the day instead of dawn, dusk, or night.
- Be noisy.
- See the bear before it sees you.
- Stay on the trail.
- Avoid dead animals.
- Secure your food and equipment properly.

Even if you take precautions to avoid a bear, you may still find yourself sharing a campsite or hiking trail with one. Nevertheless, the likelihood of being killed or attacked by a bear is very low. Between 1900 and 2009, there were only 59 incidents during which people were killed by noncaptive black bears (*Ursus americanus*) in North America, and only 63 people were killed. Of those 63 deaths, 49 occurred in Canada and Alaska, and 14 occurred in the lower 48 states. Almost all (91%) incidents involving a death occurred when people were in parties of one or two people. The National Park System is also fairly safe from bear attacks, and there are few incidents of grizzly bears injuring people. For example, Yellowstone National Park received more than 104 million visitors between 1980 and 2015, but only 38 people were injured by grizzly bears in the park. In addition, only eight people were killed by grizzly bears in Yellowstone National Park in 145 years (1872–2015). Interestingly, during this time period, six people were killed by falling trees, and five people were killed after they were struck by lightning in Yellowstone National Park. The rarity of deaths caused by bear attacks is put into perspective when the number of deaths caused by other animals is revealed. Between 1999 and 2007 in the United States, hornets, bees, and wasps were responsible for 509 deaths, and dogs were responsible for 250 deaths.

The best strategy for surviving a bear attack varies depending on many factors, including the species of bear, the time when the bear is encountered (e.g., while feeding, walking with cubs), and how the bear reacts to a person's presence. Many bears will turn away and leave an area when approached by people. When agitated, bears often make warning gestures such as teeth clacking, grunts, and paw slaps. Take such warnings as a signal to back away slowly. Never run: many bears can run at least 35 mph for short distances. People cannot outrun a charging bear. Even Usain Bolt, the fastest man in the world, who ran the 100 meter race in 9.58 seconds (23.3 mph), cannot outrun a bear. Climbing a tree is also not a good strategy, because bears are excellent climbers and may follow people trying to escape up a tree.

Once a bear decides to charge, some experts suggest that people should stand their ground. This may cause the bear to stop its advance and move away. Sometimes a bear will make a bluff charge. If the bear continues to move forward and approaches to within 30 feet, bear spray should be deployed. Bear sprays contain capsaicinoids, the ingredient that gives red peppers their kick. The Environmental Protection Agency currently allows bear sprays to contain up to 2% capsaicinoids. Smith et al. (2008) examined 83 incidents when bear spray was used on brown bears, black bears, and polar bears. Undesirable bear behavior was stopped 92% of the time when red pepper spray was used on brown bears, 90% of the time when it was used on black bears, and every time it was used on polar bears. Only 2% of the people involved in the bear spray incidents were injured by a bear, and the injuries they suffered were relatively minor.

If a bear does not stop its approach and makes physical contact, a drop and play dead scenario is the next move. People should lie on their stomachs and protect themselves by clasping their hands over their necks with their arms protecting their faces. If the bear does not stop its initial attack, experts suggest fighting back by punching and kicking. Such tactics, of course, may do little to prevent serious injury. The estimated bite forces measured at the canine teeth for polar bears, brown bears, panda bears, sun bears, Asian black bears, and American black bears are 1,646.7 Newtons (N), 1,409.7 N, 1,298.9 N, 883.2 N, 858.3 N, and 744.3 N, respectively. With the addition of claws stretching up to six inches long, dense fur, and thick layers of skin and fat, a bear is a formidable assailant and can inflict serious injury. Injuries to the head, arms, and legs are most common in people attacked by grizzly bears and sloth bears.

Unfortunately, trouble for people who survive bear attacks may not end when the bear leaves. Bear bite wounds can be deep and become infected with multiple harmful bacteria that are difficult to treat with antibiotics. Bears may also harbor the rabies virus, but the good news is that these animals are not a common reservoir for this virus that is almost 100% fatal.

The likelihood of meeting a bear in the wild is low, and an unintentional human-bear encounter will usually not result in any harm to either party. The risk of injury is lessened further with proper preparation and attentiveness to one's surroundings. Viewing a bear in its native environment is an experience to cherish, as long as it is done from a safe distance and with a can of bear spray ready.

SUMMARY

Preventability (81)

Encounters with bears can be prevented by avoiding places frequented by bears. If you do hike or camp in areas where bears are known to live, then you should take precautions (e.g., carry bear spray, secure food) to reduce the risk of a poor outcome.

Likelihood (3)

Bears do not actively seek out humans, and the chance of a bear attack is low.

Consequence (74)

An attack by a bear can sometimes be stopped by playing dead, but should a bear continue its attack, severe physical injury is likely.

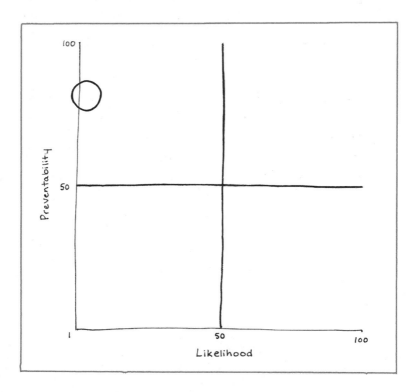

REFERENCES

Christiansen, P., & Wroe, S. (2007). Bite forces and evolutionary adaptations to feeding ecology in carnivores. *Ecology, 88*, 347–358.

Frank, R. C., Mahabir, R. C., Magi, E., Lindsay, R. L., & Haas, W. D. (2006). Bear maulings treated in Calgary, Alberta: Their management and sequelae. *Canadian Journal of Plastic Surgery, 14*, 158–162.

Herrero, S,. Higgins, A., Cardoza, J. E., Hajduk, L. I., & Smith, T. S. (2011). Fatal attacks by American black bear on people: 1900–2009. *Journal of Wildlife Management, 75*, 596–603.

Kunimoto, D., Rennie, R., Citron, D. M., & Goldstein, E. J. C. (2004). Bacteriology of a bear bite wound to a human: Case report. *Journal of Clinical Microbiology, 42*, 3374–3376.

Lehtinen, V. A., Kaukonen, T., Ikäheimo, I., Mähönen, S.-M., Koskela, M., & Ylipalosaari, P. (2005). Mycobacterium fortuitum infection after a brown bear bite. *Journal of Clinical Microbiology, 43*, 1009–1009.

Moen, G. K., Støen, O.-G., Sahlén, V., & Swenson, J. E. (2012). Behaviour of solitary adult Scandinavian brown bears (Ursus arctos) when approached by humans on foot. *PLOS ONE, 7*, e31699.

National Park Service. (n.d.). Bear inflicted human injuries and fatalities in Yellowstone. Retrieved from https://www.nps.gov/yell/learn/nature/injuries.htm

National Park Service. (n.d.). Reacting to a bear encounter. Retrieved from https://www.nps.gov/yell/learn/nature/bearreact.htm

National Park Service. (n.d.). Staying safe around bears. Retrieved from https://www.nps.gov/subjects/bears/safety.htm

Patil, L., Dutta, D., & Bement, A. (2015). *Educate to innovate: Factors that influence innovation: Based on input from innovators and stakeholders.* Washington, DC: National Academies Press.

Smith, T. S., Herrero, S., Debruyn, T. D., & Wilder, J. M. (2008). Efficacy of bear deterrent spray in Alaska. *Journal of Wildlife Management, 72*, 640–645.

Walroth, R., Brown, N., Wandeler, A., Casey, A., & MacInnes, C. (1996). Rabid black bears in Ontario. *Canadian Veterinary Journal, 37*, 492.

42. BEES

Insects and other animals play a critical role in producing food for human consumption. Bees are a major actor in pollinating fruits and vegetables as they fly from flower to flower collecting pollen and nectar. We (and other animals) also love honey. But despite their importance for food production, bees cause fear in many people because of the perceived danger of stings.

News reports have publicized the invasion of Africanized "killer bees" into North America. Killer bees are hybrids of African and European honeybees that were imported to Brazil in the 1950s to improve honey production. When some of the bees escaped into the wild, they thrived, reproduced, and moved north. These bees have now been found throughout the southern U.S. Although the venom in killer bees is not more potent than that of other honeybees, killer bees are more aggressive, and they are more likely to attack, attack in higher numbers, and continue an attack for a longer period of time.

Honeybees and bumblebees are usually not aggressive, especially when they are away from their hives and nests. The female honeybee has a barbed stinger that is a modified organ used for laying eggs (an ovipositor). Male honeybees, also known as drones, lack stingers. When a honeybee stings, the stinger hooks under the skin of its victim to prevent the stinger from coming out. Therefore, when the bee flies off, the stinger and internal organs attached to it usually get left behind. This injury results in the death of the bee. So a honeybee can sting only once. On the other hand, bumblebees have stingers that are not barbed and therefore, they can sting more than once. This is also the case for wasps and yellow jackets, although these animals are not bees.

After a stinger pierces the skin, it injects a concoction of venom made in the venom gland and Dufour's gland. Even a detached stinger can deliver venom, because the venom gland will continue to pump. The primary component in bee venom is a peptide named melittin. Melittin is responsible for the pain caused by a bee sting, and it also destroys red blood cells. Other components of bee venom affect cell membranes and mast cells, causing inflammation, itching, and redness.

Although unprovoked bees are unlikely to attack, bees do kill about 50 people each year in the U.S., and between 0.3% and 8.9% of the population is allergic to bee venom. For people allergic to bee venom, a bee sting is a life-threatening event because they can go into anaphylactic shock. An allergic reaction usually starts with hives and coughing, but as it progresses, a person may have dizziness, nausea, trouble breathing, loss of consciousness, and even death. Anyone who is allergic to bee stings should stay away from bees and carry an autoinjector that administers a dose of the drug epinephrine, which activates the heart and opens bronchial passages to improve breathing. Anaphylaxis is a medical emergency that requires immediate treatment.

There are ways to stay safe and reduce the chance of a bee sting or attack. First, do not disturb a beehive or swat at bees. Bees that become alarmed release a pheromone that attracts other bees, which may result in more numerous attackers. If bees do attack, protect your head and face and run away. Find shelter where bees cannot gain entry, but be sure you have an exit plan. Jumping into a river, lake, or pool is unlikely to help because the bees will just wait for you to come up for a breath. A long-held belief is that clothing of certain colors, perfumes, soaps, and shampoos attract bees. However, there has been no testing of various cosmetics or colors on the aggressive behavior of bees, so avoiding specific clothing or products may not do you much good.

If you are stung, the stinger should be extracted as soon as possible to reduce the amount of venom injected under the skin. Your first inclination might be to grab the stinger and pull it out. Don't do this. Grabbing the stinger will likely result in squeezing the venom sac, which will then inject more venom. Instead, try scraping the stinger off with a credit card or other object. Ice applied to the sting, medication to reduce pain, and an antihistamine to reduce swelling are generally recommended for bee stings.

You love the honey and food that bees help produce, but you fear bee stings. Most of us have no need to worry about a bee sting—just a little pain, and not much compared to the stings of some other insects. But if you are allergic to bees, avoid them and carry an epinephrine autoinjector just in case.

You might also have heard that honeybees are dying off in large numbers due to something called colony collapse disorder (CCD). This phenomenon, in which most of the worker bees die off for reasons that are still unclear, was first detected in the winter of 2006–2007. For a while CCD caused great consternation and angst among scientists and spawned several campaigns to save the bees. However, reported cases of colony collapse have decreased significantly. But this doesn't mean that bees are out of danger. There are thousands of species of bees, some of which are being edged toward extinction by pesticide use and habitat destruction. The rusty patched bumblebee, for example, was recently added to the endangered species list. Unlike the western honeybee, rusty patched bumblebees are native to North America. Native bees, of which there are more than 4,000 species in the United States, play an important role in pollinating native plants and flowers. In fact, some plants can only be pollinated by one particular species of bee. If the pollinator goes extinct, the plant will too. So spare a little worry for the bees, too.

SUMMARY

Preventability (23)

Being aware of your surroundings is the best way to prevent a bee sting. People who are allergic to bee stings should always carry an epinephrine-containing autoinjector.

Likelihood (37)

If you take a walk outside, especially in the spring and summer, you are likely to encounter bees. However, bees are not normally aggressive and will not attack unprovoked.

Consequence (38)

For most people, a bee sting will cause temporary discomfort and mild pain. Certainly, the consequences of a bee sting for someone who is allergic to bee venom or an attack by a swarm of killer bees are significantly higher.

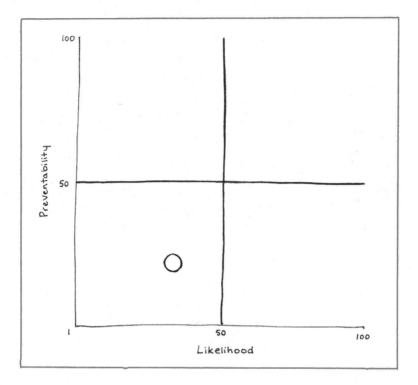

REFERENCES

Bilò, M. B. (2011). Anaphylaxis caused by Hymenoptera stings: From epidemiology to treatment. *Allergy, 66*, 35–37.

Greene, A., & Breisch, N. L. (2005). Avoidance of bee and wasp stings: An entomological perspective. *Current Opinion in Allergy and Clinical Immunology, 5*, 337.

U.S. Department of Agriculture. (n.d.). Bee pollination. Retrieved from https://www .fs.fed.us/wildflowers/pollinators/animals/bees.shtml

U.S. Environmental Protection Agency. (n.d.). Colony collapse disorder. Retrieved from https://www.epa.gov/pollinator-protection/colony-collapse-disorder

U.S. Fish and Wildlife Service. (2018, February 28). Rusty patched bumble bee (Bombus affinis). Retrieved from https://www.fws.gov/midwest/endangered/insects/rpbb/

43. DOGS

When people think of scary animals, they often mention sharks, snakes, and spiders. Dogs usually do not make the list, even though a fear of dogs is not uncommon, and many people feel anxious around dogs. Some people develop these fears after they have been bitten or knocked down by a dog or after they have seen a dog attack. The fear is reinforced by news reports of vicious dogs or city bans on specific breeds of dogs.

Perhaps dogs should be on the most-feared list. Statistics show that dogs kill more people in the United States than sharks, snakes, and spiders combined. In the United States between 1999 and 2012, dogs killed 250 people, while spiders killed 70 people, venomous snakes (and lizards) killed 59 people, and marine animals killed 10 people. Dogs also bite more than 4.5 million people in the United States and send 800,000 people to the doctor's office each year. Nevertheless, people love their dogs. In the United States, there are approximately 70 million dogs; 1 dog for every 4.5 people.

Most dogs make great pets and companion animals. Dog ownership may even have health benefits. For example, having a dog can reduce a person's stress, blood pressure, and cholesterol levels, and walking a dog provides people with a chance to exercise and socialize with others. However, when a dog bites, there are serious consequences, especially for children, who are more frequently bitten by dogs than adults. These bites can inflict significant wounds by puncturing or lacerating skin and underlying muscle tissue of a victim.

In addition to causing physical damage, dog bites can transmit disease. Rabies is a deadly viral disease that is transmitted through the bite of an infected animal such as a dog, fox, bat, or raccoon. Rabies kills more than 59,000 people worldwide each year, with 99% of the cases caused by dog bites. Most of these deaths are to children in Africa and Asia. In the United States, animal control and vaccination efforts have eliminated the spread of rabies by domestic dogs, and cases of human rabies are rare.

All dog bites have the potential to cause bacterial infections. The statement that a dog's mouth is cleaner than a human's mouth is false. A dog's mouth is filled with bacteria of different types that can enter a wound and cause infection. The bacteria may result in local infections or life-threatening systemic infections such as sepsis and meningitis. A dog bite should be washed with soap and water immediately. Serious wounds or those that become swollen or painful should be treated by a health care professional. A person bitten by an unknown dog or by a dog that looks sick should also visit a doctor for treatment recommendations.

Even if a dog doesn't bite, it can still transmit diseases that cause human illness. Tapeworms, hookworms, and roundworms are three parasites that can infect dogs and can be passed on to humans through contact with stool from an infected animal. Various bacteria (e.g., *Campylobacter, Brucella, Capnocytophaga, Leptospira*) that cause gastrointestinal problems or more serious symptoms can also be passed from dog to human. And let's not forget ringworm, which is caused not by a worm, but by the fungus *Microsporum canis*. Ringworm is a common, contagious fungal infection of the skin that people can contract after touching their dogs (and cats). The scaly, red patches on the skin caused by ringworm can be treated effectively with antifungal medication and rarely result in significant illness, but it's not fun.

Bites and diseases are not the only hazards posed by dogs. People are literally falling over their dogs and injuring themselves. Between 2001 and 2006 in the United States, an estimated average of 86,629 people each year were injured (e.g., fractures, contusions, abrasions) and treated in emergency departments each year in falls associated with dogs and cats. The most common injuries involved falling or tripping over a dog (31.3%) and being pushed or pulled by a dog (21.2%). Dog bites and other dog-related injuries don't just hurt a person's body; they hurt pocketbooks too. The Insurance Information Institute reports that dog bites and injuries account for more than one-third of all homeowner's insurance liability claims (over $600 million). In 2016, the average cost paid for a dog bite claim was $33,230.

At parks, on the street, in homes—dogs are everywhere, and it is impossible to avoid them completely. To reduce the possibility of dog-to-human infections, people should wash their hands after petting dogs or cleaning up after them. Everyone, especially children, should know how to act when approached by a dog and how to stay safe in the presence of a dog. Dog owners should also always maintain control of their dogs, obey leash laws in public-use areas, and ensure that their canine companions have adequate veterinary care.

SUMMARY

Preventability (77)

Dog owners must take responsibility for their pets by ensuring that their animals have the proper vaccinations and are kept under control at all times.

Likelihood (55)

If you own a dog, you likely have been scratched or bitten by your pet. More severe injuries or transmission of rabies occur less often.

Consequence (55)

Dogs can transmit diseases that can be cured with medication or diseases that can kill (rabies). Most injuries caused by dogs are minor, but attacks by aggressive dogs can be life threatening.

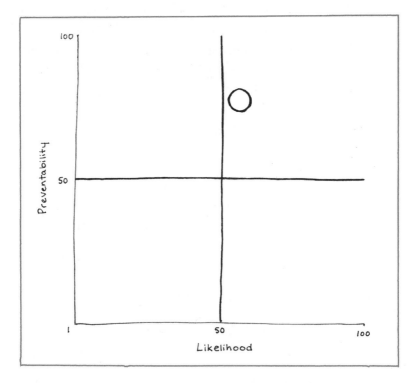

REFERENCES

American Veterinary Medical Association. (n.d.). Dog bite prevention. Retrieved from https://www.avma.org/public/Pages/Dog-Bite-Prevention.aspx

Butler, T. (2015). Capnocytophaga canimorsus: An emerging cause of sepsis, meningitis, and post-splenectomy infection after dog bites. *European Journal of Clinical Microbiology and Infectious Diseases, 34,* 1271–1280.

Centers for Disease Control and Prevention. (2009). Nonfatal fall-related injuries associated with dogs and cats—United States, 2001–2006. *MMWR, 58,* 277–281.

Centers for Disease Control and Prevention. (2017, August 23). Human rabies. Retrieved from https://www.cdc.gov/rabies/location/usa/surveillance/human_rabies.html

Insurance Information Institute. (2017, April 3). Spotlight on: Dog bite liability. Retrieved from https://www.iii.org/issue-update/dog-bite-liability

Mubanga, M., Byberg, L., Nowak, C., Egenvall, A., Magnusson, P. K., Ingelsson, E., & Fall, T. (2017). Dog ownership and the risk of cardiovascular disease and death—a nationwide cohort study. *Science Reports, 7,* 15821. Retrieved from https://www.ncbi.nlm.nih.gov/pmc/articles/PMC5693989/

World Health Organization. (2017, September). 10 facts on rabies. Retrieved from http://www.who.int/features/factfiles/rabies/en/

44. SHARK ATTACK

Despite what the movie *Jaws* might lead you to believe, sharks are not roaming the oceans looking for a human snack. In fact, according to the International Shark Attack File, in 2017, there were 88 unprovoked shark attacks worldwide, and only five of those attacks were lethal. There may be additional attacks that go unreported, especially in underdeveloped areas. But with the millions of people who swim, surf, snorkel, and dive in the ocean and the few cases of reported shark attacks, the likelihood of being injured or killed by a shark is very low. You have a better chance of drowning in the surf than being attacked by a shark. Nevertheless, many people worry that every time they step off the sand and into the water, sharks are lurking nearby, ready to bite.

Sharks have the anatomy and physiology to make them the top predators in the sea. Some sharks, such as the great white, can grow to lengths of 20 feet and weigh more than 4,000 pounds. But not all sharks are aggressive toward humans, and only a few shark species are responsible for the majority of attacks. It is often difficult to identify the species of shark responsible for an attack because people have other things to worry about when they are trying to avoid being eaten. Nevertheless, white sharks (*Carcharodon carcharias*), tiger sharks (*Galeocerdo cuvier*), and bull sharks (*Carcharhinus leucas*) cause most of the injuries, both fatal and nonfatal.

With skeletons made of cartilage instead of bone, sharks can move easily through the water. The lack of a swim bladder helps sharks move through the water column without the danger associated with pressure changes. Large muscles are capable of propelling some sharks through the water in bursts as fast as 15 mph. With an impressive array of sensory systems, sharks process a large amount of information about their environment. The ability of sharks to detect minute amounts of chemicals (e.g., to smell blood) in the water attests to their acute chemosensory (olfactory) abilities. Some sharks can respond to the presence of amino acids in the micromolar and sub-nanomolar range. Sharks also possess taste buds in their mouths and gill arches that provide information about a food's taste.

Sharks have a good sense of vision and often have large eyes to provide detailed images of their environment. Shark vision in low light conditions is enhanced by a light-reflecting membrane called the tapetum, located behind the retina. Color vision, however, is likely lacking in sharks, because their retinas do not have any cone photoreceptors or contain only one type of cone photoreceptor.

The sound and movement of struggling prey is very effective in attracting the attention of sharks. The inner ear of a shark is similar to that in other fish, and sharks can hear sounds ranging in frequency from about 20 to 100 Hz. Movement in the water causes disturbances in water pressure that sharks can detect with a lateral line system, which is a series of special cells along the length of a shark's body that respond to vibration. The lateral line system can provide sharks with information about water current (direction, speed), prey, predators, and other sharks.

In addition to having the senses of touch, taste, smell, hearing, and vision, sharks have the ability to detect electrical fields in the water. The receptors for electroreception (ampullae of Lorenzini) are concentrated in a shark's head and can detect weak electrical fields emitted by other animals. Electroreception is used to find and capture prey and may also be used to navigate through the ocean using the Earth's magnetic field.

Knowledge about the sensory abilities of sharks has been used to develop methods to repel or prevent shark attacks. Chemical shark repellents were first developed during World War II. Most of the chemicals were poisons that failed to prevent an attack, but eventually killed the shark. Rotten shark flesh, copper salts, ammonium acetate, and nigrosine dye met with mixed success. More recent research has shown that toxins from the glands of fish (*Pardachirus*, a genus of sole) and secretions from the sea cucumber may repel some species of sharks. Electrical repellents, such as systems that emit electrical signals and are worn by scuba divers or attached to nets, show some promise in deterring sharks. Similarly, devices that hide or camouflage people in the water may be effective. For example, a person can hide in a floating bag that prevents a shark from seeing or smelling a potential victim. Even auditory repellents have been developed: the makers of SharkStopper claim that their system, which combines killer whale calls with modulated frequencies, can repel sharks including great white, bull, and tiger sharks.

Analysis of 5,034 shark attacks since the early 1900s shows that men are the targets of most attacks, accounting for 81% of the fatal shark attacks and 80% of the nonfatal shark attacks. Sharks most commonly bite the legs of people swimming, bathing, or wading in shallow water. Certainly, a shark encounter can be frightening and an actual attack horrific. With sharp, serrated teeth and strong jaws, sharks are capable of inflicting significant damage to a human body with even a small nibble. As sharks bite into flesh, they often shake their heads and roll. Such action can easily remove large sections of skin and muscle and even entire limbs.

In the unlikely event that you are attacked by a shark, you can take several steps to improve your chances of survival. First, remain calm. Most shark attacks are the hit-and-run variety, as the shark bites and then releases its victim. If the shark comes back for another taste, then fight back, targeting the shark's eyes and gills. If you suffer any wounds, get out of the water as soon as possible, alert others nearby, and seek medical assistance. Rapid treatment of wounds, especially to prevent excessive blood loss, is an important step to improve the chances for survival following a shark attack. Shark bites can become infected, and proper wound care is essential to avoid complications during recovery.

Avoiding a shark attack is always better than dealing with an actual attack. This includes knowing if sharks frequent the water you will be using. Stay out of the water if you are bleeding and away from fishermen or boats chumming the water with fish parts that may attract sharks. It is also a good idea to swim in areas with good light so that you (and the sharks) can see clearly.

SUMMARY

Preventability (83)

If you want to avoid sharks, stay out of the ocean.

Likelihood (3)

The chance of being bitten by a shark is low.

Consequence (78)

Even a nibble by a shark can cause significant tissue damage; a bite from a large shark can be lethal.

REFERENCES

International Shark Attack File. (n.d.). Yearly worldwide shark attack summary. Retrieved from https://www.floridamuseum.ufl.edu/shark-attacks/yearly-worldwide-summary/

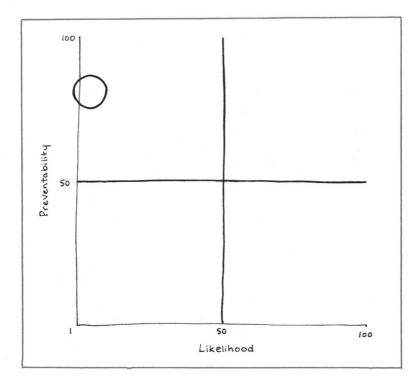

Hart, N. S., & Collin, S. P. (2015). Sharks senses and shark repellents. *Integrative Zoology*, *10*, 38–64.

Hart, N. S., Theiss, S. M., Harahush, B. K., & Collin, S. P. (2011). Microspectrophoto-metric evidence for cone monochromacy in sharks. *Naturwissenschaften*, *98*, 193–201.

Ricci, J. A., Vargas, C. R., Singhal, D., & Lee, B. T. (2016). Shark attack-related injuries: Epidemiology and implications for plastic surgeons. *Journal of Plastic and Reconstructive Aesthetic Surgery*, *69*, 108–114.

45. SPIDERS

Spiders are found in houses, schools, offices, backyards, gardens, jungles, and forests. We all share our homes with spiders. But even with spiders as housemates, many people fear spiders and worry about the dangers these arachnids pose to their health. An estimated 3.5–6.1% of the population suffers from arachnophobia, the unreasonable, irrational fear of spiders. Many other people are less afraid but still apprehensive about spiders. There are approximately 47,000 species of spiders, but few spiders can harm people. All spiders have a valuable role in the ecosystem, so there is little to fear and much to be appreciated about these eight-legged creatures.

Humans are not spider food, so spiders do not hunt people. It is true that almost all spiders are venomous, but the venom of most spiders poses little danger to humans. Moreover, most spiders will bite people only in self-defense. Perhaps the most well-known spider capable of injuring people is the black widow (*Latrodectus mactans* or *Latrodectus hesperus*). The female black widow can be identified by a red hourglass shape on its black abdomen. Often found in garages or under logs and rocks, black widow spiders are not aggressive, but they will bite if they are significantly disturbed. When poked repeatedly, black widow spiders usually just move away; only when they are pinched do these spiders bite. The danger of a black widow bite comes from the injected venom, called latrotoxin, a neurotoxin that causes the massive release of the neurotransmitter acetylcholine from the nerve terminals of a victim. Latrotoxin can cause swelling around the puncture wound, pain, cramping, high blood pressure, headache, dizziness, nausea, and vomiting. Although black widow spider bites can be lethal, deaths caused by these spiders are very rare. For example, in 2013, of the 1,866 black widow spider bite cases reported to the American Association of Poison Control Centers, there were no deaths.

Another spider capable of injuring people is the brown recluse (*Loxosceles reclusa*), also known as the fiddleback spider because of the violin-shaped mark on its back. These spiders can be found indoors in garages, basements, beds, clothing, attics, and closets. But like black widow spiders, brown recluse spiders are not aggressive. In one home in Kansas, 2,055 brown recluse spiders were found in a six-month period, and no one in the house was bitten. Although brown recluse spiders do not bite often, they have venom that can cause extensive necrosis around the wound and sometimes fever, chills, and shock. The bite wound may also become infected and take weeks or months to heal, but fatalities from brown recluse spider bites are rare.

Unlike black widow and brown recluse spiders, the Sydney funnel-web spider (*Atrax robustus*) has a bit of a mean streak and is regarded as aggressive. Fortunately (unless you're Australian), Sydney funnel-web spiders are found only in eastern and southern Australia. When approached, the Sydney funnel-web spider will raise its front legs in an attack posture. This spider's fangs are formidable, and its neurotoxic venom (atratoxin) is potent. Atratoxin causes pain and, if it spreads, a patient can experience life-threatening symptoms affecting the nervous and circulatory systems. A total of 13 people have died from funnel-web spider bites, but antivenom is so effective that no deaths from these spiders have been reported since 1981 when the antivenom was introduced.

South American wandering spiders (e.g., *Phoneutria nigriventer, Phoneutria fera*) also take up an aggressive posture when approached. Bites from *Phoneutria* species usually cause only mild pain and swelling. However, two of 422 people admitted to the hospital (both children) after being bitten by *Phoneutria* spiders showed severe symptoms, and one of these children died. *Phoneutria fera* lives in the Amazon far away from people and generally poses little risk to humans.

There is no reason to panic when you see a spider. Few spiders can harm people, and they are useful to have around the house because they eat insect pests. To further relieve any anxiety about being bitten by a spider, shake out your shoes, gloves, and clothing before putting them on. If you are bitten by a spider, apply an ice pack to the location of the bite and, in the unlikely chance of a more serious condition, seek medical attention. If you can safely trap the spider, an expert may be able to identify it in case antivenom is needed.

Spiders have no reason to bite people, and they prefer to be left alone where they can go about their business of building webs, burrowing, and hunting for prey. Although it is possible to encounter a potentially dangerous spider, the vast majority of spiders are harmless. Some spiders are even tasty: deep-fried tarantula is a delicacy in parts of Southeast Asia.

SUMMARY

Preventability (15)

Watch where you put your hands.

Likelihood (21)

Spiders are everywhere, but they are rarely aggressive.

Consequence (27)

Most spiders are not capable of harming people, but there are a few that can cause intense pain. Children and people who have underlying health problems can suffer more severe symptoms.

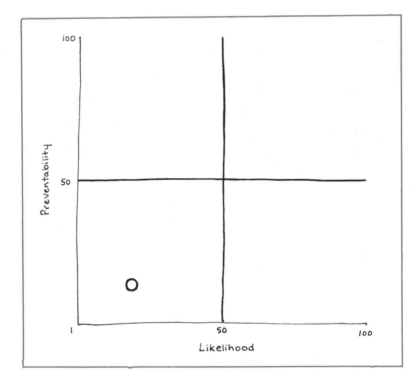

REFERENCES

Bucaretchi, F., de Deus Reinaldo, C. R., Hyslop, S., Madureira, P. R., De Capitani, E. M., & Vieira, R. J. (2000). A clinic-epidemiological study of bites by spiders of the genus Phoneutria. *Revista do Instituto de Medicina Tropical* de *São Paulo, 42*, 17–21.

Eichenberg, C., & Walters, C. (2012). Virtual realities in the treatment of mental disorders: A review of the current state of research. In C. Eichenberg, *Virtual reality in psychological, medical and pedagogical applications.* InTech. Retrieved from https://www.intechopen. com/books/virtual-reality-in-psychological-medical-and-pedagogical-applications

Isbister, G., Gray, M., Balit, C., Raven, R., Stokes, B., Porges, K., . . . Fisher, M. (2005). Funnel-web spider bite: A systematic review of recorded clinical cases. *Medical Journal of Australia, 182*, 407–411.

Mowry, J.B., Spyker, D.A., Cantilena Jr, L.R., McMillan, N. & Ford, M. (2014). 2013Annual Report of the American Association of Poison Control Centers' National Poison Data System (NPDS): 31st Annual Report, Clinical Toxicology, 52, 1032–1283.

Natural History Museum Bern. (2017). *World spider catalog.* Version 18.5. Retrieved from http://wsc.nmbe.ch

Nelsen, D. R., Kelln, W., & Hayes, W. K. (2014). Poke but don't pinch: Risk assessment and venom metering in the western black widow spider, Latrodectus hesperus. *Animal Behavior, 89*, 107–114.

Vetter, R. S., & Barger, D. K. (2002). An infestation of 2,055 brown recluse spiders (Araneae: Sicariidae) and no envenomations in a Kansas home: Implications for bite diagnoses in nonendemic areas. *Journal of Medical Entomology, 39*, 948–951.

46. TICKS

Ticks really tick off a lot of people. These small, spider-like, parasitic arachnids bite their animal hosts and after they latch onto the skin of their victim, they feast on blood. Ticks can sense an animal's body temperature, scent, and breath as they lie in wait on leaves or in grass for a passing host. Often ticks attach themselves to body parts that the host cannot see, such as the scalp, back, and legs. Mammals, birds, reptiles, and amphibians can all provide blood meals for ticks.

A tick bite often causes local skin irritation with redness, swelling, and itching. Some people are allergic to components in tick saliva that can send a victim into life-threatening anaphylactic shock and, strangely, lead to a meat allergy. Not all ticks transmit disease, but those that do can spread serious infections caused by bacteria, viruses, and protozoa.

Perhaps the most well-known tick-borne disorder is Lyme disease. Lyme disease is named after the city of Lyme, Connecticut, where an outbreak of the illness was discovered in 1975. The Centers for Disease Control and Prevention (CDC) reports that there were 26,203 confirmed cases and 10,226 probable cases of Lyme disease in the United States in 2016. The disease is caused by a bacterium called *Borrelia burgdorferi*. Deer and mice are carriers of *B. burgdorferi*, and the bacterium is transferred to ticks (e.g., *Ixodes scapularis*, black-legged tick, or *Ixodes pacificus*, Western black-legged tick) when they feed on the blood of these animals. Infected ticks then transmit the bacteria to humans (and other animals) when they bite. Symptoms of Lyme disease usually start with a gradually expanding rash at the site of the tick bite. As the bacteria spread through the body, a person may experience joint pains, general aches, chills, fever, and headache. Several weeks after the infecting bite, people with Lyme disease may experience a stiff neck, facial palsy, tingling or numbness in the extremities, headache, sore throat, and severe fatigue. Untreated Lyme disease may result in pain and swelling of the large joints, heart abnormalities (Lyme carditis), and neurological symptoms such as confusion and memory problems. Early treatment of Lyme disease with appropriate antibiotics often results in rapid and complete recovery, but late-stage Lyme disease is more difficult to treat, and symptoms may continue for many months.

Southern tick-associated rash illness (STARI) is sometimes mistaken for Lyme disease because both disorders are transmitted by tick bites and both result in circular rashes. STARI also causes some of the same symptoms as Lyme disease such as fatigue, headache, and body pains. However, STARI has been linked to the lone star tick (*Amblyomma americanum*); these ticks do not harbor *B. burgdorferi*, the bacteria associated with Lyme disease. The pathogen responsible for STARI is not known.

Another well-known tick-borne disease is Rocky Mountain spotted fever (RMSF). This disease is caused by bacteria in the rickettsia group. In the United States, the American dog tick (*Dermacentor variabilis*), Rocky Mountain wood tick (*Dermacentor andersoni*), and brown dog tick (*Rhipicephalus sanguineus*) can become infected with rickettsia bacteria. The bites of these infected ticks can cause fever, headaches, rash, nausea, and pain. Approximately 3,500 cases of RMSF were reported to the CDC in 2014. The initial illness associated with RMSF can leave some people with lingering health effects such as hearing loss, paralysis, and other neurological problems.

Different bacteria are responsible for several other tick-borne diseases, including anaplasmosis, African tick-bite fever, and tularemia. Symptoms of these diseases usually include fever, fatigue, headache, and muscle pain and can progress to serious illness involving the nervous, respiratory, and cardiovascular systems.

Ticks can also carry viruses that cause illness in people. Bourbon virus, Colorado tick fever, and Heartland virus have all been linked to tick bites and result in fever, headaches, body pains, and fatigue. Unfortunately, there are no medications or vaccines to prevent these viruses.

Babesiosis is a tick-borne disease caused by protozoan parasites (*Babesia microti*). These single-celled parasites target and reproduce in red blood cells of the host organism. In the United States, babesiosis is transmitted by the same ticks responsible for Lyme disease. People infected with *B. microti* may feel tired, lose their appetite, and have fever, nausea, sweats, and body aches. In healthy people, the infection may resolve itself, but victims who have spleen problems or take immunosuppressant medications may have serious complications and health risks.

If diseases caused by bacteria, viruses, and protozoa weren't enough, ticks have another way to transmit disease: neurotoxic saliva. Many species of ticks release a chemical neurotoxin into their saliva when they bite. This chemical attacks the nervous system, causing tick paralysis, which often starts in the feet and legs and moves progressively higher in the body. When this happens, removal of the tick, at least some species, usually results in quick and complete recovery. But if the tick is not removed and the paralysis affects breathing, a person can die.

The best way to prevent tick-borne diseases is to avoid tick bites. Long-sleeved pants and shirts, boots, and hats should be worn by people traveling through areas where ticks are found. Insect repellents, including those containing DEET or permethrin, can also be effective in warding off ticks. When appropriate, people should check their bodies, especially the scalp, underarms, and legs, to ensure that they are free of ticks.

If a tick is found on your skin, it should be removed quickly and properly. Ticks should be removed by grasping them as close to their mouthparts as possible. For example, tweezers can be inserted between the tick's mouth and host's skin and pulled straight out. It is important to remove the head of the tick and avoid squeezing or pulling the tick by its body. After the tick is removed, wash the bite area with soap and water.

Many people like to get outdoors and commune with nature. To ensure that you don't return home with any unwanted blood-sucking ticks, wear appropriate clothing, apply insect repellent, and do a body check.

SUMMARY

Preventability (78)

Dress appropriately, use insect repellent, and do body checks when you are in areas shared by ticks.

Likelihood (22)

Most ticks do not carry diseases, and a tick bite does not necessarily transmit disease. Rapid removal of a tick can reduce the likelihood of disease transmission, and appropriate antibiotic treatment for bacterial infections can resolve some tick-borne illnesses.

Consequence (67)

A tick bite can cause symptoms ranging from mild skin irritation that clears up in several days to severe health problems.

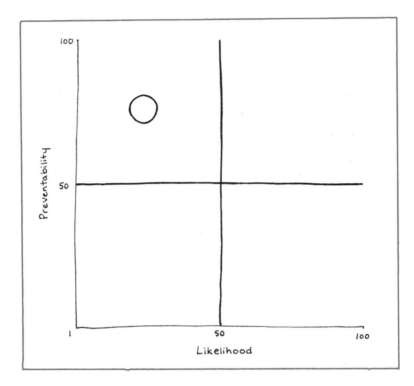

REFERENCES

Cabezas-Cruz, A., Mateos-Hernández, L., Pérez-Cruz, M., Valdés, J. J., de Mera, I. G. F., Villar, M., & de la Fuente, J. (2015). Regulation of the immune response to α-Gal and vector-borne diseases. *Trends in Parasitology, 31*, 470–476.

Centers for Disease Control and Prevention. (2017, July 25). Tickborne diseases of the United States. Retrieved from https://www.cdc.gov/ticks/diseases/index.html

Centers for Disease Control and Prevention. (2018, January 19). Lyme disease. Retrieved from https://www.cdc.gov/lyme/index.html

Pecina, C. A. (2012). Tick paralysis. *Seminars in Neurology, 32*, 531–532.

47. MOSQUITOES

osquitoes have been called the most dangerous animal on
Earth. This is obviously not because of their huge teeth, but
because of the deadly diseases they spread. These insects
are capable of spreading a host of human diseases, including malaria,
dengue, yellow fever, chikungunya, Zika, Japanese encephalitis, and
West Nile virus. Billions of people are at risk from mosquito-borne
diseases: 2.5 billion people (40% of the world's population) are at risk
for contracting dengue alone. Dengue virus infects approximately
400 million people each year.

Male mosquitoes eat flower nectar, but female mosquitoes feed
on the blood of other animals to produce eggs. Mosquito bites can
be itchy and unpleasant, but the bite itself is rarely dangerous. The
problem is that mosquitoes usually bite more than one animal, and
in so doing they can acquire and then distribute human diseases.
When mosquitoes infected with viruses or parasites bite, they inject
a small amount of saliva containing the infectious agent into their
blood meal host. When *Anopheles* mosquitoes infected with *Plasmodium* protozoan parasites (*P. falciparum*, *P. vivax*, *P. malariae*, *P. ovale*)
bite, the result is malaria. The parasites release toxic substances into a
person's bloodstream that kill red blood cells and result in symptoms
including fever, nausea, chills, headache, and general malaise. The
parasites can invade and damage the brain, liver, kidney, and lungs.

Many people who have contracted malaria do not show symptoms of the disease for several weeks after they are bitten by an infected mosquito. Malaria can be cured if it is diagnosed and treated quickly. However, malaria that affects the brain is especially dangerous and lethal. The U.S. Centers for Disease Control and Prevention estimates that worldwide there were 212 million cases of malaria and 429,000 people died of malaria in 2015.

Yellow fever, dengue, Zika virus, and chikungunya are viral diseases spread by *Aedes* mosquitos. The virus that causes Japanese encephalitis and the West Nile virus are spread primarily by *Culex* mosquitoes. These diseases share some symptoms such as fever, headache, and joint and muscle pain. In addition to this shared set of symptoms, each of the different viruses throws in its own particular unpleasantness. For example, people with yellow fever may experience low blood pressure, skin rashes, and liver and kidney failure that can be fatal. Untreated, dengue can affect the central nervous system, circulatory system, and respiratory system and cause depression, seizures, breathing problems, and shock. With prompt and proper management, death from these infections is not common. However, symptoms and suffering can persist for years after the initial sickness.

People who live or travel in tropical areas of Asia, Africa, South America, Central America, and the Pacific are at the highest risk of yellow fever, dengue, chikungunya, and Japanese encephalitis. But North America is not safe from these viruses: West Nile virus and Zika virus have both been found in the United States. West Nile virus is spread when mosquitoes feed on infected birds, such as crows, or other animals; the virus is then transmitted to people through the bite of infected mosquitoes. Although the majority of people who are infected with West Nile virus remain free of symptoms, other people may experience flu-like symptoms, fatigue, sensitivity to light, and rashes several days after becoming infected. A small proportion (1 in

150) of people infected with West Nile virus will develop encephalitis, meningitis, or paralysis, and about 1 in 10 of these people will die. Likewise, many people infected by the Zika virus remain symptom free or suffer only mild symptoms. Recently, Zika virus has been linked to the development of Guillain-Barré syndrome, a neurological disorder that damages nerves and muscles and can cause paralysis. As most people have heard by now, women infected with Zika virus while they are pregnant are at risk of giving birth to babies with serious brain defects, including microcephaly.

Governmental agencies and commercial companies around the world have taken many steps to protect the public from mosquito-borne illnesses. Effective mosquito control takes into account mosquito physiology and biology, life cycle, feeding habits, and mechanisms by which viruses spread. Professionals and the general public can help prevent the spread of mosquito-borne diseases by eliminating the breeding grounds (e.g., standing water) where mosquitoes lay eggs and hatch. Insecticides to kill larval and adult mosquitoes and reduce the risk of disease may also be used. Research using genetic modification methods shows some promise for controlling mosquito populations, but it is controversial.

The best efforts by professionals to prevent mosquito-borne diseases are often not enough. Individuals can take some responsibility for their own health and protect themselves if they live in or travel to areas with a high prevalence of mosquito-borne diseases. For example, people can be vaccinated against yellow fever and Japanese encephalitis. However, there are no vaccines for other diseases such as Zika and malaria. Unfortunately, the ingredients (e.g., preservatives, animal proteins) in some vaccines cause allergic reactions in some people. Prophylactic drugs to protect against malaria are available, but their effectiveness is variable, and they may interact poorly with other drugs or medications.

Everyone who will be in an area that has a high incidence of disease spread by mosquitoes should take protective measures. These steps start with knowing what diseases pose a potential risk and when mosquitoes are most likely to bite: some mosquitoes bite primarily during the day, while others are most active at dawn, dusk, or evening. Insect repellents applied to the skin can significantly reduce the chance of a mosquito bite (see chapter about DEET). People can reduce the risk of contracting a disease by applying insect repellents to long-sleeved shirts, long pants, and hats that they wear and by sleeping under mosquito nets.

For many people, mosquitoes and their bites are not just a simple annoyance; instead they pose a serious health threat.

SUMMARY

Preventability (53)

Insecticides and insect repellents can reduce the risk of mosquito-borne illnesses, but mosquito management has proved to be difficult in many parts of the world.

Likelihood (82)

The high incidence of mosquito-borne disease is a global health threat.

Consequence (88)

A mosquito bite may cause minor, local skin irritation, or it can transmit life-threatening disease.

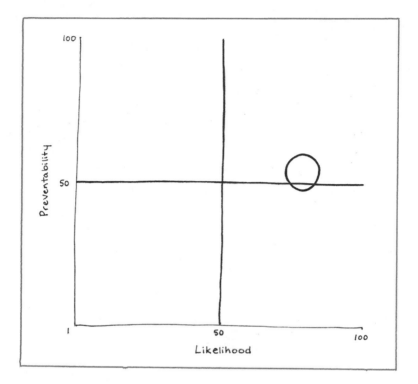

REFERENCES

Centers for Disease Control and Prevention. (2017, August 2). West Nile virus. Retrieved
    from https://www.cdc.gov/westnile/symptoms/index.html
Centers for Disease Control and Prevention. (2018, May 10). Malaria. Retrieved from
    https://www.cdc.gov/malaria/
World Health Organization, Regional Office for South-East Asia. (n.d.). Dengue.
    Retrieved from http://www.searo.who.int/entity/vector_borne_tropical_diseases/
    data/data_factsheet/en/

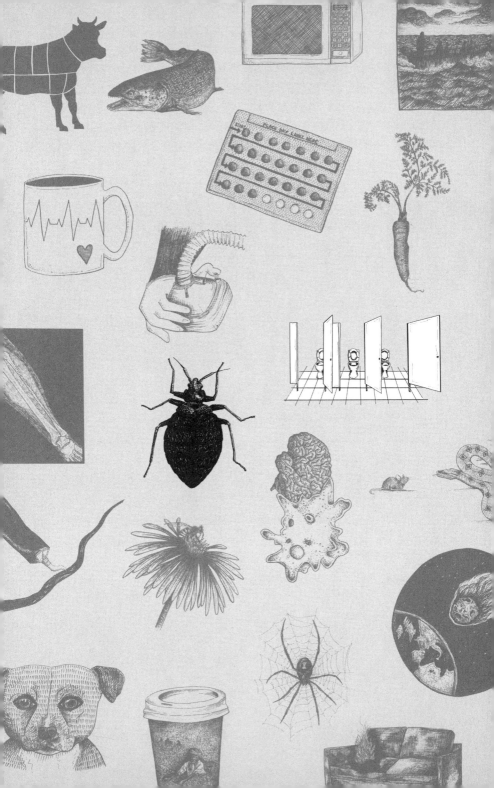

Travel

48. ELEVATORS

With 325 million passenger trips each day (119 billion trips each year) in the United States and billions more worldwide, you would think that elevators are a fairly safe way to travel. And you would be correct: only approximately 27 people each year are killed by elevators.

The two most common types of elevators are those that use a hydraulic system and those that use a cable system. Hydraulic elevators lift and lower passenger cars with fluid. The elevator car is attached to an arm that is moved by pumping fluid (e.g., oil) in and out of a reservoir. To raise the car, fluid is pumped by a motor into the arm, and the car goes up. To lower the car, a valve is opened and fluid moves back into the reservoir. Elevators that use a cable system have steel ropes attached to the elevator car and a counterweight. A motor connected to a pulley system moves the ropes to raise and lower the car. Both types of elevators require a control system to tell the elevator what to do.

Fortunately, visions of an out-of-control elevator car plunging to the ground are mostly a product of Hollywood imagination. Elevator safety regulations have been established by the American Society of Mechanical Engineers and International Building Codes. The likelihood of an elevator falling down a shaft is very low because of several safety mechanisms built into the design of elevators. First, multiple steel cables, usually six to eight, each with the ability to hold the car and counterweight by itself, are attached to an elevator car. If a single cable breaks, the other cables will prevent the car from falling. The counterweights also serve as a safety measure because they are a bit heavier than an empty car. Even without any other cables attached to an empty car, or a car with just a few people, the counterweights would move down and the elevator would be pulled up. Second, friction brakes under an elevator car engage gradually when a car moves too quickly. As an elevator car falls and builds up speed, the brakes work to slow the car. Third, in case of a power outage, electromagnetic brakes engage to hold the elevator in place. Fourth, automatic brakes engage if an elevator car gets too close to the top or bottom of an elevator shaft. The last line of safety is a shock absorber at the bottom of an elevator shaft. There is also no need to worry that an elevator has too many people on it: elevator doors will remain open and the car will not move if it is overloaded.

Although plunging to the bottom of the shaft is exceedingly unlikely, elevators can malfunction, and people can be injured by elevators due to electrical or mechanical failures. For example, problems with an elevator's cables can cause the car to drop in the shaft before safety mechanisms take over. The sudden drop and stop can cause injuries. Defective wiring in an elevator raises the risk of electrocution. But the majority of elevator injuries occur when people slip, trip, or fall when they enter or exit an elevator. This can happen when the elevator floor is not level with the building floor. The elderly are especially at risk for elevator injuries, with approximately 2,640 injuries each year (one-third of all elevator injuries) occurring in people 65 years and older in the U.S. Children age 4 years and younger suffer approximately 824 injuries each year, with the majority (70.3%) of injuries caused when an elevator door closes on a body part. Elevator malfunctions may trap people inside. Usually, people are freed after a short time, although there are reports of people being confined inside an elevator for more than 24 hours.

People who work in or near elevator shafts account for 50% of all deaths associated with elevators. These workers include elevator installers and repair and maintenance technicians. The majority (56%) of these deaths occur when workers fall into open elevator shafts. From 1992 to 2009, 89 people died while using an elevator at work and from 1997 to 2010, 91 passengers died while using an elevator while they were not at work. Falls into elevator shafts, when an elevator door opens and there is no car, accounted for about half of all deaths.

Simple common sense practices should reduce the risk of elevator deaths and injuries. For example, before you enter an elevator, wait for passengers to leave the elevator. If there are too many people in the elevator, wait for the next car. Don't try to stop a closing elevator door with your hands or feet. If you are already on the elevator and want to hold the door open for someone, use the door open button. As you enter or exit an elevator car, watch your step and look down to ensure the surfaces are level and that, indeed, the car is there. After you are on the elevator, make sure that your clothing, backpack, keys, and bags are clear of the closing door. In the event that an elevator stops while you are riding, stay in the car, remain calm, and use the elevator emergency telephone or alarm or your own phone to alert authorities. Do not try to pry the doors open or climb out of the elevator car. Use the stairs, not an elevator, if there is an earthquake or fire in the building.

In fact, you should take the stairs instead of an elevator whenever you can. Using the stairs is good exercise and better for your health.

SUMMARY

Preventability (85)

You can often take the stairs instead of the elevator—and for a bit of exercise, you probably should.

Likelihood (2)

The safety mechanisms built into elevators make an elevator falling out of control highly unlikely.

Consequence (95)

Severe injury or death is the likely outcome of the unlikely event that an elevator car falls from a significant height.

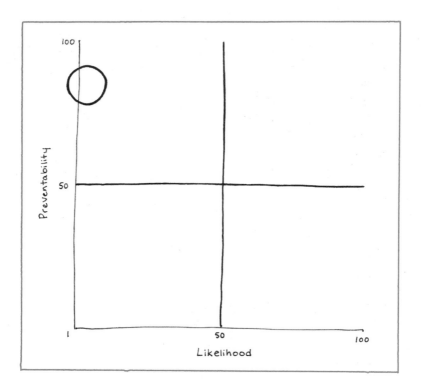

REFERENCES

Consumerwatch.com. (n.d.). Elevators. Retrieved from http://consumerwatch.com/
  workplace-public-safety/elevators/
Elevator Escalator Safety Foundation. (n.d.). Fun facts. Retrieved from https://www
  .eesf.org/fun-facts/
O'Neil, J., Steele, G. K., Huisingh, C., & Smith, G. A. (2007). Elevator-related injuries
  to children in the United States, 1990 through 2004. *Clinical Pediatrics, 46*, 619–625.
Paumgarten, N. (2008, April 21). Up and then down: The lives of elevators. *New Yorker.*
Steele, G. K., O'Neil, J., Huisingh, C., & Smith, G. A. (2010). Elevator-related injuries
  to older adults in the United States, 1990 to 2006. *Journal of Trauma and Acute Care
  Surgery, 68*, 188.

49. PUBLIC RESTROOMS

When you've got to "go," sometimes there is no other place than a public restroom. And when you are finished, you hope that you don't leave with bacteria or a virus that you didn't have when you entered.

Some people have a special public toilet ritual they use in hopes of avoiding germs. For example, many women do not sit on the toilet seat, instead preferring to squat over the seat. Although this method will prevent skin-to-toilet seat contact, it puts pressure on pelvic muscles that may make urination difficult, prevent full emptying of the bladder, and increase the chances of contracting a bladder infection. Another common practice in public restrooms is to cover the toilet seat with a layer of toilet paper. The thought is that the toilet paper will create a protective shield between a person's buttocks and the germ-infested toilet seat. But think again. That thin buffer zone may expose a person to more germs, not fewer. The absorbent, textured nature of toilet paper makes a great environment for bacteria. Given that a roll of toilet paper is usually conveniently located right next to the toilet, bacteria launched from a flushed toilet do not have far to travel to land on the toilet paper. The smooth, cool surface of a toilet seat makes it more difficult for bacteria to find a home. Although many bacteria and viruses do not survive for a long time outside their natural environment, this is little solace to those lined up to use the facilities in a crowded stadium or movie theater.

The toilet seat is not the only location inside a public restroom where germs may be present. Researchers have found many different types of bacteria on bathroom floors, stall doors, faucet handles, toilet handles, and soap dispensers. Most of the bacteria found inside public restrooms originates from human skin, although some are from the human gut. Bacteria normally found in soil have been found on bathroom floors and on toilet flushing handles. This suggests that some people transferred bacteria from the bottom of their shoes to the flush handle by using their feet to flush the toilet. Disease-causing bacteria such as *E. coli*, *Streptococcus*, and *Staphylococcus aureus* are found on surfaces in public restrooms, but a person's skin and immune system usually prevent an infection. To get into the body, these bacteria need to enter through an open cut or mucous membrane, which shouldn't be touching a toilet seat in the first place. Therefore, sitting on a toilet seat is not likely to cause an illness.

Infectious materials are dispersed inside a public restroom by a "toilet plume." Think of a toilet plume as a small aerosol geyser containing the contents of toilet bowl water that erupts with every flush. The droplets in the plume may spread infection when bacteria and viruses land on restroom surfaces or are inhaled. Putting the toilet lid down before flushing may reduce the dispersion of germs. Unfortunately, some public toilets do not have lids. In this case, the best strategy might be to step away from the toilet before flushing, get out of the way, and hold your breath. Also, keep your belongings off the floor and away from the toilet.

The ultimate protection against restroom contamination is hand washing, which reduces the chances of diarrhea by about 30% and respiratory infections by 16%. Just about everywhere in a public restroom is a potential resting place for bacteria and viruses. So avoid touching any surfaces where germs may live by using a clean paper towel to flush the toilet and to open the stall door as you enter and leave. When you finish your business, make sure you wash your hands with soap and warm water. Use another paper towel to turn off the sink and open the restroom door. Some public restrooms are equipped with trash cans near door exits to discard soiled paper towels.

Unfortunately, some public restrooms have removed paper towel dispensers and installed electric hand dryers. Fear that hand dryers may spread germs has led researchers to examine how these devices work. Jet air dryers do disperse more virus particles and bacteria at further distances than either warm air dryers or paper towels. Jet air dryers blasted virus particles up to 3 meters from the device. These experiments illustrate the power of a jet air dryer, but because research subjects rinsed their gloved hands with a virus-laden or bacteria-laden mixture prior to using the dryer, the results do not simulate a real-life scenario, in which people should wash their hands before using the dryer.

Careful hand washing should eliminate most of the risk associated with bacteria and viruses lurking in a public restroom. Just make sure you wash your hands properly: 20 seconds in warm water with soap. And don't touch the door on your way out of the restroom.

SUMMARY

Preventability (33)

Sometimes you've just got to go, and a public restroom is the only facility to use. Reducing the risk of picking up bacteria or viruses in a public restroom is fairly simple: wash your hands.

Likelihood (21)

As long as you wash your hands after you use the restroom, you are not likely to become infected with a microorganism that will make you sick.

Consequence (22)

Some bacteria and viruses found in public restrooms can make you ill, but most are not lethal.

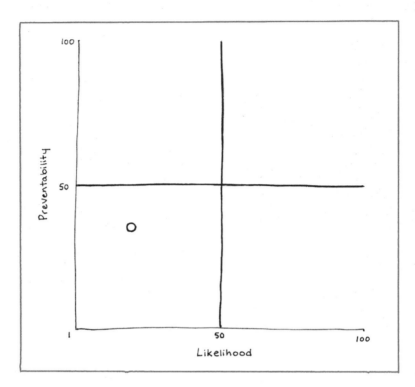

REFERENCES

Best, E. L., Parnell, P., & Wilcox, M. H. (2014). Microbiological comparison of hand-drying methods: The potential for contamination of the environment, user, and bystander. *Journal of Hospital Infection, 88*, 199–206.

Ejemot, R. I., Ehiri, J. E., Meremikwu, M. M., & Critchley, J. A. (2008). Hand washing for preventing diarrhea. *Cochrane Database of Systematic Reviews*, CD004265.

Flores, G. E., Bates, S. T., Knights, D., Lauber, C. L., Stombaugh, J., Knight, R., & Fierer, N. (2011). Microbial biogeography of public restroom surfaces. *PLOS ONE, 6*, e28132.

Gibbons, S. M., Schwartz, T., Fouquier, J., Mitchell, M., Sangwan, N., Gilbert, J. A., & Kelley, S. T. (2015). Ecological succession and viability of human-associated microbiota on restroom surfaces. *Applied Environmental Microbiology, 81*, 765–773.

Johnson, D. L., Mead, K. R., Lynch, R. A., & Hirst, D. V. L. (2013). Lifting the lid on toilet plume aerosol: A literature review with suggestions for future research. *American Journal of Infection Control, 41*, 254–258.

Kimmitt, P. T., & Redway, K. F. (2016). Evaluation of the potential for virus dispersal during hand drying: A comparison of three methods. *Journal of Applied Microbiology, 120*, 478–486.

50. PUBLIC TRANSPORTATION

Planes, trains, buses, and subways are inexpensive, safe, and usually convenient forms of public transportation. Millions of people use public transportation to get to work, school, or vacation. However, some people worry that when they disembark, they take along more than their luggage or baggage—they worry that they will pick up a germ that will make them sick. A survey of people from 12 different countries revealed that 12% of the respondents avoid public transportation because they are worried about becoming sick due to poor hygiene. Perhaps these people are concerned that crowded, enclosed, poorly ventilated public transportation systems provide a good environment for the transmission of pathogens from person to person. That doesn't seem like such an unreasonable concern.

One heavily used public transportation system is the New York City subway system. Its subway cars and stations have never had a reputation for cleanliness. Indeed, when swabs from NYC subway turnstiles, exits, ticket kiosks, benches, handrails, doors, and seats were taken, researchers found hundreds of different species of bacteria. Most (57%) of these bacteria turned out to be harmless, but 12% of species were known to cause human disease. These dangerous pathogens included *Yersinia pestis* (bubonic plague), *Bacillus anthracis* (anthrax), and methicillin-resistant *Staphylococcus aureus* (MRSA).

Contamination of the NYC subway system with fecal matter was also suspected because of the detection of *E. coli* bacteria. The London and Boston subway systems also get poor marks for cleanliness, because potentially dangerous bacteria have been found in their systems too.

One particular bacterium (*Staphylococcus*), often found on the skin, has received a good deal of attention because this microbe can spread disease, and some strains are resistant to antibiotics. For example, MRSA infections are difficult to treat and can cause life-threatening symptoms. MRSA has been found inside public buses in several cities, and researchers in Portland, Oregon, discovered six different strains of *Staphylococcus* in public buses and trains. The highest concentrations of *Staphylococcus* bacteria were found on bus and train floors (97.1 colonies/sample) and cloth seats (80.1 colonies/sample). Handrails (9.5 colonies/sample), seats and armrests at bus stops (8.6 colonies/sample), undersides of seats (3.8 colonies/sample), windows (2.2 colonies/sample), and vinyl seats (1.8 colonies/sample) had significantly fewer bacterial colonies by comparison. Although some of the bacteria were resistant to the antibiotics penicillin and ampicillin, the good news is that none of the bacteria were identified as MRSA. The bad news is that the strains of bacteria that were found on the buses and trains can still cause human illness. Surface areas inside mass-transit vehicles are not the only places where *Staphylococcus* can be found. Air samples taken from public metro stations in Shanghai found *Staphylococcus* strains that were resistant to antibiotics.

Tuberculosis is another bug with the potential to be passed from traveler to traveler. Active tuberculosis can be spread through the air when an infected person coughs or sneezes. Infections caused by the tuberculosis bacterium can result in respiratory problems and spread to other organ systems such as the kidneys and brain. People who use public buses and trains have been shown to be at risk for contracting tuberculosis.

People who use public transportation are also at a greater risk of getting sick with an acute respiratory infection. In fact, people who use public buses or trams were six times more likely to get sick five days after using the bus or tram than people who did not use these vehicles. Interestingly, occasional riders were slightly more susceptible to getting an acute respiratory infection than riders who used buses or trams regularly. Regular riders may develop immunity to viruses that make others ill.

Bus, train, and subway rides are relatively brief. On the other hand, on plane trips, passengers can be in close proximity to each other for several hours. High-efficiency particulate air (HEPA) filters installed on airplanes help reduce bacteria, fungi, and large viruses in the air, but low cabin humidity may make people more susceptible to getting sick. Aircraft passengers are many times more likely to catch a cold than those who do not fly. For example, catching a cold is estimated to be 15 times more likely after taking a flight between San Francisco and Denver than after staying on the ground. In addition to the common cold, tuberculosis, SARS, influenza, measles, malaria, dengue, and food poisoning have been spread on commercial airlines.

The spread of in-flight pathogens may take place directly by person-to-person contact or indirectly by contact when an infected passenger contaminates surfaces by coughing, sneezing, or touching objects. Armrests, seats, seatbelt buckles, air vents, headrests, pillows, entertainment touchscreens, tray tables, blankets, magazines, and pillows are a few of the possible landing spots for airborne microbes. Airplane bathrooms can harbor large numbers of pathogens too.

Each of us sheds millions of bacteria into the air every hour, and we are exposed to an assortment of microbes every day, so it is impossible to avoid other peoples' germs. Yet we usually stay healthy, and even places like the New York subway have not been responsible for any epidemics (yet). Our immune system usually does a good job combating pathogens we encounter in our daily lives. Nevertheless, there are still ways to improve the odds of staying healthy. At the top of this list is to wash your hands with soap and warm water after you get off a bus, train, or plane. While traveling, it is especially important to wash your hands before you eat any food, such as that delicious in-flight meal. If you can't wash your hands with soap and water, wear gloves or use an alcohol-based hand sanitizer or antibacterial gel to clean your fingers and palms. You can also use some hand sanitizers to wipe down the surfaces (e.g., armrests, tray tables, screens, windows) near your seat, although you should be prepared for some strange looks from other passengers. After you find your seat, make sure that it is clean. If your seat is not clean, ask to change to another location. Similarly, if the person sitting next to you appears ill, try to move to another seat. Finally, when you get to your destination, change your clothes and put them in the wash, because some pathogens can hitch a ride on your clothing.

SUMMARY

Preventability (76)

Many people rely on public transportation to get from place to place. Although riding on buses, trains, subways, and planes may be unavoidable, people can take steps to reduce their exposure to potentially dangerous microbes.

Likelihood (31)

People are not likely to encounter potentially dangerous pathogens on public transportation.

Consequence (26)

Most bacteria and viruses found on public transportation will not cause serious health problems.

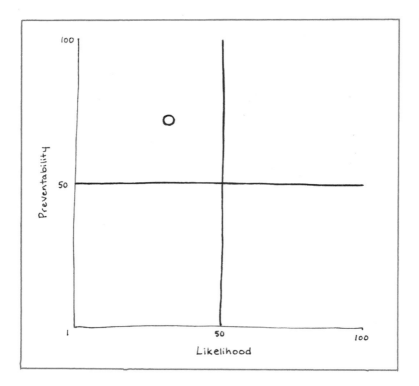

REFERENCES

Afshinnekoo, E., Meydan, C., Chowdhury, S., Jaroudi, D., Boyer, C., Bernstein, N., . . .
    Mason, C. E. (2015). Geospatial resolution of human and bacterial diversity with
    city-scale metagenomics. *Cell Systems, 1,* 72–87.
Conceição, T., Diamantino, F., Coelho, C., de Lencastre, H., & Aires-de-Sousa, M.
    (2013). Contamination of public buses with MRSA in Lisbon, Portugal: A possi-
    ble transmission route of major MRSA clones within the community. *PLOS ONE,
    8,* e77812.
Edelson, P. J., & Phypers, M. (2011). TB transmission on public transportation: A review
    of published studies and recommendations for contact tracing. *Travel Medicine and
    Infectious Disease, 9,* 27–31.
Groth, M. (2016). Joining forces for progress. *Hygiene Matters.* Report 1016/17.
    Retrieved from http://reports.essity.com/2016-17/hygiene-matters-report/servicep
    ages/downloads.html
Hocking, M., & Foster, H. D. (2004). Common cold transmission in commercial aircraft:
    Industry and passenger implications. *Journal of Environmental Health Research, 3,* 7–12.
Hsu, T., Joice, R., Vallarino, J., Abu-Ali, G., Hartmann, E. M., Shafquat, A., . . . Hut-

tenhower, C. (2016). Urban transit system microbial communities differ by surface type and interaction with humans and the environment. *mSystems, 1,* e00018-16.

Lutz, J. K., van Balen, J., Crawford, J. M., Wilkins, J. R., Lee, J., Nava-Hoet, R. C., & Hoet, A. E. (2014). Methicillin-resistant Staphylococcus aureus in public transportation vehicles (buses): Another piece to the epidemiologic puzzle. *American Journal of Infection Control, 42,* 1285–1290.

Mangili, A., & Gendreau, M. A. (2005). Transmission of infectious diseases during commercial air travel. *Lancet, 365,* 989–996.

Staveley Head. (2017). London under the microscope. Retrieved from http://www.stave leyhead.co.uk/assets/under-the-microscope/index.html

Troko, J., Myles, P., Gibson, J., Hashim, A., Enstone, J., Kingdon, S., . . . Van-Tam, J. N. (2011). Is public transport a risk factor for acute respiratory infection? *BMC Infectious Disease, 11,* 16.

Yeh, P. J., Simon, D. M., Millar, J. A., Alexander, H. F., & Franklin, D. (2012). A diversity of antibiotic-resistant Staphylococcus spp. in a Public Transportation System. *Osong Public Health and Research Perspectives, 2(3),* 202–209.

Zamudio, C., Krapp, F., Choi, H. W., Shah, L., Ciampi, A., Gotuzzo, E., . . . Brewer, T. F. (2015). Public transportation and tuberculosis transmission in a high incidence setting. *PLOS ONE, 10,* e0115230.

Zhou, F., & Wang, Y. (2013). Characteristics of antibiotic resistance of airborne Staphylococcus isolated from metro stations. *International Journal of Environmental Research and Public Health, 10,* 2412–2426.

51. PUBLIC SWIMMING POOLS

Not all of us can afford to have a private swimming pool. Instead, we turn to public pools to cool off and exercise. Nothing is more refreshing than a dip in a pool on a hot summer day, unless it is accompanied by mouthful of water polluted with fecal matter and other human grime. Unfortunately, this may be the case more often than we would like to believe. Some public pools might be compared to cesspools because of the contaminated water people swim in. Sweat, urine, fecal matter, oil, and dirt can all end up in the pool water when we take a swim.

Several potential contaminants lurk in the blue waters of public pools. In 2012, the Centers for Disease Control and Prevention (CDC) tested the water from public pool filters in the metro Atlanta area. Of the 161 water samples tested by the CDC, 93 (58%) tested positive for *Escherichia coli* bacteria. The presence of *E. coli* in the water indicated that swimmers deposited fecal matter in the water. Ingestion of *E. coli* can cause severe gastrointestinal problems and other health issues. In addition to finding *E. coli* in the water samples, the CDC researchers detected *Pseudomonas aeruginosa* in 95 (59%) of the samples, *Giardia intestinalis* in two (1%) of the samples, and *Cryptosporidium* species in one (0.6%) of the samples, all microbes that can cause human illness such as skin problems, conjunctivitis, diarrhea, nausea, fever, and respiratory problems. *Cryptosporidium* parasitic infectious outbreaks linked to swimming pools increased from 16 outbreaks in 2014 to 34 outbreaks in 2016.

People expect pool owners and operators to keep their facilities clean, but this is often not the case. The CDC found that 78.5% of water areas reported health violations, and 12.3% of these violations were serious enough to cause an immediate closure of the facility. To help reduce the risk of illness and injury at public pools, the CDC issued the Model Aquatic Health Code (MAHC), which describes best practices for pool design, maintenance, operation, and inspection. However, the MAHC guidelines are voluntary, and it is up to local municipalities to regulate and inspect public pools. For whatever reasons, such as insufficient funds, lack of trained staff, or outright negligence, public pools may not be as clean or as safe as they should be.

The blame for poor pool water quality does not fall only on the owners and operators of pools. Swimmers must take some responsibility for keeping their public pools clean. A 2012 survey commissioned by the Water Quality and Health Council revealed that 43% of swimmers do not shower before they enter a pool. Because showering can reduce the number of microbes on a person's body, skipping a shower dumps potentially dangerous bacteria into the pool water where other people can ingest it while they swim. The survey also found that 19% of the respondents admitted to urinating in the pool; 11% of the respondents said they swam with a runny nose; 8% of the respondents said they swam with an exposed rash or cut; and 1% said they failed to report when children soiled their diaper or bathing suit while in the pool. All of these behaviors can contaminate the water with microbes that can sicken people.

Disinfection of pool water with chemicals such as chlorine is the primary way to reduce the transmission of infection. In appropriate concentrations, these chemicals kill dangerous bacteria and viruses in pool water. Maintenance of proper water pH levels with acids, such as hydrochloric acid, ensures that chlorine remains effective in killing pathogens. When used or stored improperly, these chemicals can cause burns or respiratory problems. Even when used as recommended, pool disinfectants form other chemicals (disinfection by-products) when they interact with urine, sweat, and skin cells in the water. Chlorine, for example, produces chloramines that produce the noxious smell in indoor pools and irritate eyes. Some of these chemical by-products are mutagenic or carcinogenic, and chronic exposure to these chemicals may increase the risks of developing bladder cancer, asthma, and other respiratory illnesses.

Swimming is one of the best forms of exercise for people of all ages. It's a full-body workout without the wear and tear of other exercises such as running. But if you swim in a pool, some simple steps will help protect you and others from picking up an unwanted infection. Start with good hygiene before you dive into the pool. Take a shower to wash off bacteria before it gets into the water. If you are swimming with children, make sure they shower, especially if they have used the toilet or had their diapers changed. Children should take bathroom breaks from the pool so they aren't tempted to use the pool as their toilet. Adults should also use the bathroom and refrain from using the pool as a communal toilet. Infants in the pool should have their diapers checked often to make sure they aren't soiled. Diapers are not effective in keeping pathogens out of the pool. If you have diarrhea, do not go into the pool. Most importantly, do not swallow pool water. Keep your mouth closed—you never know what someone else has left behind in the pool.

SUMMARY

Preventability (89)

Proper pool maintenance and good hygiene practices will prevent many of the health risks associated with public pools.

Likelihood (6)

Although pools may be contaminated, the likelihood of becoming ill after swimming in a public pool is low.

Consequence (27)

The symptoms associated with most infections that people contract after using a public pool are mild to moderate and temporary.

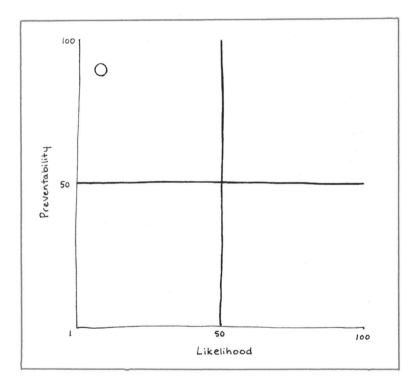

REFERENCES

Amburgey, J. E., & Anderson, J. B. (2011). Disposable swim diaper retention of Crypto-sporidium-sized particles on human subjects in a recreational water setting. *Journal of Water and Health, 9*, 653–658.

Centers for Disease Control and Prevention. (2009). Pool chemical-associated health events in public and residential settings—United States, 1983–2007. *Morbidity and Mortality Weekly Report (MMWR), 58*(18), 489–493. Retrieved from https://www.cdc.gov/mmwr/preview/mmwrhtml/mm5818a1.htm

Centers for Disease Control and Prevention. (2013). Immediate closures and violations identified during routine inspections of public aquatic facilities—network for aquatic facility inspection surveillance, five states. *Morbidity and Mortality Weekly Report (MMWR), 65*(5), 1–26.

Centers for Disease Control and Prevention. (2013). Microbes in pool filter backwash as evidence of the need for improved swimmer hygiene—Metro-Atlanta, Georgia, 2012. *Morbidity and Mortality Weekly Report (MMWR), 62*(19), 385–388. Retrieved from https://www.cdc.gov/mmwr/preview/mmwrhtml/mm6219a3.htm

Centers for Disease Control and Prevention. (2016). Model Aquatic Health Code. Retrieved from https://www.cdc.gov/mahc/index.html

Centers for Disease Control and Prevention. (2017, May 18). Crypto outbreaks linked to swimming have doubled since 2014. Retrieved from https://www.cdc.gov/media/releases/2017/p0518-cryptosporidium-outbreaks.html

Richardson, S. D., DeMarini, D. M., Kogevinas, M., Fernandez, P., Marco, E., Lourencetti, C., . . . Villanueva, C. M. (2010). What's in the pool? A comprehensive identification of disinfection by-products and assessment of mutagenicity of chlorinated and brominated swimming pool water. *Environmental Health Perspectives, 118*, 1523–1530.

Wiant, C. (2012). New public survey reveals swimmer hygiene attitudes and practices. *International Journal of Aquatic Research and Education, 6*, 201–202.

52. AIRPORT BODY SCANNERS

Traveling by plane has become a real struggle for many people. After purchasing an expensive ticket and the slow trek to the airport, travelers face long lines to check baggage, crowded planes, and terrible in-flight food (if there is any to be had at all). And, of course, there is the unpleasant task before boarding a flight: the dreaded security line.

"Take out all electronics. Put liquids in a clear plastic bag. Take off your shoes." That's the mantra that everyone hears from security personnel as they snake through mazes at airports throughout the country. Then the words that put fear into many travelers: "Please step into the scanner." Anxiety sweeps over many people who are afraid that they will be exposed to damaging levels of radiation as they pass through the scanner.

Travelers and their baggage are exposed to several sources of radiation in an airport. First, luggage is screened with an X-ray machine. As luggage moves into the machine, X-rays are sent from one side to the other. Detectors in the machine measure the energy absorbed by different objects, and an image can be constructed based on an object's density. Different materials such as metals, food, and paper absorb different amounts of energy and can be displayed in different colors to machine operators. Fortunately for travelers and screening personnel, X-ray machines have lead walls and curtains to minimize radiation escaping from the machine.

People must undergo screening too. Most airport metal detectors use pulse induction technology. Pulse induction scanners emit high-frequency, short pulses of electrical current. The electrical current sets up a magnetic field that is altered when a metallic object is placed in its path. These scanners alert security officers to suspicious objects a person may be carrying. Pulse induction technology does not use X-rays.

Some airports around the world employ whole-body scanners, which come in two types: those that use backscatter technology and those that use millimeter wave technology. Airports in the U.S., Australia, the European Union, and some other countries have phased out backscatter technology in favor of the newer millimeter wave technology. Backscatter whole-body scanners use low levels of ionizing radiation that bounce off objects to detect potentially dangerous items. Even though backscatter technology uses low levels of radiation, the possibility that exposure to this level of radiation could contribute to cancer is non- zero. The U.S. Food and Drug Administration (FDA), however, insists that the health risks posed by backscatter scanners are so low that people do not need to restrict the number of times they pass through the scanner. The FDA maintains that a person needs to be scanned more than a thousand times in a year to exceed the annual radiation dose limit.

The driving force that led to the removal of these backscatter body scanners may not have been the possible health risks of the technology. Rather, there was a public outcry about privacy: backscatter scanners can produce graphic images of the human body. Some critics even called the backscatter scanner a virtual strip search. The Transportation Security Administration (TSA) safeguards to protect traveler privacy, such as blurring of faces and deleting images, did little to lessen the fears that someone's essentially naked body would show up as an image on the internet. The Department of Homeland Security was sued because of the perceived invasive nature of the full-body scans. Backscatter imaging devices were removed from all U.S. airports by June 2013 due to privacy concerns.

Millimeter wave whole-body scanners use nonionizing radiation and do not have the health or privacy concerns associated with backscatter scanners. Low-intensity electromagnetic waves with frequencies between those of radio and infrared are emitted by millimeter wave whole-body scanners. These waves bounce off surfaces but do not significantly penetrate the body surface. The reflected energy is received by detectors to produce images of items on the body. The locations of detected items are displayed on a simple outline of the human body and then analyzed by security personnel for their potential danger.

Most travelers in the United States can opt out of a full-body scan, but they will be given a thorough pat down by security personnel. Some passengers are required to undergo body scanners if their boarding pass shows that they have been chosen for enhanced screening. Travelers will know that they have been selected for this extra special treatment if SSSS is printed on their boarding pass.

SUMMARY

Preventability (83)

In many countries, travelers can avoid body scanners by requesting pat-down search.

Likelihood (7)

Normal operation of body scanners is not likely to expose people to dangerous levels of radiation.

Consequence (7)

Normal operation of body scanners should not result in any significant health risks.

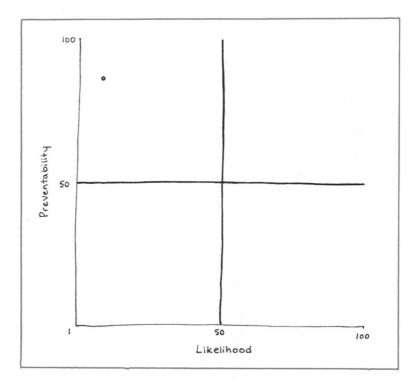

REFERENCES

Australian Government. (2017). Body scanners. Retrieved from http://travelsecure.infra
structure.gov.au/passenger-screening/body-scanners.aspx

European Commission. (2017). Aviation security: Commission adopts new rules on the
use of security scanners at European airports [press release]. Retrieved from http://
europa.eu/rapid/press-release_IP-11-1343_en.htm?locale=en

National Academies of Sciences, Engineering, and Medicine. (2015). *Airport passenger
screening using backscatter X-ray machines: Compliance with standards.* Washington, DC:
National Academies Press.

TSA. (n.d.). Security screening. Retrieved from https://www.tsa.gov/travel/security
-screening

U.S. Food and Drug Administration. (2017). Products for security screening of people.
Retrieved from https://www.fda.gov/radiation-emittingproducts/radiationemitting
productsandprocedures/securitysystems/ucm227201.htm

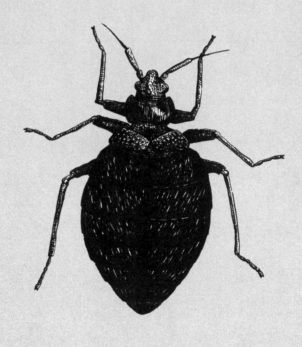

53. BEDBUGS

It's been a long, difficult day of travel. You've trudged to the airport, subjected yourself to the scrutiny of the TSA, eaten terrible airline food, been tormented by a toddler kicking the back of your airplane seat, collected your luggage, and found a taxi that battled through rush-hour traffic to get you to your hotel. All you want to do is take a shower and go to sleep. You crawl into bed to get a few hours of rest. The next morning you wake up and look in the mirror. What are those itchy, red spots on your face, neck, arms, and shoulders? Could these be bedbug bites? You run to the bed and throw off the top sheet. Are those small bloodstains? What are those other dark spots? Bedbug fecal matter! To confirm your horror, you lift the mattress. And there they are: bedbugs!

Bedbugs (*Cimex lectularius*, the common bedbug) are found all over the world. The insecticide DDT effectively reduced the bedbug population in the United States after World War II, but the pests have made a bold comeback due to global travel and the restrictions on the use of some chemical treatments. The insects are found in just about all places you will find people. In 2015, the National Pest Management Association and the University of Kentucky surveyed employees of pest management companies about their experiences identifying and managing bedbug infestations. Survey respondents reported finding bedbugs in houses, hotels, apartments, nursing homes, offices, college dormitories, schools, day care centers, hospitals, medical clinics, retail stores, libraries, movie theaters, laundromats, restaurants, airplanes, and ambulances. Bedbugs are not fussy about their living space and can hide not only in beds, but also in furniture, clothing, closets, picture frames, and toys and behind wallpaper. Spending extra money on an upscale, expensive hotel is no guarantee that the place will be bedbug free. The bugs can be transported from place to place inside luggage, clothing, and used mattresses.

These flat, reddish brown, 4–5 mm long, parasitic insects are most definitely pests, but they are remarkable in several ways. For example, although bedbugs thrive in temperatures of 70–80°F, they can live in cold climates and in environments where the temperature reaches 120°F. Young (nymphs) and adult bedbugs can also live without a meal for several months. When bedbugs do feed, they release saliva with analgesics to reduce pain so the victim will not feel anything, and anticoagulants to increase blood flow. Female bedbugs need blood to produce eggs.

Fortunately, unlike lice, bedbugs do not spread diseases through their bites. Bedbug bites do cause local itching and swelling in many people, but some people show no symptoms of a bite. Other people who are allergic to bedbug saliva must seek medical attention if they are bitten. Furthermore, if the bite area is scratched and not kept clean, an infection can develop. In most cases, the skin affected by a bedbug bite clears in one to two weeks. Lasting damage of a bedbug infestation can be psychological (stress, anxiety, and loss of sleep) and financial.

Some simple steps can reduce the chances of an encounter with bedbugs. First, always check the bed in a hotel or motel room (or any other place you sleep) for signs of bedbugs. Look for small stains on all bedding material and furniture. Second, examine the entire bed (i.e., mattress, box springs, headboard, and bedding) for bedbugs and their fecal matter. Third, keep suitcases closed and off hotel floors and beds. Fourth, check the Bedbug Registry (http://www.bedbugregistry.com/) for recent reports of bedbugs before you travel. In large numbers, bedbugs may be detected by a berry, herbal, or musty smell. So, that smell of your hotel room may not come from the previous human tenants. While traveling, when possible, keep your bags and coats off upholstered seats in trains and planes or, at the very least, examine the surfaces before placing your belongings there. At home, vacuum your bed weekly and dispose of the vacuum bag promptly. Also, check all used furniture, bedding, and clothing for bedbugs before these items are brought inside a house.

The course of action to get rid of bedbugs depends on the level of infestation. Washing clothing and bed sheets in hot water and drying them in a hot dryer can kill the bugs. Freezing infested items for several days can also kill bedbugs. Dogs trained to recognize the smell of bedbugs can confirm the existence of an infestation. Large numbers of bedbugs likely will require professional treatment, which could include heating rooms to at least 122°F and the application of insecticides. Unfortunately, bedbugs are developing resistance even to newer insecticides.

So, next time you see that lovely, used couch on the side of the road, just leave it. Unless you want to take a chance of bringing home some less lovely *Cimex lectularius* with you.

SUMMARY

Preventability (47)

Checking hotel beds for signs of bedbugs should be routine for all travelers. However, it is difficult to check other surfaces (e.g., taxi seats, car trunks) where bedbugs may live.

Likelihood (43)

Bedbugs can be found in many different locations.

Consequence (12)

Bedbugs do not transmit disease, but they can cause skin irritation and psychological distress.

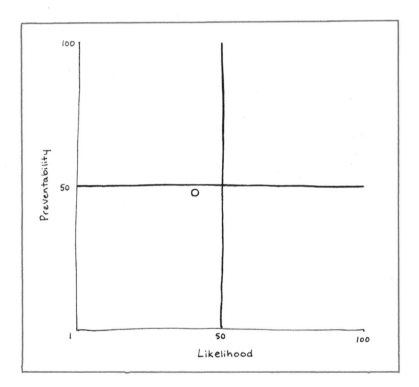

REFERENCES

Ashbrook, A. R., Scharf, M. E., Bennett, G. W., & Gondhalekar, A. D. (2017). Detection of reduced susceptibility to chlorfenapyr- and bifenthrin-containing products in field populations of the bed bug (Hemiptera: Cimicidae). *Journal of Economic Entomology*, *110*, 1195–1202.

Potter, M. F., Haynes, K. F., & Fredericks, J. (2015, November–December). Bed bugs across America: The 2015 bugs without borders survey. *Pestworld*, 4–14.

U.S. Environmental Protection Agency. (2016). Introduction to bed bugs. Retrieved from https://www.epa.gov/bedbugs/introduction-bed-bugs

54. CRUISE SHIPS

Traveling on a cruise ship should be a relaxing, enjoyable experience. Unfortunately, cruise ship travelers may have to contend with more than seasickness and sunburn. With thousands of people in the confined space of these floating cities, some health issues that are common on dry land can get out of control on the high seas.

Worldwide, cruise ships host approximately 23 million passengers each year, with Carnival (21.3%) and Royal Caribbean (16.7%) lines hosting the most travelers. In the United States, passengers tend to be older, as people 50–59 years old and 60-plus years old are 22% and 26% of all cruise ship passengers, respectively. Older travelers and those with underlying health issues may be at increased risk for contracting infections and suffering from injuries (e.g., falls) during a cruise.

Travelers usually are not concerned about a cruise ship sinking, but some are worried that they may catch a virus that hitches a ride on the cruise. In addition to the common cold virus, noroviruses can spread quickly throughout a cruise ship. Noroviruses are the source of most nonbacterial gastroenteritis infections (the stomach flu). Gastroenteritis typically causes symptoms such as vomiting, diarrhea, abdominal cramps, headache, fever, and muscle aches that usually last one to three days. Norovirus usually isn't dangerous, but it is unpleasant. It's probably not how you want to spend your honeymoon. Treatment for gastroenteritis involves managing symptoms of the illness and could include drugs to control diarrhea and vomiting. Dehydration should also be prevented by drinking nonalcoholic fluids.

Norovirus spreads through person-to-person contact and in aerosolized particles when someone coughs or sneezes. Any surface that comes in contact with the virus can transmit the virus to someone who touches it. The lounge chair, buffet spoon, slot machine handle, shuffleboard paddle, and anything else on the ship can potentially transmit disease. Although ships may be cleaned, it is not possible to disinfect every inch of a large cruise liner and kill the norovirus where it is hiding.

Fortunately, the CDC's Vessel Sanitation Program (VSP) works with the cruise ship industry to reduce the risk of gastrointestinal illnesses on cruise ships. The VSP has jurisdiction over all ships with a U.S. port that carry 13 or more passengers and have a foreign itinerary. These vessels are inspected unannounced at least twice each year. The SHIPSAN ACT has a similar function for controlling diseases on ships cruising waters in the European Union. During an inspection, VSP inspectors check a ship's (1) medical facilities to ensure medical logs and documentation of illnesses are in order; (2) potable water systems; (3) swimming pools and whirlpool spas for proper filtration, disinfection, safety, and maintenance; (4) galleys and dining rooms for suitable food protection, employee health, and hygiene; (5) child activity centers for properly equipped diaper-changing stations, toilets, and disinfection facilities; (6) hotel accommodations for proper infection control procedures; (7) ventilation systems; and (8) common areas for pest management, cleanliness, and maintenance. Inspected ships are scored on a 100-point scale, with a minimum of 86 points necessary for a passing grade. Passengers can check the scores of specific vessels on the CDC VSP website. When an outbreak of a gastrointestinal illness occurs on a cruise ship, the VSP works with the ship's crew to determine the cause and magnitude of the illness and to develop a plan to contain and stop the illness. The VSP can also ask cruise lines to notify port authorities about the outbreak and to delay a ship's next voyage.

In 2016, the CDC reported 13 outbreaks of gastrointestinal illness on international cruise ships participating in the VSP. Of these 13 outbreaks, 10 were caused by norovirus alone, one by combined norovirus and *E. coli* bacteria, one by *E. coli* alone, and one by an unknown agent. In some of these incidents, 10% of all passengers on board had symptoms (vomiting, diarrhea) of gastroenteritis. Given the large number of passengers who travel on these cruise ships, the likelihood of contracting acute gastroenteritis is small. According to a CDC report, of the 73.6 million passengers and 28.3 million crew members who sailed between 2008 and 2014 on cruise ships under the VSP, only 129,678 passengers and 43,132 crew members contracted acute gastroenteritis. This is equivalent to only 0.18% of passengers and 0.15% of crew members. Almost all (92%) of the illnesses were caused by norovirus.

Outbreaks of other infectious diseases such as rubella, chicken pox, hepatitis, and Legionnaires' disease have also been reported on cruise ships. For example, in 2008, passengers returning to the United Kingdom after a cruise around the world were affected by an acute hepatitis E infection likely caused by contaminated food. A total of 83 cases of Legionnaires' disease (six deaths) have been linked to cruises taken between 1977 and 2012.

Cruise ship passengers face special health challenges depending on their destination. For example, people traveling to parts of Asia, the Caribbean, Africa, and Central America may be exposed to mosquitoes that carry dengue fever, malaria, chikungunya disease, and Zika virus. Travelers on shore excursions to various locations should also be cautious of water and raw food contaminated with bacteria and viruses.

The best way to stay healthy on a cruise is to have good hygiene practices. Wash your hands with soap and warm water frequently, especially before all meals and after using the bathroom. Alcohol-based hand sanitizers can also be used if running water is not available. To reduce the spread of contamination by person-to-person contact, Eilif Dahl of the Norwegian Centre for Maritime Medicine suggests using a fist bump instead of a handshake as a greeting on cruise ships. Passengers traveling to areas with mosquitoes and other bugs should apply insect repellents and wear long sleeves and long pants to reduce the chance of bites. The risk of contracting an illness from contaminated food and water can be reduced by eating only cooked food and peeled fruits and vegetables and drinking beverages from sealed packages without ice. Finally, it is a good idea to pack your own first aid kit, because a ship's medical facility may not stock the supplies you need.

SUMMARY

Preventability (98)

No one needs to take a cruise; there are many other ways to travel.

Likelihood (14)

Cruise ships can harbor infectious pathogens, but most cruise ships travel from port to port without a problem.

Consequence (37)

Contracting an infectious disease on a cruise ship can spoil your vacation or possibly send you to the hospital.

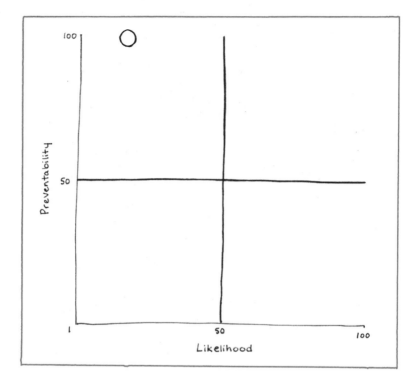

REFERENCES

Centers for Disease Control and Prevention. (2017, July 18). About the Vessel Sanitation Program. Retrieved from https://www.cdc.gov/nceh/vsp/desc/aboutvsp.htm

Cruise Market Watch. (2017). Growth of the ocean cruise line industry. Retrieved from http://www.cruisemarketwatch.com/growth/

Dahl, E. (2016). Cruise tap versus handshake: Using common sense to reduce hand contamination and germ transmission on cruise ships. *International Maritime Health*, *67*, 181–184.

Freeland, A. L., Vaughan, G. H., Jr., & Banerjee, S. N. (2016). Acute gastroenteritis on cruise ships—United States, 2008–2014. *MMWR, Morbidity and Mortality Weekly Reports*, *65*, 1–5. doi:http://dx.doi.org/10.15585/mmwr.mm6501a1

Mouchtouri, V. A., & Rudge, J. W. (2015). Legionnaires' disease in hotels and passenger ships: A systematic review of evidence, sources, and contributing factors. *Journal of Travel Medicine*, *22*, 325–337.

Said, B., Ijaz, S., Kafatos, G., Booth, L., Thomas, H. L., Walsh, A., Ramsay, M., & Morgan, D. (2009). Hepatitis E outbreak on cruise ship. *Emerging Infectious Diseases*, *15*, 1738–1744.

SHIPSAN ACT. (n.d.). Retrieved from http://www.shipsan.eu/

55. AMUSEMENT PARK RIDES

Apocalypse, Banshee, Blazing Fury, Thunderbolt, Pandemonium, California Screamin', Invertigo, Mind Eraser, Exterminator, Coastersaurus: these are not your grandma's merry-go-rounds. Are these dire-sounding contraptions harmless fun or death traps? All amusement park rides, whether a roller coaster, a drop ride, a Ferris wheel, or a water slide, are designed to entertain and excite. When you get on a ride, you should only feel like you're going to die—you shouldn't actually be in peril. And, fortunately, ride design and safety have come a long way since the early days of roller coasters when cars sometimes flew off their tracks or failed to stop. But rides have become bigger and faster over the years, while at the same time amusement park attendance has skyrocketed. With approximately 335 million visits each year to amusement parks in the United States, the thrill business is soaring.

Keeping an amusement park ride safe requires careful maintenance to protect against electrical, mechanical, and weather-related issues that may affect safety. The costs of inspections, maintenance, and repairs to a ride are far less than the costs of bad publicity and lawsuits following an injury or death at a park. But this is really the strongest incentive that parks have to make sure their facilities are safe. It may surprise you to learn that safety regulations for amusement rides in the United States are inconsistent and largely voluntary.

Although the U.S. Consumer Product Safety Commission (CPSC) regulates food, clothing, and prizes sold on site, it has no authority or jurisdiction over the safety of rides that are permanently fixed to a site within an amusement park or water park. There is more federal oversight on a stuffed animal or a T-shirt sold at the park than there is over the roller coaster that goes 100 miles per hour. Instead of federal officials, local or state authorities create their own regulations for fixed-site rides. Amusement park operators can also choose to follow their own policies or voluntary standards such as those detailed in ASTM F24 Committee on Amusement Rides and Devices. The ASTM F24 committee works with the amusement park industry and other organizations, such as the International Association of Amusement Parks and Attractions, to create standards for ride safety. Currently 34 of 50 states in the U.S. reference ASTM F24 standards in state regulations.

A comparison of state ride safety regulations reveals inconsistent requirements for inspections, oversight boards, insurance, accident reporting, and accident investigations. For example, only 12 states have a ride safety advisory board, and only nine states require that ride operators must be at least 18 years old. A total of 13 states do not require that rides be registered, and seven states do not require that rides are insured. Some states require that ride owners must report accidents that cause severe injury or death or a visit to the emergency room or doctor, but other states do not compel ride owners to report any accidents. When accidents do occur, only 26 states require that owners preserve the accident scene for an investigation. Presumably, in those states without such a requirement, an accident scene can be cleaned up and the ride be put back in action without an investigation into the cause.

And accidents do happen. In August 2016, the National Safety Council issued a report for the International Association of Amusement Parks and Attractions that estimated the number of injuries on fixed-site amusement park rides in the United States that occurred between 2003 and 2015. Based on ridership data from a limited number of amusement parks, the National Safety Council reported 1,508 injuries (0.8 injuries per million patron-rides) in 2015. Of these 1,508 injuries, the majority (63%) occurred on family and adult rides, while 29% occurred on roller coasters and 8% on children's rides. Of those injuries, 5.5% were serious enough to require a hospital stay longer than 24 hours. The Amusement Safety Organization has compiled data on the areas of the body that were injured and the names of the amusement parks and rides causing the injuries in accidents. They report substantially more significant injuries than the National Safety Council, although the source of these data is unclear. Of course, if injuries incurred on rides that move from place to place, such as in carnivals and fairs, are included in the count, the numbers are larger. For example, the examination of U.S. hospital emergency department records from 1990 to 2010 revealed that an estimated 92,885 children (17 years old or younger) sought treatment for injuries involving amusement rides.

Accidents on amusement park rides can be the result of many factors. Some accidents are caused by problems with the ride itself (brake failure, abrupt stops, collisions, malfunctions, defective or worn parts) or by operator error. Other accidents may be attributed to rider negligence or inattention, such as standing up on a ride, unlocking a safety restraint, or failing to keep hands and arms inside a ride. The design of some rides, especially roller coasters that generate high speed and high gravitational force, may contribute to head, back, and neck injuries. Regardless of the cause, amusement park accidents can be catastrophic. In fact, the CPSC reported that between 1987 and 2004, 46 people were killed by fixed-site rides, and 13 people were killed by mobile rides (the sites of rides causing 8 additional deaths were unknown).

The easiest way to reduce the chance of an injury on an amusement park ride is to follow the rules. These rules are designed to keep riders safe, so when you are told not to stand up, don't stand up. If a person does not meet the age, height, and weight requirements of a ride, do not let that person on the ride. Many rides list warnings in the boarding areas, but riders should be aware of their own health conditions that may increase their risk of injury. For example, people who have preexisting neck, back, or heart problems, high blood pressure, or who are pregnant, should probably avoid high-speed rides with rapid twists, turns, and sudden stops. You can observe a ride prior to boarding to get an idea what to expect.

Although the likelihood of an injury or death on a trip to the amusement park is low, following the rules and knowing your limitations will further reduce risk and maximize the thrills instead of the spills.

SUMMARY

Preventability (97)

Injuries caused by amusement parks rides are almost 100% avoidable: just don't ride them. However, some people make amusement parks into destination vacations and feel compelled to experience all of the thrills these places have to offer.

Likelihood (2)

The likelihood of suffering an injury on an amusement park ride is very low.

Consequence (67)

Bumps and bruises are much more common than catastrophic injuries.

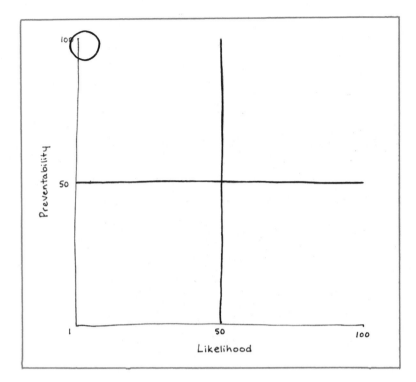

REFERENCES

ASTM International (n.d.). Committee F24 on Amusement Rides and Devices. Retrieved from https://www.astm.org/COMMITTEE/F24.htm

Braksiek, R. J., & Roberts, D. J. (2002). Amusement park injuries and deaths. *Annals of Emergency Medicine, 39,* 65–72.

CPSC. (n.d.). Consumer Product Safety Act. Retrieved from https://www.cpsc.gov/Regulations-Laws--Standards/Statutes/Summary-List/Consumer-Product-Safet-Act

Saferparks. (2017, April). U.S. federal and state amusement ride regulation. Retrieved from http://www.saferparks.org/regulation/agencies

Saferparks. (2018). Safety regulations for U.S. amusement rides. Retrieved from http://www.saferparks.org/regulation

Thompson, M. C., Chounthirath, T., Xiang, H., & Smith, G. A. (2013). US pediatric injuries involving amusement rides, 1990–2010. *Clinical Pediatrics, 52,* 433–440.

Miscellaneous

56. PIRATES

The times of swashbuckling pirates in schooners who roam the high seas searching for victims to plunder are long gone. But pirates still do exist in this day and age. Modern-day pirates, armed with small guns, automatic weapons, or even rocket-propelled grenades, now use motorized skiffs or speed boats to attack and terrorize. Unlike pirates of yore, modern pirates are not the model for popular Halloween costumes.

Article 101 of the United Nations Convention on the Law of the Sea (1982) defines piracy as:

(a) any illegal acts of violence or detention, or any act of depredation, committed for private ends by the crew or the passengers of a private ship or a private aircraft, and directed:
   (i) on the high seas, against another ship or aircraft, or against persons or property on board such ship or aircraft;
   (ii) against a ship, aircraft, persons or property in a place outside the jurisdiction of any State;
(b) any act of voluntary participation in the operation of a ship or of an aircraft with knowledge of facts making it a pirate ship or aircraft;
(c) any act of inciting or of intentionally facilitating an act described in subparagraph (a) or (b).

With this definition in mind, it is clear that piracy is still an issue today. The International Maritime Organization (IMO) and International Chamber of Commerce's International Maritime Bureau (ICC-IMB) track the incidence of piracy and armed robberies against ships. For the 10-month period from January 1 to October 30, 2017, the IMO logged 151 separate acts of piracy or armed robbery. The number of such acts against ships reported by the ICC-IMB compares favorably to the IMO numbers: 121 actual and attempted attacks between January and September 2017. Many additional attacks likely go unreported.

The majority of incidents reported by the IMO and ICC-IMB involved attacks on tankers, bulk carriers, and container ships. In some cases, the pirates fled when an alarm was raised, but in other cases pirates boarded vessels, stole property, or assaulted or kidnapped crews. In one case, pirates armed with guns tried to board the ship but aborted the attack when a Philippine navy boat and air force helicopter approached. Cruise ships, some capable of carrying thousands of passengers, travel at high speeds and are difficult to attack. Between 2002 and 2012, only 13 of 3,806 ships attacked were passenger ships. Only one passenger ship was included in the 2017 IMO incident report. Sailing yachts, on the other hand, are relatively easy to attack and have few defenses against pirates: 82 yachts were attacked between 2002 and 2012.

The coast of Somalia was a prime location for pirates between 2008 and 2011, with hundreds of attacks and billions of dollars in stolen cargo. But after 2011, security (e.g., armed crew) was added to ships plying Somalia's coastal waters, and the number of attacks in the region dropped significantly. In 2010, the economic cost of Somali piracy was $7 billion. It dropped to $1.7 billion in 2016. Although piracy around Somali waters has returned to some degree, examination of IMO and ICC-IMB reports shows that recent piracy is concentrated in four areas: (1) the Singapore Strait,

(2) the Sulu and Celebes Seas, (3) the Gulf of Aden, and (4) the Gulf of Guinea.

The purpose of a pirate attack influences the consequences to crew and cargo. If pirates are interested in stealing cargo only, and the ship's crew offers no resistance, then the loss will likely be only economic. If the pirates want the cargo and the ship, they may have no need for the crew, and the life of the crew may be in jeopardy. Holding crew for ransom is not uncommon, and some people have been held hostage by pirates for more than a year.

Vessel owners and crew can use online resources (e.g., IMB Piracy Reporting Center) to monitor the seas and ports for reports of piracy and avoid hot spots. But regardless of attempts to stay away from waters frequented by pirates, ships may still encounter them. Several lines of defense can be used by crew and ships to discourage, repel, or evade pirates. Larger ships can simply increase their speed to outrun and evade a slower pirate boat. A show of force by armed guards may also discourage pirates from launching an attack. Rimming ships with razor wire and electric fences can prevent pirates from boarding a vessel. Some ships are equipped with water cannons that can be turned on pirates to repel them. Other nonlethal technologies, such as long-range acoustic devices that blast sound waves and "pain rays" that fire microwaves, may provide some measure of defense. If all else fails, and pirates do gain access to a ship, the crew can retreat to a secure safe room where they can wait for rescue.

In the future, ships may be navigated remotely without the need of a crew. These crewless or drone ships could be monitored and controlled from anywhere. Pirates could still overrun a crewless ship or hack into the ship's control systems, but there would be no risk of loss of life.

SUMMARY

Preventability (88)

If you decide to sail, you need to plan your trip to stay out of dangerous waters.

Likelihood (2)

Few people will ever encounter pirates on the open seas.

Consequence (83)

An encounter with pirates may result in a simple robbery or could
escalate to a kidnapping or murder.

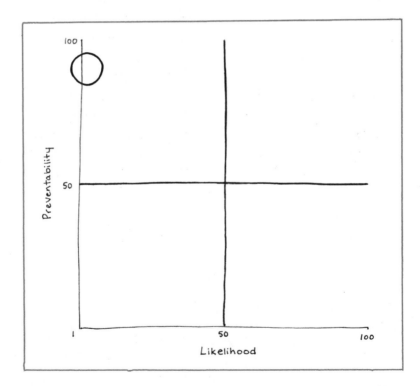

REFERENCES

International Chamber of Commerce, Commercial Crime Services. (n.d.). IMB Piracy Reporting Centre. Retrieved from https://www.icc-ccs.org/index.php/piracy-reporting-centre

International Maritime Organization. (n.d.). Piracy reports. Retrieved from http://www.imo.org/en/OurWork/Security/PiracyArmedRobbery/Reports/Pages/Default.aspx

Nikolić, N., & Missoni, E. (2013). Piracy on the high seas—threats to travelers' health. *Journal of Travel Medicine, 20*, 313–321.

Oceans Beyond Piracy. (2016). The state of maritime piracy 2016: Assessing the economic and human cost. Retrieved from http://oceansbeyondpiracy.org/reports/sop/summary

57. TOYS MADE IN CHINA

I f you have children, you likely have toys around the house that were made in China. China produces 90% of all toys sold in the United States. The poor working conditions of Chinese toy factories have raised ethical and moral issues about supporting companies who manufacture their products in China. For example, the China Labor Watch organization published a report in 2016 that described the deplorable work environments in four factories that produced toys (e.g., Thomas the Tank Engine, Hot Wheels, Barbie dolls) for companies including Disney, Mattel, Fisher-Price, and McDonald's. The factories were found to have many labor law violations such as excessive work hours, lack of safety protection measures, refusal to pay insurance, inadequate wages, and the absence of procedures to handle worker complaints.

If poor working conditions in Chinese toy factories are not enough to tarnish the reputation of companies who build their products in China, then perhaps forced labor and child labor in these factories will do the trick. The U.S. Department of Labor lists toys made in China as products it believes are made by child labor or forced labor. Certainly, China is not the only country that subjects its workers to unacceptable work environments and employs underage labor, but the magnitude of toy exports from China highlights the problem with these products.

Besides being made in sweatshops and with underage labor, many toys made in China may pose risks to the health of you and your family. The European Union is alarmed by the volume of unsafe products manufactured in China. The EU Rapid Alert System for Dangerous Products reports that China leads all nations by far in attempts to import dangerous products into the EU. The most-notified dangerous products to the EU from China are clothing articles and toys. In the United States, the Consumer Product Safety Commission (CPSC) oversees consumer products and evaluates injuries and incidents to protect public safety. Several hundred products are recalled each year by the CPSC. We examined the list of products recalled by the CPSC from January 1 to December 31, 2017, and found 75 products intended for children were recalled (see table below). Of these 75 products, 60 (80%) were manufactured in China. The products were recalled because they posed risks for choking, burns, strangulation, mold, falls, and lacerations.

The United States and China have made efforts to reduce the levels of lead in toys made in China. Lead is a heavy metal that can damage many organs of the body, and it is especially dangerous because it is a neurotoxin that can harm the nervous system. Children are particularly at risk because they are growing rapidly, and the toxicity of lead can affect brain development. In the United States in 2007, 17.6 million toys (42 different recalls) were recalled because of excessive lead levels. In 2008, the Consumer Product Safety Improvement Act was passed to improve the safety of children's products sold in the U.S. Since 2008, the number of toys recalled because of high levels of lead has been reduced significantly. In fact, the 2017 CPSC recall list did not include high levels of lead as a cause for the recall of any Chinese-made toys. However, examination of items recalled in 2015 and 2016 revealed several children's products (e.g., jewelry, water bottles, chairs, swings) made in China were recalled by the CPSC because they contained excessive levels of lead. Therefore, millions of toys in many homes are likely contaminated with lead.

Lead is not the only chemical found in toys made in China to worry about. Bisphenol A (BPA, a chemical used to harden plastic found in many products; may harm nervous, endocrine, and reproductive systems), phthalates (chemicals used to increase the softness and flexibility of plastic; may cause liver, reproductive, and kidney problems), and chromium and cadmium (heavy metals linked to cancer and organ damage) are found in many products intended for children. Although the safety of BPA is still in question, some states and cities have banned the sale of various products containing it. Phthalates, chromium, and cadmium have also been restricted or banned in some countries, but toys, especially older ones, may still contain these chemicals.

You can minimize the risks posed by toys made in China by following a few easy steps:

- Throw away old toys that may contain lead, or have the toys and children's metal jewelry tested for lead.
- Purchase toys made in the United States or European Union, countries with more strict regulations than those in China.
- Purchase toys made from wood, natural fibers, or bamboo instead of plastic.
- Stay up to date on toy recalls from the CPSC.
- Test your children's blood levels for lead.
- Avoid toys made with PVC (polyvinyl chloride), which contains phthalates.

SUMMARY

Preventability (78)

It will take some searching and research to find toys that are not made in China. Testing of toys for lead content is also possible.

Likelihood (35)

Not all toys made in China contain chemicals that pose health risks.

Consequence (58)

Although the neurological consequences of lead exposure are well known, the health effects of BPA are still unclear.

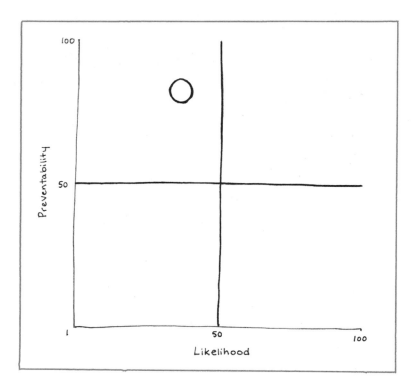

REFERENCES

China Labor Watch. (2016, November 15). An investigation into four toy sweatshops. Retrieved from http://www.chinalaborwatch.org/report/122

Consumer Product Safety Commission. (n.d.). Toy recall statistics. Retrieved from https://cpsc.gov/Safety-Education/Toy-Recall-Statistics

Kavilanz, P. (2017, March 6). This Michigan toymaker pledged never to go to China. CNN Money. Retrieved from http://money.cnn.com/2017/03/06/smallbusiness/manufacturing-toys-american-plastic-toys/index.html

Office of the European Union. (2016). Rapid Alert System for dangerous products: Working together to keep consumers safe. Retrieved from https://ec.europa.eu/con-

sumers/consumers_safety/safety_products/rapex/alerts/repository/content/pages/
rapex/reports/docs/rapex_annual_report_2016_en.pdf

Snyder, M., & Carfagno, B. (2017, March 23). Chinese product safety: A persistent challenge to U.S. regulators and importers, U.S.-China Economic and Security Review Commission, Staff Research Report. Retrieved from https://www.uscc.gov/Research/chinese-product-safety-persistent-challenge-us-regulators-and-importers

U.S. Department of Labor, Bureau of International Labor Affairs. (2016, September 30). List of goods produced by child labor or forced labor. Retrieved from https://www.dol.gov/ilab/reports/child-labor/list-of-goods/

CPSC Recalls of Products Intended for Children (January 1–December 31, 2017)

Product Name	Hazard	Company	Recall Date	Manufacturing Location
Toddler bed	Entrapment	Land of Nod	12/28/2017	Vietnam
Children's sleepwear	Burn	Wohali Outdoors	12/21/2017	China
Children's step stool	Fall	Squatty Potty	12/19/2017	China
Fireworks	Burn	Matrix Fireworks	12/19/2017	China
Toddler mattress	Burn	Dream on Me	12/12/2017	United States
Children's pajamas	Burn	One Stop Shop	12/8/2017	China
Clay craft kit	Mold	Toys "R" Us	11/29/2017	China
Children's pajamas	Burn	Woolino	11/21/2017	China
Fireworks	Burn	Wholesale Fireworks	11/15/2017	China
Jackets	Choking	OshKosh B'gosh	11/8/2017	Indonesia
Bicycles	Fall	Norco	11/7/2017	China
Rain ponchos	Strangulation	JW Crawford	11/3/2017	China
Children's sleepwear	Burn	Little Mass	11/1/2017	United States
Children's sleepwear	Burn	Dondolo	11/1/2017	Colombia
Children's sleepwear	Burn	VIV&LUL	11/1/2017	China
Baby gyms	Strangulation	Plan Toys	10/25/2017	Thailand
Infant motion seats	Burn	Fisher-Price	10/24/2017	China

Product Name	Hazard	Company	Recall Date	Manufacturing Location
Musical toys	Choking	Kids Preferred	10/19/2017	China
Infant wiggle balls	Choking	Toys "R" Us	10/5/2017	China
Playtex plates/ bowls	Choking	Playtex Products	10/3/2017	China
Nightlights	Electrical shock	Skip Hop	9/28/2017	China
Strollers	Fall	Delta Enterprise Corp.	9/25/2017	China
Fireworks	Burn	Fireworks Over America	9/20/2017	China
Bib/ bootie sets	Choking	DEMDACO	9/20/2017	China
Bracelet/ storybooks	Laceration	Studio Fun International	9/7/2017	China
Toddler sweaters	Choking	L.L. Bean	9/7/2017	Jordan
Nightgown/ pajama sets	Burn	ASHERANGEL	9/5/2017	China
Stacking toys	Choking	Hallmark Marketing Co.	8/31/2017	China
Infant rompers	Choking	Fabri-Tech	8/29/2017	China
Rattles	Choking	BRIO	8/15/2017	China
Girl's dresses	Choking	Laura Ashley	8/15/2017	China
Children's swimsuits	Choking	Meijer	8/8/2017	China
Children's robes	Burn	Richie House	8/3/2017	China
Pajamas	Burn	Sweet Bamboo	8/2/2017	China
Building sets	Choking	Panelcraft	8/1/2017	China
Activity toys	Choking	Manhattan Toy	7/20/2017	China
Stuffed toys	Laceration	TOMY	7/13/2017	China
Infant coveralls	Choking	Burt's Bees	6/29/2017	India
Fireworks	Burn	American Promo- tional Events	6/27/2017	China

Product Name	Hazard	Company	Recall Date	Manufacturing Location
Children's robes	Burn	Little Giraffe	6/15/2017	China
Safety gates	Strangulation	Madison Mill	6/7/2017	United States
Playwear	Choking	Lila + Hayes	6/6/2017	Peru
Children's robes	Burn	Kreative Kids	6/1/2017	China
Spinner toys	Choking	Hobby Lobby	5/23/2017	China
Ride-on toys	Fall	Dynacraft	5/23/2017	China
Scooters	Fall	Pulse Performance Products	5/19/2017	China
Plush toys	Choking	Douglas Company	5/17/2017	China
Science kits	Burn	Little Passports	5/12/2017	China
Nightlights	Fire	AM Conservation Group	5/10/2017	China
Strollers/ car seats	Fall	Combi USA	5/4/2017	China
Child backpack carrier	Fall	Osprey	4/27/2017	Vietnam
Booties	Choking	Zutano	4/25/2017	China
Remote-controlled cars	Fire	Horizon Hobby	4/25/2017	China
Motorized caster boards	Fall	Razor	4/20/2017	China
Water- absorbing toys	Ingestion	Target	4/13/2017	China
Sweatshirts/ jackets	Choking/ laceration	Fred Meyer	4/4/2017	China
Infant caps	Choking	Sock and Accessory Brands	3/30/2017	China
Toy trolleys	Impact	Juratoys	3/29/2017	China
Magnetic games	Choking/ ingestion	Target	3/29/2017	China
Bibs	Suffocation	Discount School Supply	3/22/2017	China
Sleepwear	Burn	LIVLY	3/14/2017	Peru

Product Name	Hazard	Company	Recall Date	Manufacturing Location
Sweatshirts	Strangulation	RDG Global	3/9/2017	China
Rattles	Choking	Kids II	3/2/2017	China
Jackets	Choking	Dillard's	2/28/2017	China
Pool slides	Fall	S.R. Smith	2/28/2017	United States
Toddler swings	Fall	Little Tikes	2/23/2017	United States
Toy frogs	Chemical injury	Moose Toys	2/22/2017	China
Strollers	Fall	Britax	2/16/2017	China
Toy wands	Laceration	Feld Entertainment	2/9/2017	China
Nightlights	Fire	Walt Disney Parks/Resorts	2/2/2017	China
Electric scooters	Fall	Pulse Performance Products	1/24/2017	China
Mobiles	Choking	RH Baby & Child	1/17/2017	China
Electric skateboards	Fire	Boosted	1/12/2017	China
Toy shovels/ tools	Lead	Active Kyds	1/10/2017	India
Sweatshirts	Choking	Walt Disney Parks/Resorts	1/4/2017	China

58. ASTEROID STRIKE

Hurtling toward the city of Chelyabinsk, Russia, at a speed of 19 kilometers per second (68,400 kph or 42,502 mph), the 12,000 metric ton space rock did not make it to the surface of the Earth. Instead, the asteroid broke into small pieces and, with the energy of 500 kilotons of TNT, burst into a fireball approximately 30 kilometers above the ground. The blast broke windows and damaged buildings. Although some injuries were caused by the shock wave, flying glass, and falling debris, no residents around Chelyabinsk were killed. This is the scenario that played out on February 15, 2013. About a century earlier (June 30, 1908), an asteroid exploded over the Siberian skies (the Tunguska event), destroying 2,150 square kilometers of forest. Because the area was sparsely populated, there were no casualties. The dinosaurs were not so lucky when a giant asteroid made contact with Earth just off the Yucatan Peninsula in Mexico approximately 65 million years ago. This asteroid, estimated to have had a diameter of 10–15 kilometers, created the Chicxulub crater, with a diameter of 180 kilometers. The impact, with a force of 10-100 trillion megatons, resulted in a massive tidal wave and sent up a global dust cloud that resulted in the extinction of many life forms.

Our home planet is showered with tons of dust and sand-sized particles from space every day. Most of these materials burn up in the Earth's atmosphere and pose no threat. On occasion, an asteroid does make it through the atmosphere. Depending on its size, an asteroid that makes it to the surface can cause minimal local damage or wipe out most life on the planet. The Earth Impact Database lists only 190 confirmed impact craters on Earth dating from 2.4 billion years ago to the present. For example, about 50,000 years ago, an asteroid weighing 300,000 tons crashed into northern Arizona and created the Barringer crater, 1 kilometer wide and 750 feet deep. The shock-wave, heat, and shrapnel created by this impact would have destroyed all life within 1.5 miles.

The destructive effects of an asteroid's impact on Earth are related to the size of an asteroid. Asteroids with diameters greater than 10 kilometers will result in mass extinctions and likely the total annihilation of all humans. Impacts by smaller asteroids (1–3 kilometers diameter) will likely cause massive death, infrastructure damage, and global climate change. Asteroids with diameters between 100 and 300 meters will cause regional damage and set up devastating tsunamis. Even smaller asteroid impacts can cause many deaths if they strike populated areas.

Asteroid impacts generate several damaging forces including heat, tsunamis, pressure waves, cratering, shrapnel, earth shaking, and wind blasts. Wind blasts and pressure shock waves will likely cause most of the human casualties when asteroids (15–400 meters in diameter) impact the Earth. A 200-meter asteroid striking the city of London would be expected to kill approximately 8.7 million people. With enough warning of an impending asteroid strike, it may be possible to evacuate a city to minimize casualties.

Predicting where and when an object from space will impact Earth is tricky business. The Center for Near Earth Object Studies (CNEOS) at the Jet Propulsion Laboratory (California Institute of Technology) and the Spaceguard Project (Powys, United Kingdom) have created an impact monitoring system to track the orbits of hazardous asteroids. Based on the analysis of an asteroid's orbit, the Sentry system makes a prediction about the time and location of the asteroid's impact.

The CNEOS Sentry system currently lists 70 potential Earth impact events within the next 100 years. The asteroid with the highest likelihood of impact (predicted to be between the years 2185 and 2198) has a 99.84% chance of missing the Earth. The other 69 objects have an even greater chance of missing our planet. All 70 objects currently have a 0 on the Torino Impact Hazard Scale. The Torino Scale rates the likelihood and consequences of an asteroid impact. A 0 rating indicates that the likelihood of a collision is essentially zero or that the object is so small that it will burn up in the atmosphere or cause little damage if it hits the ground.

So, currently, no asteroids of any significance have been detected that are on a collision course with Earth within the next 100 years. Nevertheless, NASA's Planetary Defense Coordination Office is still scanning the skies for asteroids and comets that pose a danger to Earth. If a potentially dangerous object is on its way to Earth, given enough time to prepare and deploy a plan, it may be possible to prevent an impact. The key is timing. The sooner an object is detected, the sooner its velocity or direction can be changed, so the Earth can avoid a strike. A system to slow an asteroid by hitting it with another object or by using the gravitational force of another large object placed near the asteroid could work as a defense mechanism.

Exploding a nuclear bomb or ramming a spaceship into an approaching asteroid may not save the Earth from an asteroid's impact if the asteroid is large or porous. Even if the asteroid did break up, the remaining pieces might still rain down and cause havoc. Detonating a nuclear explosion (or two or three) near an asteroid instead of on it may create enough force to alter the asteroid's direction. The sooner an asteroid's course can be altered, the less it has to be moved to avoid a collision with the Earth.

The technology and capability to create and deliver the energy needed to deflect large asteroids are beyond our current capabilities. With decades of planning (and billions of dollars, euros, yen, yuan, and rubles), scientists and engineers might be able to detect approaching asteroids and mount an effort to deflect such objects in order to save life on Earth. In the meantime, it appears that we will not go out as the dinosaurs did, at least not anytime soon.

Feel free to keep an eye on approaching asteroids and comets with NASA's Asteroid Watch Widget (https://www.jpl.nasa.gov/asteroidwatch/asteroid-widget-instructions.cfm).

SUMMARY

Preventability (1)

No technologies are currently available to stop or alter the trajectory of an asteroid. There is also no action an individual can take that would alter the likelihood or consequences of an asteroid striking the Earth.

Likelihood (1)

The chance of a catastrophic asteroid strike on the Earth within the lifetime of anyone reading this book is extremely low.

Consequence (100)

A large asteroid strike has the potential to wipe out all human life on Earth.

REFERENCES

Borovička, J., Spurný, P., Brown, P., Wiegert, P., Kalenda, P., Clark, D., & Shrbený, L. (2013). The trajectory, structure and origin of the Chelyabinsk asteroidal impactor. *Nature, 503*, 235–237.

Chapman, C. (2003, January). How a near-earth object impact might affect society. Global Science Forum, OECD, Workshop on Near Earth Objects: Risks, Policies, and Actions, Frascati, Italy.

Farinella, P., Foschini, L., Froeschlé, C., Gonczi, R., Jopek, T. J., Longo, G., & Michel, P. (2001). Probable asteroidal origin of the Tunguska Cosmic Body. *Astronomy and Astrophysics, 377*, 1081–1097.

Hildebrand, A. R., Pilkington, M., Connors, M., Ortiz-Aleman, C., & Chavez, R. E. (1995). Size and structure of the Chicxulub crater revealed by horizontal gravity gradients and cenotes. *Nature, 376*, 415–417.

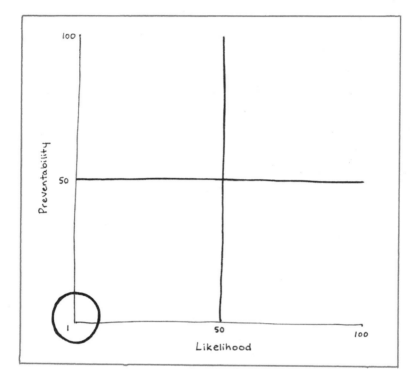

Planetary and Space Science Centre. (2018). Earth Impact Database. Retrieved from http://www.passc.net/EarthImpactDatabase/index.html

Popova, O. P., Jenniskens, P., Emel'yanenko, V., Kartashova, A., Biryukov, E., Khaibrakhmanov, S., . . . Mikouchi, T.; Chelyabinsk Airburst Consortium. (2013). Chelyabinsk airburst, damage assessment, meteorite recovery, and characterization. *Science, 342,* 1069–1073.

Rumpf, C. M., Lewis, H. G., & Atkinson, P. M. (2017). Asteroid impact effects and their immediate hazards for human populations. *Geophysical Research Letters, 44,* 2017GL073191.

Rumpf, C. M., Lewis, H. G., & Atkinson, P. M. (2017). Population vulnerability models for asteroid impact risk assessment. *Meteoritics and Planetary Science, 52,* 1082–1102.

CONCLUSION

In this book we have reviewed a number of issues that you might reasonably choose to worry about. We have done this with the express goal of understanding what is and what is not worth the burden of concern you might put into it. As part of this exercise we have assigned a worry index to each topic, although, as we have gone to some lengths to point out, these are just our own estimates and not a rigorously defined scale. Nevertheless, we think they provide an interesting starting point for weighing the relative risks of these subjects. Because humans (like most primates) are quite visual, it is often easier to understand data in graphic form. Therefore, we have presented a plot in each chapter representing the worry index in three dimensions: preventability, likelihood, and consequence.

Now that we have done the hard work of assigning a score to each entry, we present the combined graph that shows how the worry indexes for each topic compare to each other. As you may recall, in our opinion, the things most worth worrying about are those which (a) are likely to happen, (b) will be serious if they do happen, and (c) can be prevented by some action on your part. Addressing these topics will make the biggest difference for the least effort. These most worry-warranting items show up as large circles in the top right quadrant of the graph. Because they are the most important, we have labeled them.

You may be surprised by the topics in the "recommended to

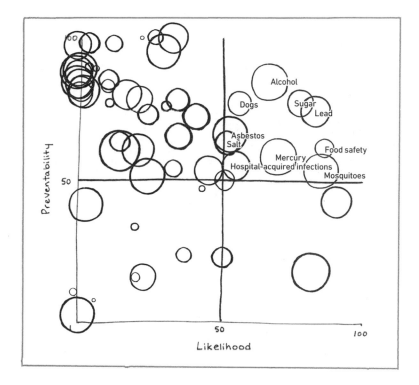

worry about" zone. With the possible exception of hospital-acquired infections, there is nothing on the list that most of us didn't already know about. Because they are so familiar, however, we may not be giving them the level of attention that they deserve. Many people are worried about snakes, but for most of us, dog bites are a much more pressing concern. Likewise, as a society we have a very cavalier attitude about alcohol. But drinking can have very serious consequences. And, critically, these consequences are highly preventable. Sugar and lead (both sweet!) also rank high on the worry scale. You probably already knew you needed to worry about these issues, but they might not seem as urgent as they really are. In some ways, the lack of novelty in the top-ranking worry issues can be sort of a letdown. It's a bit of an anticlimax to hear, again, that you need to watch your salt, sugar, and alcohol intake. All we can say is that we sympathize with you.

If you're feeling let down by the top right quadrant, there are some interesting features in other quadrants. For example, the bottom right section of the graph has two big scary circles. These correspond to antibiotics in feed animals and medical errors. What makes these issues so troubling is that they are likely to happen, the consequences can be very serious, and you can't do much to stop them. We recommend that you do not spend your time and attention on these issues exactly because you can't do much about them. But we freely admit that there isn't much comfort there.

Another interesting feature is what we refer to as the zone of uncertainty. As it happens, for some subjects the risks are poorly characterized, either because the data don't exist or because different studies have produced conflicting results. In these cases, we have assigned a score of 50. It seems wrong to say that you shouldn't worry about some of these things, because they could be quite dangerous. On the other hand, if the potential to harm hasn't been proven, it seems irresponsible to stir up anxiety. This is exemplified by BPA, which we have given a score of 50, 50, 50, and which appears smack dab in the middle of the chart.

The best news about this plot is that most of the points fall on the left-hand side. That means they are unlikely to cause you any problems (as long as you are the average person in each case). This might be because we have chosen a very skewed distribution of topics to review. Perhaps if we had chosen different topics, we would have seen a different result. But another likely explanation is that there aren't as many things to worry about as we tend to imagine. At least, not as many things in the category of topics that we have focused on in this book.

It is worth pointing out that all of the topics addressed in this book are higher-order issues. That is to say, they are only the sorts of things that you worry about when all of your more fundamental needs are being met. You only think about BPA leaching into your food when you have enough food, and you only worry about flame retardants in your mattress when you have a mattress to sleep on. So if you have the opportunity to worry about these things at all, you are in a privileged position. This is not to say that these issues are trivial or not worth considering, only that they should be considered in perspective.

This actually takes us in a bit of a philosophical direction. We have optimized worrying in a way that makes sense to us. But you should not take this at face value. Instead, take some time to consider what your priorities are for your life. It is natural (and good) to want to minimize personal pain and suffering, and to prolong your life span. The instinct to survive and to protect our loved ones is important. However, sooner or later we will all have to confront the fact that no matter how careful we are, immortality is unachievable.

We are living in a unique time in human history, which means we have unique problems that our ancestors never had to deal with. In centuries past, no one had to worry about PFAs or GMOs or artificial coloring in their food. There is a temptation to look back on those times and imagine that they were better. We romanticize the simplicity of the past, and in some ways maybe it was better. But in many meaningful respects it wasn't. People didn't live as long, and they didn't live as well. They didn't have as many choices, and they didn't have as much information with which to make choices. They didn't worry about exposure to pesticides, but they could be driven to starvation by locusts. They didn't get hospital-acquired infections because there were no hospitals; if you could afford to get medical treatment, you were likely to be prescribed elemental mercury. The world is a dangerous and worrisome place, but it always has been. That is just part of the human condition.

This being the case, how do you want to balance quality of life with quantity of life? Worrying about things will cost you time, effort, stress, and often money. Is it worth it? How do you want to spend your limited life resources? Clearly, there is no one right answer to this question. But there is an argument to be made that, in addition to making you stressed out and sick, worrying about small things can distract you from worrying about life's major issues like finding a purpose, finding love, and learning to forgive. Unfortunately, we can't help you with that; you're going to have to find a different book.

This book is about navigating life's everyday hazards, and on that, we can offer some advice. During the writing of this book we repeatedly came across the same advice in different contexts. It turns out there are some simple practices that will help you to minimize your risk on several fronts simultaneously. Adopting these habits will kill multiple (figurative) birds with one stone:

1. Wash your hands frequently.
2. Eat fewer processed foods.
3. Eat more vegetables.
4. Keep the dust down in your home.
5. Read and follow directions.
6. Communicate extensively with your physician.

Finally, if you come across something disturbing, don't worry about it—do something about it.

APPENDIX A

DO-IT-YOURSELF

When you begin to research a topic, you must keep one very important thing in mind: not all sources of information are equally credible and not all opinions are equally educated. To put it more bluntly, anyone can say anything. This has always been the case, but it is especially important to keep in mind in the internet age. We are lucky to live in a time when practically anyone, anywhere can look up any strange idea they have using their phone. The internet is an incredible resource, but it is also the source of profound misinformation and deception. If you're going to use it for research (and you should), you need to be able to identify good sources.

When it comes to credibility, expertise is important. There are all kinds of experts, but in general, education is important; experts will have lots of it. A PhD is the most advanced degree you can get in most scientific fields. A person who holds a PhD has completed four years of undergraduate education and at least four years of graduate education, usually longer. Original research is a required component of a PhD. Contrary to what most people believe, research is actually the most challenging and time-consuming part of the degree. After completing a PhD, many scientists also go through postdoctoral training—a few more years of research under the supervision of a senior scientist. People with this level of training have a high level of expertise, but in a very narrow field. A PhD qualifies a person to speak with authority in the field in which they have been trained. But a PhD in immunology, for example, does not convey any expertise in economics. Good scientists do not extend themselves outside their area of expertise. That is not to say that they will never venture beyond the bounds of their own discipline—that is exactly what we have done in this book. It does mean that they respect and rely upon the opinion of other experts and provide sources and citations.

People with PhDs do not practice medicine (legally); they have doctorates, but they are not physicians. An MD, on the other hand, is a medical doctor—someone who has completed four years of undergraduate training and four years of medical school. To practice medicine, an MD also needs to complete a residency in a specialty (e.g. pediatrics, neurology, dermatology). Many specialists also complete fellowships after their residencies. Some MDs are also researchers, but not all of them. MDs are experts in the treatment of human diseases, and those who do research are experts in their research domains. A heroic few are both MDs and PhDs, but their area of expertise is still their research area. There are other kinds of professional degrees (JD, PharmD, etc.) that may also confer expertise. If you are wondering what the mystery letters after someone's name mean, a quick internet search should tell you.

Beyond taking the word of an expert, you can also consult scientific sources. There are several different kinds of scientific sources, such as articles in the popular press, fact sheets published by governmental and nongovernmental organizations, popular science books, and primary sources. Again, these are not all created equal. Primary sources are original research articles or reviews that have been published in a scientific journal. These articles (often called papers) present data from experiments conducted by the authors as well as some interpretation of the results. Importantly, journal articles are peer reviewed. Peer review is the process by which several other scientists who are experts in the field read through and make comments on the paper before it is published. The peer reviewers may question the way that the data were collected or analyzed, or the interpretations that are drawn by the authors. A paper cannot be published in a scientific journal until the reviewers are satisfied with its scientific merit. This is far from a perfect process, but it is the current gold standard. In addition, papers that are published in a scientific journal must guarantee that any research that has been conducted on animal or human subjects has been reviewed by the appropriate oversight committee.

Given these factors, it might seem like primary sources should be the first place you look for information. However, this may not be the case. Journal articles are written for a very specific audience, and they will typically assume a high level of background knowledge and training. They are difficult to read and understand (although, if you want to try, we have included some advice in Appendix B). Plus, they can be expensive, although you can usually access them for free through a state university's library if you live nearby. A better first source is often an agency fact sheet. For example, the American Cancer Society and the American Heart Association produce fact sheets on topics related to cancer and cardiovascular health, respectively. The trick here is being able recognize a reputable organization. We suggest that you stick to well-known nonprofits such as the American Cancer Society, American Heart Association, American Medical Association, and the Mayo Clinic, and governmental organizations such as the Centers for Disease Control and Prevention (CDC), the National Institutes of Health (NIH), and the National Aeronautics and Space Administration (NASA). The World Health Organization (WHO), a United Nations agency, is also a good source.

If you are inclined toward conspiracy theories, or if you come from a group with good historical reasons to feel wary of the government, you might not find the idea of trusting government scientists very appealing. However, consider the alternative. For the most part, research is very expensive, which means you need someone with deep pockets to pay for it. The government funds science because it is a public good—it is good for everyone in society. Publicly funded research at universities is allocated based on grants, which are based on proposals, which are reviewed by other scientists for merit. Once a grant has been given, the funding agency requires periodic reporting. Titles and abstracts for publicly funded projects are also freely available, even before publication. When research that is funded by the NIH is published in a scientific journal, it must be made freely available within one year. Furthermore, when government labs conduct studies, they make their data publicly available and provide a description of their data collection and analysis techniques. Because taxpayers fund science, the requirement for transparency is high. On the other hand, when organizations in the private sector fund research, these requirements do not exist. This can lead to real or perceived conflicts of interest. The tobacco industry, for example, produced data for many years suggesting that smoking was not dangerous. For this reason, we suggest that you take fact sheets and other publications produced by privately funded think tanks with a grain of salt. It may not be obvious where the funding is coming from or what conflicts of interest may exist.

Of course, many news and popular science outlets publish stories about science. The quality of reporting in the popular media is highly variable. Misunderstanding and exaggeration abound, but there are some outlets (e.g., *Scientific American*, *Science Magazine*) that are generally high quality. If you read something in a popular source, it is best to verify that what is claimed is true. Incidentally, that applies to popular science books, including this one. Popular science books are not peer reviewed and may be strongly biased or even false. We have tried to keep our own personal biases out of this book, and we are not aware of any conflicts of interest. We certainly have no intention to present false or misleading information. Nevertheless, as they say, trust but verify.

It is not recommended that you believe much of what you find in a personal blog, unless you can verify the credentials of the author. In the course of writing this book we found many, many instances of misunderstanding and misapplication of scientific evidence in blogs. Remember, personal experiences do not always translate into population-level effects, and sincerity of belief is irrelevant to objective truth. Just because something has been liked and reposted hundreds of times on social media doesn't mean anyone has checked it for accuracy.

Once you have identified your sources, consider the following. First, scientists speak in probabilities, not certainties. It is unusual for a scientist to say something *will* happen; rather, they will say that it is *likely* to happen. Then they will tell you how likely it is. This can be frustrating, but it's important to understand. Exposure to a substance may be statistically proven to cause cancer, but that doesn't mean that it will cause cancer in everyone, all the time. There are typically many factors that contribute to diseases and other real-world phenomena. Scientists try to quantify the extent to which any one factor will affect the probability of an outcome, and some factors will drive the risk more than others. For example, eating bacon and smoking cigarettes are both known to be carcinogenic. But smoking cigarettes increases the probability that you will develop cancer much more than eating bacon does. This is an important point when it comes to evaluating relative risk. If you're going to prioritize decreasing your cancer risk, you need to work on your smoking habit first. Of course, there will be some people who eat a pound of bacon every morning and smoke two packs of cigarettes every day and live to be 100. Statistically, this is going to happen sometimes, but most of the time it won't.

Second, you will find a diversity of scientific opinion on almost any topic. This is actually a good thing. It is useful to get a wide variety of opinions, and it is rare for one person to have all the right answers to any question. But when you are drawing conclusions, scientific consensus (what most scientists think) will be the most useful indicator. Has scientific consensus ever been wrong? Yes, notably it has. But these cases are notable because they are unusual. The great majority of the time, the opinion of the field will settle closer to the truth than the opinion of any individual.

Finally, there is no one thing to blame for everything. Conversely, no one thing will fix everything. The temptation to believe that the right diet plan or the right vitamin supplement can solve everything is understandable, but in the end, it isn't true.

APPENDIX B
READING A SCIENTIFIC PAPER

Before you read a scientific paper, you might want to ask yourself if you're prepared for a difficult task, because it will likely not be an easy read. Primary scientific literature is written by scientists for other scientists and assumes a certain level of background understanding. This doesn't mean that you can't read it, but it does mean that you need to prepare.

Scientific publications are written for a very specific purpose: to disseminate research findings. Correspondingly, they are written in a very specific and (mostly) standardized format. Specifically, you will find the following sections in a scientific journal article: title, abstract, introduction, methods, results, discussion, and references. Depending on the journal, the order might be switched up a bit (it is currently trendy to put methods at the end) and you may find some additional sections such as keywords, acknowledgments, or an informal summary. It is important to note that some journals allow a supplement, extra documents that are important to understanding or supporting the paper but which don't fit in the body of the main article. The supplement is there for a reason; don't overlook it.

Here we discuss what you will find in the different sections of a research paper. The abstract summarizes the purpose, methods, results, and conclusions of the researchers in one paragraph. The abstract will let you know if you want to continue reading, because it provides information about the rationale and major results of the study.

The introduction provides readers with background information that sets the stage for the experiment. Authors discuss previous work in the field and alert readers to what is known and what knowledge gaps still exist. The introduction aligns the research project within the broad context of the field. Authors often use the introduction to propose a hypothesis that frames the motivation for performing the study.

The methods section lets readers know how the researchers performed their experiment by detailing the materials and explaining the procedures used to answer the research question. This section should be sufficiently detailed so that any reader can repeat the experiment exactly. The exact materials used in the research should also be included. Methods should also describe the statistical tests used to analyze the results so readers can assess the significance of the findings.

The results section contains the data obtained from the experiments, which are presented in figures, graphs, illustrations, photographs, and tables to show what was found. All experimental data, even those data that are unexpected or contrary to the authors' hypothesis, should be discussed. Each table should have its own title and description and each figure should have its own title and caption. Some authors write lengthy figure captions that provide readers with extensive information about the data. The meaning of the data should not be discussed in this section; instead, this is left for the next section of the paper, which is aptly named discussion.

The discussion is where authors provide evidence (based on their data) that strengthens or weakens their original hypothesis and answers the questions outlined in the introduction. It also includes interpretations of the data and comparisons to other studies. Many authors conclude the discussion section with a statement about future research that would be useful to move the field forward.

All work cited in a scientific paper must appear in the references section (the bibliography). References will include books, journal articles, websites, abstracts, and conference proceedings. The reference section can be extremely useful if you want to find more information about a particular topic.

If you do decide to read a scientific article, here are some tips:

- Plan to read it more than once.
- Take notes and make diagrams.
- Be prepared to look up phrases and concepts that you don't understand.
- Pay special attention to the figures.
- Don't assume all of the author's conclusions are correct, but don't assume they are incorrect.
- Remember, data can be interesting, even if you don't agree with the conclusions.
- Understand that you will need to read many papers to understand a topic; a single research paper is unlikely to give you a broad perspective on the field. .

APPENDIX C
FIRST AID KIT

Item	Approximate Cost
Adhesive bandages in different sizes (e.g., Band-Aid, Curad)	$5.00/100 bandages
Antibacterial ointment or cream	$6.00/0.5 oz
Antihistamine (e.g., Benadryl)	$12.00/100 tablets
Antiseptic wipes	$7.00/100 wipes
Cloth bandages	$7.00/roll
Cloth tape	$4.00/roll
Cotton balls	$5.00/100 balls
Gauze pads	$8.00/25 pads
Heat pack	$10.00/ea
Ice pack	$10.00/ea
Insect repellent	$7.50/ea
Iodine solution	$5.00/oz
Itch cream	$6.00/oz
Pain reliever (e.g., aspirin, ibuprofen, acetaminophen)	$10.00/500 pills
Rubbing alcohol	$6.00/16 oz
Safety pins	$5.00/100 pins
Scissors	$10.00/ea
Sunscreen	$10.00/8 oz
Surgical gloves	$10.00/100 gloves
Thermometer (oral)	$15.00/ea
Tweezers	$10.00/ea

INDEX

ABOUT THE AUTHORS

Lise A. Johnson, Ph.D., is a neural engineer, science educator, and science writer from Centennial, CO. She is the Director of Basic Science Curriculum and Assistant Professor of Physician Assistant Studies at Rocky Vista University. She is also a busy mom to two small children, whom she worries about extensively, and who inspired her to write this book.

Eric H. Chudler, Ph.D., is a neuroscientist at the University of Washington and the executive director of the Center for Neurotechnology in Seattle, WA. In addition to his research, Eric works with fellow scientists and teachers to create materials to help the public understand how the brain works. Eric has conducted workshops and given presentations to a variety of audiences including precollege students, university students, teachers, judges, and Tibetan Buddhist monks and nuns.